Religion in Prison

Equal Rites in a Multi-Faith Society

This is the first in-depth examination of relations between the Church of England and other faiths in the Prison Service Chaplaincy. It shows how the struggle for equal opportunities in a multi-faith society is politicising relations between the Church, the state and religious minorities. Drawing on a wealth of new data, it considers the increasingly controversial role of Anglican chaplains in facilitating the religious and pastoral care of prisoners from non-Christian backgrounds, whose numbers among the prison population have been growing. Comparison with the United States underlines the closeness of the tie between the state and Christian churches in English prisons, and this book argues that it is time to reconsider the practice of keeping ethnic and religious minorities dependent on Anglican 'brokering' of their access to prison chaplaincy.

JAMES A. BECKFORD is Vice President of the International Sociological Association (1998) and President-elect of the International Society for the Sociology of Religion for 1999. He is the author of four books in the sociology of religion, including *Religion and Advanced Industrial Society* (1989) and *Cult Controversies: The Societal Reaction to New Religious Movements* (1985). Professor of Sociology at the University of Warwick, he has also taught at the universities of Reading, Durham and Loyola, Chicago.

SOPHIE GILLIAT is a Research Fellow in the Department of Sociology, and Tutor at the Institute of Education, University of Warwick. She has published on the religious identity of Muslims in Britain and multi-faith issues.

Religion in Prison

Equal Rites in a Multi-Faith Society

James A. Beckford and Sophie Gilliat

CAMBRIDGE
UNIVERSITY PRESS

PUBLISHED BY THE PRESS SYNDICATE OF THE UNIVERSITY OF CAMBRIDGE
The Pitt Building, Trumpington Street, Cambridge CB2 1RP

CAMBRIDGE UNIVERSITY PRESS
The Edinburgh Building, Cambridge CB2 2RU, United Kingdom
http://www.cup.cam.ac.uk
40 West 20th Street, New York, NY 10011-4211, USA   http://www.cup.org
10 Stamford Road, Oakleigh, Melbourne 3166, Australia

First published 1998

Printed in Great Britain at the University Press, Cambridge

Typeset in Plantin 10/12 pt. [VN]

A catalogue record for this book is available from the British Library

Library of Congress cataloguing in publication data
Beckford, James A.
Religion in prison: equal rites in a multi-faith society /
    James A. Beckford & Sophie Gilliat.
        p.   cm.
includes bibliographical references and index.
ISBN 0 521 62246 8 (hb)
1. Prisoner – Religious life – Great Britain.   2. Religious work
with prisoners – Great Britain.   3. Prison Service Chaplaincy (Great
Britain)   4. Church of England – Clergy.   5. Christianity and other
religions – Great Britain.   I. Gilliat, Sophie, 1969– .
II. Title.
365'.66–dc21.   97-38738   CIP

ISBN 0 521 62246 8 hardback

To Bryan R. Wilson and to the memory
of Deirdre Green in gratitude for their
exemplary scholarship

Contents

Figures

Tables

Abbreviations

ACA   American Correctional Association
ACCA   American Correctional Chaplains Association
ACG   Assistant Chaplain General
CCJ   Council of Christians and Jews
CG   Chaplain General
CPE   Clinical Pastoral Education
HIA   Head of Inmate Activities
PSC   Prison Service Chaplaincy
RFRA   Religious Freedom Restoration Act
RRLO   Race Relations Liaison Officer

Preface

One of the reasons why prisons are such daunting places is that they are complicated and closed social systems. Another difficulty for researchers is that even within the highly centralised prison system of England and Wales the variety of prison establishments is so wide that it almost defies any attempt to make general statements about them. The pace of change in prison policies and practices is also so rapid that descriptions of prison life run the risk of being out of date before they are published. Nevertheless, our book argues that at least one structural feature of prisons in England and Wales is relatively unaffected by the differences between establishments and by the hectic pace of change. This is the chaplaincy service which is responsible for providing religious and pastoral care to inmates and staff alike.

More than 500 religious professionals, lay workers and volunteers from various religious traditions deliver religious and pastoral care on a daily basis in every one of the more than 130 prisons in England and Wales. And, although these chaplaincy workers have undoubtedly been buffeted by the winds of change in prisons, their structural position in the social system of prisons has not changed drastically since the mid-1980s. On the other hand, significant changes have taken place in the inmate population. For example, while the size of the prison population has increased dramatically since the early 1980s, the proportion of prisoners registering as members of the main Christian churches has declined sharply. There has been an even sharper increase in the number of prisoners declining to register any kind of religious affiliation; and the proportion of prisoners reporting membership of faith communities other than the Christian has grown steadily since the mid-1970s.

In this book we have tried to make sociological sense of the ways in which the Church of England chaplains, who are widely regarded as the dominant force in the Prison Service Chaplaincy and who represent nearly 80 per cent of all full-time chaplains in the prisons of England and Wales, have responded to these changing circumstances. More precisely, our analysis is focused on the Anglican chaplains' performance of their traditional role as 'facilitators' and 'brokers' for Buddhists, Hindus, Jews, Muslims and Sikhs. Our aim is to explain how and why prison chaplains from the 'national church' continue to perform this role at a time when leading representatives of some other faith communities would prefer to be less dependent on Anglican brokerage. The resulting tensions reflect broader concerns about the power and privilege of an Established Church in a society which not only shows considerable indifference towards organised Christianity but which also contains ethnic and religious minorities growing in size and capacity to mobilise their members in pursuit of, among other things, the right to participate in public life on the same basis as Christians.

These concerns are political in the sense that they touch on the differential distribution of power between faith communities and on the capacity of the Church of England to facilitate other faith communities' access to resources and power in the public sphere. There are also political questions about the claims of some individuals and organisations to represent their faith communities in negotiations with the Church of England, the Prison Service Chaplaincy and the Prison Service. In short, the provision of religious and pastoral care in prisons has become a site of controversy in which wider issues about the establishment of the Church of England, the Church's relations with other faith communities and the latter's empowerment all play a part.

Prison chaplaincy is more than a site of controversy, however. We have collected evidence of the impressive care and commitment with which chaplains and Visiting Ministers of other faiths foster religious interests among individuals and groups in prison. Levels of co-operation and mutual respect between Christians and members of other faith communities are also high in some establishments despite the difficult conditions in which many of them have to work. The dedication and goodwill of individuals are rarely in doubt. It is important to emphasise this point and to make it as clear as possible that our analysis is not primarily about individuals but is focused on the *structural* constraints within which prison chaplaincy takes place. In order to reinforce the importance of social structures we have included a chapter on prison chaplaincy in the United States. Our hope is that the comparison will underline the strong differences between what chaplains can achieve in systems regulated by different frameworks of law, rules, resources, authority and inter-faith relations.

The fact that prison chaplaincy in a religiously diverse society raises many questions about power, privilege, equal opportunities and the brokerage exercised by the Established Church means that our analysis will inevitably arouse strong feelings in some quarters. We have tried to take an objective and dispassionate view of our evidence but we also know that our interpretations of that evidence will not be shared by all readers. Our hope is that this book will at least stimulate and inform public debate about the increasingly complex and sensitive relations between the state, the Christian churches and other faith communities. We believe that prison chaplaincy should be considered as merely one, albeit important, part of this wider and long overdue debate.

The research for this book and for a broader discussion of 'The Church of England and Other Faiths in a Multi-Faith Society' was funded for two years by the General Synod of the Church of England and by the Leverhulme Trust. We are most grateful for their generous support. In addition, numerous individuals provided valuable help at various stages of the project. The original idea for research on the Church of England's relations with other faiths emerged from conversations between the Archbishop of Canterbury, Dr George Carey, and Professor David Dabydeen of the Centre for Caribbean Studies at the University of Warwick. Neither of them necessarily shares our ideas, but we have benefited enormously from their personal support and encouragement. Other people who went to great lengths to assist us include Cllr J. S. Birdi, Dr Harriet Crabtree, Mr Harish Dhokia, Rabbi Dr Julian Jacobs, Professor Robert Jackson, The Venerable Ajahn Khemadhammo, The Revd Canon Dr Christopher Lamb, Professor Jørgen Nielsen and Imam Dr Abduljalil Sajid.

The scope of our project was so wide and multi-faceted that we could not possibly have completed it if we had not also been able to draw on the expertise and personal qualities of a large group of consultants whose names appear in the Appendix. We are grateful to all of them for their support, advice and guidance.

Mr Bashir Ebrahim-Khan, the Venerable Ajahn Khemadhammo and Mr Indarjit Singh help to co-ordinate the provision of religious and pastoral care to, respectively, Muslims, Buddhists and Sikhs in English prisons. They were not only generous with valuable information and 'contacts' but also patient with our questions and misunderstandings. The Venerable David Fleming, Chaplain General of the Prison Service Chaplaincy, the Rt Rev Monsignor Joseph Branson, Principal Roman Catholic Chaplain, the Revd William Davies, Superintendent Methodist Chaplain, and the Revd Thomas Johns, Assistant Chaplain General, were no less helpful. So too was the Revd John Hargreaves, now retired Assistant Chaplain General of the Prison Service Chaplaincy. He was a mine of helpful information and a patient respondent to our awkward questions. Thanks should also go to Mrs Alanah Grundy of the Prison Service Chaplaincy office in Stafford. We are grateful to all of these individuals who have helped us conduct research on prison chaplaincy.

Thanks should also go to those chaplains and Visiting Ministers who assisted us in the initial stages of research. This usually involved a visit to the prisons in which they served, and their hospitality in terms of time and information was always generous. They are: the Revd Bryan Gracie, the Revd Nigel Dent, the Revd Hitesh Dodhia, Hajji Cassim Mohammed, Rob Yellowhammer, Dr Surindar Singh and Mrs Ranjit Kaur.

A number of institutions and organisations provided various forms of assistance at different times. It is our pleasure to acknowledge the help of the Centre for Research in Ethnic Relations at the University of Warwick, the Church of England Record Centre, the Library staff of HM Prison Service College at Newbold Revel, the Inter Faith Network for the United Kingdom and the Library staff of the University of Warwick. Thanks should also go to our colleagues in the Department of Sociology and to the Study Leave Committee at the University of Warwick.

Finally, it is a pleasure to record our sincere thanks to the hundreds of other people who completed our questionnaires, answered our interview questions, welcomed us into their places of work, took us on tours of their premises, offered us hospitality, spoke to us on the telephone or sent us information. We cannot name them because we wish to preserve the confidentiality of our communications with them, but we would like them to know that we are deeply appreciative of their willingness to help our project. We alone take responsibility for any shortcomings.

1 Equal opportunities and multiculturalism in prisons

'WE'LL DIE FOR OUR RIGHTS
IN PRISON'

Halal food row leads to jail hunger strike

Furious Muslim prisoners who claim that they are being forced to eat haram food have gone on an all-out hunger strike
since last Friday.

Hamid Quereshi and over 80 fellow prisoners at Strange-
ways Prison, in Manchester, are shocked that they are eating
food fried in bacon fat oil when they have opted for the 'halal'
menu.

(*Eastern Eye*, 14 January, 1996)

Prisons are challenging and problematic for all sorts of reasons. The mass media are full of stories about such problems as overcrowding, excessively harsh or excessively soft regimes, inconsistent sentencing policies, brutal- ity, the drain on public resources, the allegation that prisons function as 'crime factories', and so on. The history of penal policy shows that none of these problems is entirely new or peculiar to the twentieth century. In fact, penal policy seems to move in cycles or, at least, in a pendulum motion.

Nevertheless, one aspect of prison life and of prison problems has been largely ignored by journalists, politicians and academic researchers alike. This is the place of religion in prisons. Of course, many observers of prisons are aware of the importance of religion to various campaigns for reform of penal policy and practice. Historians of prisons also emphasise the centrality of evangelical Protestantism to the prototype of, for example, solitary confinement or continuous surveillance (Grünhut 1948; Fox 1952). Chaplains held considerable power and influence in English prisons throughout the nineteenth century; and religious motivations lay

1

behind many of the attempts to make prisons more disciplined and orderly institutions (Ignatieff 1978). Yet, for all this attention to early religious influences on prison regimes, very few studies have examined the provision of religion in modern English prisons. This book will examine the place of religion in prisons in detail and will explain why it has become more problematic as English society has become religiously more diverse. It will argue that these problems are a microcosm of many of the better publicised difficulties surrounding multiculturalism and equal opportunities for ethnic minorities and non-Christian faith communities in the United Kingdom and other countries.

The lack of attention to issues surrounding religion in prisons might suggest that the well-attested decline in the power and influence of prison chaplains, particularly in comparison to the mounting status of such 'caring' professionals as welfare officers and psychologists in the Prison Service, has been mirrored by the eclipse of all religion in prisons. Indeed, we shall show in chapter 2 that a declining proportion of prisoners is willing to take an active part in collective Christian activities or even to declare that they belong to any religious grouping. But at the same time religion is becoming more contentious and therefore more interesting in prisons. The fact that the overall level of prisoners' religious practice is declining should not be allowed to obscure the more important fact that a growing number of prisoners from faith communities other than Christianity are declaring themselves to be, for example, Buddhists, Hindus, Muslims or Sikhs. Moreover, these prisoners from 'other faiths'[1] are making demands on prison authorities which expose deep-rooted problems and imbalances in the prison system's provision of facilities for religious practice. These problems are a leading theme of this book.

The increase in numbers of prisoners from other faiths in English prisons has been strong since the early 1980s but is not the sole cause of problems associated with religion. It is the conjunction of a basically Christian system of prison chaplaincy and a disproportionately high rate of increase in the number of prisoners from non-Christian faith communities which presents a more serious challenge to the Prison Service's capacity to deal with religious diversity on a large scale. This type of challenge is not unique to prisons: it reflects the difficulties which are widespread in the rapid transition that the United Kingdom is making from being a country with many variations on Christianity (and a few on Judaism) to becoming a country in which varieties of Christianity and Judaism pale into insignificance compared with the more radical differences between Christianity, Hinduism, Islam, Sikhism and other smaller faith communities.

Moreover, the difficulties emerging in the Prison Service's encounter with other faiths have their parallel in the spheres of education, employment, housing and health care. The sudden and rapid growth of religious diversity, beginning in the 1960s, was experienced as a shock and a challenge in all these spheres but it was submerged by the preoccupation with diversity perceived in terms of 'race', ethnicity or skin colour. This is one of the reasons why so many journalists and politicians overlooked the fact that the number of immigrants to the United Kingdom from Ireland, Italy, Poland and other 'white' European countries was greater than that of the so-called non-white immigrants in the post-war period. The differences between the ways of life displayed by immigrants and refugees from the Caribbean, East African and South Asian regions and those of the majority of Britons were usually framed in racial or ethnic terms. As a result, the contribution of religion towards the different ways of life was relegated to a relatively insignificant role. Schemes to combat prejudice and discrimination against people from Black and Asian communities also focused on the importance of according them equal opportunities for access to such things as employment chances, public office and social services. It has taken several decades to realise that many British Asians and members of other faiths are pressing for equal opportunities and equal respect for their cultures and religions as well (Poulter 1987; Modood 1994a; Nye 1996). The delay in acknowledging that equal treatment for minorities' cultures and religions was also important may, according to Talal Asad (1990), have derived from the assumption that cultural differences would either be flattened out in a process of assimilation to a supposedly unitary British culture or would be relegated to the sphere of private life where their impact on the social order would presumably be slight. Yet, a recent survey of ethnic minorities in the United Kingdom showed that 80 per cent of Asian respondents did not think of themselves as 'black'. Instead, most of them preferred to identify themselves in religious terms as Hindus, Muslims or Sikhs (Modood 1997).

The reason why the issue of equal opportunities for religion has become so important in prisons is that it arises at a major point of tension between the state, the Church of England and other faiths. It is an issue which epitomises and, by virtue of being an extreme case of a general phenomenon, clarifies some of the underlying difficulties facing the UK's transition to a religiously mixed society. It does so by challenging taken-for-granted assumptions about the basis for societal cohesion and social justice in a society characterised by an imbalance of power between majority and minorities and by many types of diversity. The concepts of a 'multi-faith' and a 'multicultural' society need to be explored at this point since they are the terms in which discussion of these issues usually takes place. But we insist on addressing the ambiguities and implicit assumptions which often pervade these terms in order to expose their inadequacies from our point of view.

'Multi-faith'

The starting point is that both 'multi-faith' and 'multicultural' are loaded with positive connotations. They are not neutral terms of description. They usually imply that diversity of faith communities and cultures is to be welcomed. In other words, these two concepts convey the notion of diversity but they also go beyond it to suggest that diversity is a good thing. This is why 'multicultural' is often encountered in the form of the noun 'multiculturalism', meaning an outlook or an ideological position which regards the diversity of cultures as a benefit for societies. It sometimes implies that steps should be taken to promote the expression of diversity for its own sake, but this usage can be problematic, as we shall explain later.

With specific regard to religion, 'multi-faith' occurs most often in connection with activities which bring representatives of different faith communities together. 'Multi-faith worship' is the clearest instance of such usage, for this is an activity which involves the orchestration of different forms of worship from different religious traditions in a joint ceremony. It raises all sorts of theological and liturgical questions which attest to its contentious character. Even the committed advocates of multi-faith worship acknowledge the need for care and caution (Church House Publishing 1992).

But 'multi-faith' can also have a less contentious meaning, as in the designation of a room in a hospital or prison as a 'multi-faith room'. This is a weaker sense of the concept, meaning that people from different faith communities may simply share the same room for the purposes of worship. They are unlikely to participate in joint ceremonies in the room: it is merely a facility which is available to each faith community separately.

Probably the weakest sense of the term occurs in the characterisation of a country as a 'multi-faith country'. In this case, it simply means that a diversity of faith communities is found in the same place. As it happens, however, 'multi-faith' tends to be used in this particular sense only when speakers or writers wish to commend or welcome the fact of religious diversity. It is unlikely that an opponent or critic of religious diversity would use 'multi-faith' except perhaps in an ironic or sarcastic mode. In view of the term's wide range of applications and implications we shall use 'multi-faith' sparingly and only as a stylistic alternative to 'religiously diverse'.

'Multicultural'

Turning now to the term 'multicultural' we encounter even more variability of usage and problems. This is why we need to be careful about its precise denotation in this book. As with 'multi-faith', the simplest meaning is nothing more than the co-existence of different cultures in the same society. Very few societies at the end of the twentieth century are not multicultural in this sense of the term. It is even used in this way to designate societies which have a dominant culture and various subcultures or 'subaltern' cultures. This has been true, of course, of many societies at most periods of history.

Yet, even this apparently commonsensical usage of 'multicultural' entails problems. The first is that it runs the risk of implying that earlier and perhaps 'normal' human societies were 'uni-cultural'. Yet, this state of affairs may never have existed except in societies composed of a few hundred individuals living in isolation from others. For the fact is that, if culture is defined broadly as 'widely shared meanings' or 'a complete way of life', even very small, isolated societies give rise to a wide range of cultural meanings, not all of which are shared by all members. The degree to which meanings are shared is always variable; and the degree to which individual human beings use, or conform with, shared ideas is also variable. Consequently, claims that societies which are now multicultural must have been homogeneous in the past are dubious.

A further difficulty with 'multicultural' is that it tends to exaggerate the extent to which it is possible to mark out sets of shared meanings or ways of life as discrete cultures or sub-cultures. In Steve Vertovec's view, multiculturalism tends not only to exaggerate the homogeneity of cultures and of the communities which are supposedly identified by them but also to exclude such communities from the 'meaningful parts of the public domain' (Vertovec 1996: 60). He agrees with the argument that minority communities are integral to British society and therefore entitled to participate in forging the country's public culture. This can only occur, however, 'if communities feel confident enough to engage in a dialogue and where there is enough public space for them to interact with the dominant culture' (Parekh & Bhabha 1989: 27). We shall suggest that the field of relations between the Prison Service Chaplaincy and representatives of other faith communities is precisely the kind of area in which minority religions might be able to achieve a mode of effective involvement in public life but that it is important for them to do so without being patronised or co-opted by more powerful agencies.

Does this mean that the term 'multicultural' is virtually redundant since the contrast class of 'unicultural' societies is empty? Not entirely, is our answer. For, it is often overlooked by scholars who rush to denounce any suggestion that clear boundaries can be drawn around cultures and sub-cultures that some administrative practices actually create, reinforce or impose such boundaries. So, although there are good intellectual reasons for being sceptical about the unicity and boundedness of cultures, in practice some social processes create a strong impression that cultures are clear-cut entities. For example, the Prison Service of England and Wales operates with a complex categorisation of more than eighty 'permitted religions' to which prisoners may declare themselves to belong. Since the records in this system are now computerised, staff who register prisoners on reception have no latitude with regard to how sensitively they record each prisoner's religious affiliation, if any. Thus, the category 'Hindu' or 'Sikh' is clear-cut, unambiguous and definite as far as the Procrustean administrative procedures are concerned. Prisoners must simply accommodate themselves to one of the categories on offer. This encounter with rigid categories is their lived experience, and it probably influences their self-identity despite the fact that some prisoners may not be able to recognise or to categorise themselves in such an unequivocal fashion. Although scepticism about the unitary character of cultures is justified, then, it is a mistake to ignore the fact that some institutions function *as if* the boundaries separating cultures were sharp and impermeable. Prisons exemplify the kind of institutions which do not easily tolerate ambiguity or confusion of 'official' categories.

The only safe assumption to make is that cultural variation has been a feature of English society at least since early modern times (Colley1992). The justification for talking about multiculturalism in the late twentieth century is that a relatively new aspect of diversity has been introduced and that it is considered to make a significant difference to social and cultural life. In short, we believe that an important change has taken place in the nature or degree of 'normal' cultural variation in recent decades.

What is this significant change? It is not simply the fact or the extent of novelty. Much more significant is the spread of the idea that varieties of cultural meaning systems all have claims to equal respect (Taylor 1992) and that the human groups which share these relatively different cultures can also claim the same opportunities as other groups to put their cultures into practice. Diversity is not the only consideration in this sense of 'multiculturalism'. The demand for equal respect and equal opportunities is no less central to this strong version of the concept (Rex 1994).

Why is an insistence on equal opportunities thought essential to a workable notion of multiculturalism? The main reason is to prevent the diversity of cultures from simply being fêted for its own sake or as an exotic side-show[2] without giving consideration to the unequal distribution of power or life-chances among, for example, minority ethnic or faith communities. For, unless multiculturalism is allied with equal opportunities, there is a danger that 'The existence of cultural difference can . . . become a marker of the boundary between those who are accorded and those are not accorded social, legal or political rights' (Rex 1986: 10). It is unusual, however, to employ ideas of equal opportunities in connection with religion; they are usually confined to spheres such as employment, housing or health care. But there is a sound reason for considering them in relation to religion in prisons. This is because the Prison Act 1952 obliges the Prison Service to make provision for prisoners to receive the services of appropriate ministers of religion. In other words, Christian chaplains and Visiting Ministers of other faiths are officially appointed by an agency of the state to deliver pastoral and religious care to prisoners and Prison Service staff. Resources for these religious services come from the public purse. This is why issues of equal opportunities are relevant to religion in prisons.

Prisoners can choose to ignore the services on offer, and it is important to emphasise that our concern in this book is not primarily with the positive or negative value of religion. Recognising that it is a statutory requirement for the Prison Service of England and Wales to make provision for religious personnel, we merely investigated how public resources were deployed for this purpose. Moreover, it seems to us that the notion of equal opportunities in the field of religion should include the right of prisoners not only to take no part in religious or pastoral activities but also to be protected against undue pressure to associate with members of their own faith communities. However, we have collected no evidence that exploitative forms of 'fundamentalism' have benefited from a multiculturalist ethos in prison (Yuval-Davis 1992). Nevertheless, we believe that religious care should be available to all prisoners equally, regardless of their particular faith if such provision is made at all. If the provision is not perceived to be even-handed, accusations may be made about discrimination. As we shall argue throughout this book, the fact that responsibility for administering the provision of religion to prisoners rests mainly with clergy of the Church of England gives rise to difficult questions about the equality of opportunities for non-Christians to have access to religious personnel and care. The conventional wisdom that religion is a private matter and therefore outside the public sphere in which consideration of equal opportunities is normally relevant does not apply to the special circumstances of prisons. In fact, as we shall now argue, the question of multiculturalism and equal opportunities for access to religious services is especially challenging in prisons.

Why are prisons especially challenging sites for multiculturalism? In addition to the 'racial', ethnic and cultural diversity of the prison population in England and Wales (Genders & Player 1989; FitzGerald & Marshall 1996), other factors help to make relations between some faith communities politically sensitive. In the first place, prisoners are by definition deprived of certain rights and opportunities enjoyed by the rest of the population. And, as was argued above, prisoners' identities are subjected to various pressures. This is a situation in which the demand for respect for the distinctiveness of the cultures with which prisoners identify themselves is likely to be strong. Symbols of belonging and of commitment to revered sources of collective identity tend to be highly prized and vigorously defended, especially if prisoners believe that disrespect is deliberately shown to them. It is as if the confined nature of prison life increases sensitivity to matters of individual and collective respect. For example, prisoners have sometimes reacted violently to Prison Officers who touched their sacred texts while conducting routine searches of cells. Perhaps the individual prisoners' exposure to daily indignities and deprivation sharpens their sensitivity to perceived offences against symbols of their collective identity. Moreover, the Prison Service's race relations policy makes it an offence to discriminate on grounds of religion, among other things, so that there is a measure of official backing for demands that religion should be respected.

Another reason for the heightened significance of relations between faith communities in prisons is the fact that, at least in some basic respects, most prisoners are subject to the same conditions, the same regulations and the same discipline. In these circumstances, if prisoners perceive that privileges or penalties are given to certain categories of prisoners for no legitimate reason, feelings of resentment will be strong. The provision of opportunities, facilities or resources for practising religion and the ways of life associated with religion can be the occasion of resentment if equality of respect is not perceived for all religious practices. The resentment may be felt by members of religious minorities towards the Christian majority and their chaplains. No less sensitive, however, is the issue of competition and resentment between minority groups, especially when it comes to special diets and release from work without loss of earnings on religious holidays.

Finally, multicultural issues in prisons take on added significance when the focus is on equal respect for religions. This is because religions claim to represent a level of reality which is ultimately true and irreducible to any other meaning system. Religions are about absolutes. Consequently, religious believers who perceive that their particular religion does not receive the same degree of respect as do others may feel seriously disadvantaged and offended. No compromise is possible when it comes to matters of absolute significance for the believers. They find it unacceptable to have to put up with what appears to be at best *relative* or conditional respect for their religion. Some prisoners actually become more serious about their religion precisely because they object to perceived slights against its value or integrity.

For all the above reasons, then, considerations of equal respect are serious in prisons, especially when they concern religion and culture. No doubt this is why the European Prison Rules specify that 'The religious beliefs and moral precepts of the group to which a prisoner belongs shall be respected' (Loucks 1994: 48). If grievances centre on the suspicion that prison authorities do not accord equal respect to the religious faiths of all prisoners, there is the potential for dissatisfaction, resentment and possibly unrest. This is one more strand in the complex web of competition and manipulation which characterises many of the social relationships in prisons. As we shall show in this book, however, many of the grounds for grievance in relation to religion are different for Christians and members of other faiths.

So far, we have discussed the concepts of 'multi-faith' and 'multiculturalism' in largely abstract terms, but the truth is that they are part of the daily experience of prisoners, chaplains, prison officers and prison officials. They are experienced, for example, as claims for recognition of the need for prisoners to wear, to eat, to possess and to do (or to be excused from doing) certain things as requirements of their religious faith. The claims are sometimes based on comparisons with provisions already made for members of other religious groups or inmates of other prisons. In other words, multiculturalism is a field of broadly political or ideological struggle. Since it is about competition and relativities it is never static but is, at best, in a state of provisional equilibrium. As we shall show in this book, Christian chaplains and Visiting Ministers of other faiths are crucial to the process of making claims for equal respect, countering them or acceding to them. Negotiation is constant. Multiculturalism is not abstract in the context of prisons: it is a daily reality. This does not mean that there is any clear agreement about the meaning or value of multiculturalism. There are only the Prison Service's official statements about 'race' relations and about the treatment of 'permitted' religions. In the absence of agreement or policy, it is only a mild exaggeration to describe religion as something of a political 'battleground' (Wallerstein 1990) in prisons. At this writing, there are no signs that the 'battle' is subsiding; but there is widespread concern to prevent matters from deteriorating further.

It is important to stress that our usage of 'multiculturalism' in the sense of demands for equal respect for religious faiths is only one specific application of broader and more ambitious notions of multiculturalism.

Contrary to the situation in Sweden, for example, where it is the state's policy to promote multiculturalism through schemes for creating equality, freedom of choice between immigrant and indigenous cultural forms and partnership between all communities (Ålund & Schierup 1992), the situation in English prisons is less a matter of official policy and more a matter of political struggle between contending interest groups. This is why we characterised multiculturalism as a 'field of struggle'. Moreover, our interest in the multicultural aspects of religion in prisons is not part of a concern with trying to preserve minority cultures for their own sake. And it is certainly not our intention to suggest that better 'management' of religion in prisons could or should contribute towards the control of 'difficult' minorities. Our first concern is with the ways in which issues of equal respect arise in the relations between prison authorities, Christian chaplains and representatives of other faiths (principally Visiting Ministers).

Secondly, we are concerned with the ways in which the struggle for equal respect for other faiths in prison feeds into the wider issues of political empowerment and of full participation for religious minorities in the nation's public life. This is the very opposite of marginalising religion or of ghettoising it. The question, by contrast, is how far religion can serve as a vehicle or medium of political *and* cultural values – not just for the sake of peaceful coexistence or frictionless assimilation of minorities into majority cultures. But there is no implication in this question that religion and culture are the only effective avenues through which minorities can pursue their rights and their interests. Nor are we suggesting that political and social problems are 'really' cultural or religious. We want to resist such a 'culturalist' claim. Indeed, we assert that many of the difficulties facing ethnic or religious minorities in prisons stem from the material and political realities of their communities outside prisons, including overt racism, institutionalised racism and generalised discrimination. Our view is that it is desirable for communities of interest to have equal opportunities to participate fully in public life and to pursue their interests by whatever legal means they see fit to choose. Religion is only one of these means but it can be pursued alongside other strategies and does not indicate that the most significant problems are necessarily religious or cultural. Indeed, the rejection of a distinction between politics, religion and culture is a feature of some non-Christian religions.

One other aspect of debates about multiculturalism must be discussed at this point. It concerns a distinction between the public sphere and the private sphere, which is central to some versions of the concept. Thus, multiculturalism is sometimes said to involve a defence of the rights of minorities to equal opportunities for participation, without discrimination, in public life and for the practice of their own cultures in private life (Rex 1994). But, as Parekh (1990) and Modood (1994b) among others have argued, this relegation of culture to the private sphere is a form of discrimination against minorities whose cultures do not distinguish between public and private in the same way. Indeed, there is a secularist bias in claims that religion properly belongs only to the private sphere. Thus:

Multiculturalism which states that public recognition of minority cultures is essential to equal citizenship, combined with a denial of an equivalent public recognition of religion, can only convey the message that religious identity has and ought to have less status than other forms of group identity. (Modood 1994b: 8)

For this reason we prefer to think of a multicultural society as one in which minorities have equal opportunities to participate in public life and to follow their own cultural practices in public as well, within the usual conditions imposed for the sake of public order and safety.

Relevant examples in the context of prisons would include recognising the right of Buddhists, Hindus, Jews, Muslims, Sikhs and of other religious minorities in the United Kingdom:

(a) to be routinely involved by right in discussions about the strategy for providing religious care to prisoners belonging to their own faith communities, i.e. not by concession, co-option or exception;
(b) to have their requirements for religious and pastoral care in prisons met as a matter of routine rather than as a special concession, and;
(c) to receive the same opportunities as the Christian majority to observe their religious and cultural practices in prisons.

Negotiation, challenge, tension and conflict are endemic in such situations. For example, eating ritually pure food, meeting regularly with appropriate religious specialists or having a suitable place for religious meditation are not simply a matter of private taste or preference as far as many Buddhists, Hindus, Jews, Muslims and Sikhs are concerned. They see it as a matter of their right to practise their religion and of their right to have the same opportunities to do so as have most Christians. In their eyes it is unfair discrimination to deny these rights, regardless of the fact that their faiths are not in the majority and are not representative of the population of this country. Chaplaincy in prisons is therefore a site on which all the political challenges, conflicts and negotiations of a multicultural society can be observed in miniature, as it were. It is essential to add that prison chaplaincy can also be a site on which remarkable co-operation, consensus, mutual respect and sensitive understanding have occurred between faith communities. The successes are just as interesting as the problems and failures.

Participation in public life

It is a mistake to think of 'ethnic minorities', 'minority cultures' or 'other faiths' as unitary or monolithic phenomena. They are all cross-cut by such markers of difference as gender, social class, generational differences, 'theological' schools and regional origins (Vertovec 1994). It follows, then, that if policies which aim to generate equal respect and equal opportunities for minorities are to be successful they must take due account of these differences. Another implication is that it is unrealistic to expect that complex, differentiated communities can be adequately represented in the public sphere by single organisations or representatives. Since power and authority are distributed across many different, and often competing, organisations pursuing the interests of minorities in different ways, their involvement in the nation's public life is also likely to take different forms. Religious organisations and activities are just one avenue through which communities may engage in public life; but they are often high-profile and contentious in the eyes of some journalists and politicians (Commission on British Muslims and Islamophobia 1997). The challenge for us was to understand how, if at all, the provision of religious care for members of other faith communities in prison contributed towards the participation of these communities in public life.

The phrase 'participation in public life' is vague and general. It can refer to a host of very different things. We deliberately favoured a broad characterisation of this central object of our research because we wanted our inquiry to be wide-ranging. We were primarily interested in the access that other faith communities have to facilities funded from the public purse for religion in prisons. This access is conditional upon faith communities having the power, prestige and know-how to be taken seriously as collectivities in their own right and as collectivities that deserve a voice and visibility in the public sphere.

The sort of things that count as evidence of participation in public life are partly objective in the sense of, for example, collective membership of public decision-making groups; being consulted by public officials as a collectivity as a matter of course; receiving official representation on public bodies; obtaining funding from statutory sources; or having the opinions of leading representatives of a faith community taken formally into account by official bodies. But the phrase also has more subjective or impressionistic meanings in the sense of, for example, feeling that a faith community's collective views are taken seriously; believing that collective sensitivities and values receive due respect outside a faith community; or being confident that access to public resources is obtained as of right instead of as a result of special pleading, patronage or tokenism.

The term 'public' is notoriously slippery. Indeed, it carries several different meanings in this discussion, but two aspects are particularly important for us. In the first place, 'public' implies difference from 'private' or personal. The significance of this distinction is that it emphasises our focus on the collective dimension of religion. Our main interest here is not in the religious beliefs, knowledge, experiences, actions or emotions of individuals in, for example, their private devotions or private study. On the contrary, our research concerns the status and activities of religious collectivities (for example, prison chaplaincy organisations) and religious categories of people (for example, Muslims) in settings to which most members of English society have access either by right or necessity rather than by choice. Religious activities in prisons are public in this first sense of being visible, collective and available on demand to all people who enter the prison system.

The second main meaning of 'public' in this context has to do with legally constituted authorities. Chaplaincies in prisons are public in this second sense of being organised and largely funded by bodies authorised by statute on behalf of the entire body politic. Here the implied difference is between private in the sense of either voluntary or 'for commercial purposes' and public in the sense of legally required and applicable to everyone. Participation in public life, in this particular sense of the phrase, is especially significant for minorities who can measure the extent to which they enjoy the same rights and opportunities as other sections of the population by their ease of access to public resources, public offices and public organisations.

It is worth mentioning, in passing, a third but less central meaning of 'public' in our research. We deliberately narrowed the focus down to the specific activities associated with the provision of religious and pastoral care in prisons. But 'the public sphere' is a wider phenomenon which only partly overlaps with these specific activities. 'The public sphere' refers to an area of social life which is neither the sphere of the family nor the state nor the world of work and commerce. The public sphere is often defined as a separate area of social life where citizens are presumed to have the freedom to exchange their opinions, mobilise themselves in campaigns or movements and organise voluntary associations. We did not directly study the involvement of other faith communities in the public sphere understood in this broad way, although there is no doubt that their contributions continue to be extensive and valuable. We were interested in a different issue. We wanted to know whether full participation in prison chaplaincies could serve to empower other faith communities to make an even more effective contribution to the public sphere if they wanted to. Put differently, the question is whether full participation in the relatively marginal activities of publicly funded chaplaincies in prisons could enhance the power of other faith communities to influence more publicly visible and more politically sensitive areas of social life.

At first glance, it may seem paradoxical or even naïve to think that other faith communities could improve their involvement in public life by mobilising themselves in pursuit of equal respect and equal opportunities for the religious activities of their co-religionists in prison. Surely, prisons are not part of public life. And would it not be foolish or politically risky for minority communities to draw attention to their members who have been convicted of serious offences? No doubt, there are members of these communities who would prefer to dissociate themselves from all questions about prisons. For example, the story of a hunger strike among Muslim prisoners with which we prefaced this chapter provoked an ironic letter to the Editor of the newspaper which had published the story. The correspondent, who had an Asian name, was amused by

the thought that here are convicts who have committed probably sins far greater than consuming 'haram' food – and yet here they are complaining about their rights as Muslims . . . If [they] had respect for their own religion they would not have dealt in illegal drugs or committed murders, robberies, fraud, etc. Far from complaining, they should genuinely attempt to try and repent for their wrong-doing and be thankful they aren't in prison in India, Pakistan or Bangladesh – or Saudi Arabia! (*Eastern Eye* 21 June 1996)

But there are also counter-arguments.

On the one hand, the extent to which a minority faith community takes seriously the question of how its members in prison are cared for in religious terms could be considered a measure of its public responsibility. If such a community takes charge of this responsibility instead of ignoring it or of leaving it to some other agency it could be said to be participating in public life. This would be a matter not only of looking after its own members but also of contributing towards public debates about religion in prisons. On the other hand, involvement in schemes for supplying religious care to prisoners would mean that minority faith communities would be likely to achieve official recognition. In so far as they were then regarded by agencies of the state as suitable points of contact and perhaps co-operation they might reach positions of influence or even power. They might bring about change in public policy or practice. The likelihood of this happening depends in large part on the Church of England's prison chaplains.

Facilitation and brokerage

As we shall see in chapter 2, the provision of religious care to prisoners is a statutory responsibility which is exercised by the Prison Service Chaplaincy. This is a division of the Prison Service staffed mainly by Church of England clergy but with small numbers of Roman Catholic and Methodist Church representatives. The Chaplain General of the Prison Service Chaplaincy, an Archdeacon of the Church of England, shares overall responsibility for this aspect of prisons in England and Wales with senior chaplains from the Roman Catholic and Methodist churches. Nevertheless, the Church of England plays the leading role in prison chaplaincy. Its chaplains are therefore in the best position to influence the kind of access that prisoners belonging to other faiths have to appropriate religious care and religious specialists. The chaplains act as 'gatekeepers' as far as the representatives of other faith communities are concerned, in the sense that they need the chaplains' invitation, permission, support and, sometimes, patronage in order to gain access to 'their' prisoners.

This book is an extended examination of these relations between Anglican prison chaplains and members of other faith communities. The focus will be on two facets of the 'gatekeeper' role: facilitation and brokerage. The term 'facilitation' refers to the various ways in which Church of England chaplains make it possible for members of other faiths to practise their religion in prisons. It is a form of enabling and is used in connection with, for example, providing copies of sacred texts or rooms in which worship can take place. 'Brokerage' is a more contentious term. Some may consider it to be a loaded term which devalues the work that the Church of England does in relation to other faith communities by implying that this work is contractual, commercial or even venal. We need to make it clear, however, that we do not wish to convey any such narrow or negative meaning. On the contrary, 'brokerage' in this context means acting as an intermediary between two other parties. A broker negotiates with one party on behalf of another, often in circumstances where it would be difficult or impossible to reach agreement without the broker's 'good offices'. In these circumstances, brokerage is an honourable and often hazardous undertaking which relies as much on goodwill and self-sacrifice as on payment. This is an important consideration because, as we shall argue at length, the relationship between Anglican chaplains and ministers of other faiths in prison chaplaincies rests partly on the customary responsibilities of chaplains (for which they are paid) and partly on their goodwill 'beyond the call of duty'.

Studies of multiculturalism and equal opportunities rarely consider the role of agents who act as the intermediaries between majority and minority communities. This is a serious omission because, as our research on prison chaplains revealed, the respect accorded to minority cultures is often mediated by people who enjoy power, privileges and authority. Of course, the active struggles conducted by minorities themselves are also important or even decisive in many cases. Nevertheless, the process of gaining equal respect and equal opportunities can be significantly advanced or retarded by influential insiders and gatekeepers.

On the other hand, our study also uncovered the limits to which prison chaplains could go in their roles as facilitators and brokers. These limits partly reflected personal attitudes and ideological views; but the organisational structures and physical surroundings in which the chaplains worked exercised even more powerful influences over their capacity to give members of other faith communities access to the resources and facilities that they required for their religious practices. The Prison Service imposes severe constraints on the chaplains' freedom of manoeuvre. In this respect it is the nature of the unstated 'contract' between the Church of England and the Prison Service which calls for close scrutiny. This is one of the few points at which the complex and subtle relationships between established church, state and nation in England can be examined in their day-to-day operations. This book is the first full-length analysis of these relationships and processes.

The Church–State relationship is thrown into even sharper relief by questions about the treatment accorded to other faiths in prison. The demands from non-Christian religions for equal respect and equal opportunities to be given to them in the state's own institutions are a test of the state's tolerance and sensitivity to 'different' interests. But the demands are an even greater challenge to the Christian church which services prisons on the state's behalf.

The Church of England is caught in a dilemma. On the one hand it clearly has a Christian mission to prisoners and prison staff but, on the other, it accepts the need to treat all people alike – including members of other faith communities. Put differently, the Church of England enjoys the privileges of being the most representative religious organisation in England and of representing the state but at the same time it acknowledges that it has a special responsibility to all people in England who call for its services. In the words of the Archbishop of Canterbury,

We are a national Church. This gives us immense privileges as well as responsibilities. The strength of being such a Church is that there is a recognisable parochial network throughout the land. People have a right to call on us and seek the sacramental ministries of our Church. (Carey 1993: 182)

This line of reasoning was taken further by two Anglican experts on relations with other faiths:

Hopefully, there is now a deeper recognition in Britain that adherents of many religions now co-exist here and that they must be given the respect and freedom traditionally enjoyed by the established church. Indeed, we would claim that only if the Church of England actively promotes the respect and freedom for others can its privileged position still be justified. (Hooker & Lamb 1993: xiii)

The question for our study was how far does the Church of England take its universalist mission in supporting individuals and organisations not associated with Christianity but actively involved with other faiths. This is a major challenge for a national church which has lost much of its hold over the majority of the nation's adults and which is witnessing the growth of non-Christian communities on its own territory – to say nothing of the growing strength of conservative evangelical denominations and of the Roman Catholic Church.

This study of religion in prisons also raises questions about the state's capacity to accommodate the demands for equal respect for other faiths among its prisoners so long as the main responsibility for prison chaplaincy remains in Anglican hands. Is it conceivable that the Church of England's brokerage is an expedient for keeping intractable problems of religious diversity under control? Would it be easier if the provision of religious and pastoral care could be administered by a religiously neutral agency? Or does the close link between the state and the Church of England in prison chaplaincy help to place a 'religious straitjacket' on 'racial' and ethnic tensions in prisons? We are unable to answer all these questions here but we raise them for the first time in the context of an empirical study of the management of religious diversity in prisons.

The focus is primarily on prisons in England and Wales where the influence of the established Church of England is still pervasive, although we shall also make some comparisons with the situation in prisons governed by the Scottish Prison Service and the Northern Ireland Prison Service.[3] Our interest in the practical implications of the link between the Church of England and agencies of the state in a country with growing religious diversity dictated such a precise focus for our work. Nevertheless, chapter 7 will broaden the analysis by considering how chaplaincy services are provided in state and federal prisons in the United States. The main reason for including material on the United States was to demonstrate the possibilities and the problems of adopting a rigorously neutral attitude towards religious differences among prisoners and, therefore, to throw the distinctiveness of the chaplaincy arrangements in England and Wales into sharper relief. We collected this material by visiting several prisons in the United States in 1995 and 1996, interviewing key chaplains and prison administrators, and analysing published and unpublished literature on the subject.

Research strategies

Triangulation

Given our interest in the social configuration of prison chaplaincy, we had to seek and listen to the views expressed by people in many different positions. We paid particular attention to Anglican chaplains for two reasons. The first was that we wished to focus on chaplains representing the *national* church. They have a statutory responsibility for all staff and inmates regardless of religious registration. Since they are therefore the principal 'brokers' for other faiths, we preferred to keep the focus of research firmly on them. The second reason was that relations between Anglican, Catholic and Methodist chaplains are thoroughly institutionalised in accordance with a Concordat signed in 1971 and refined since then. These relations are less problematic and therefore less interesting to researchers who are concerned with brokerage and empowerment in a multi-faith society. In any case, our research showed that it was the Anglican chaplains who routinely took responsibility for relations with Visiting Ministers representing other faiths. We nevertheless investigated Catholic and Methodist chaplains' opinions about the Anglicans' practice of facilitation for other faiths. In addition, we collected information from representatives of other faiths – Buddhists, Hindus, Jews, Muslims and Sikhs. We also needed to listen to staff in chaplaincy organisations as well as to leading representatives of the main faith communities. Only a form of methodological *triangulation* (Denzin 1970; Gilbert 1993) could make it possible to understand how prison chaplaincy operated as seen from these differing viewpoints. This means examining a subject from different points of view with a variety of methods. So, we made sure that we collected information from all these interested parties. And we did so by means of several conventional methods:

> interviews;
> questionnaires;
> analysis of official documents and background literature;
> on-site observation.

Equally important to the triangulation strategy was the attempt to ask respondents and informants from all groups to comment on *the same issues*. In this way, we were able to piece together a sort of Cubist picture of what some common situations look like to actors standing in different relations to them, although it was sometimes virtually impossible to recognise that informants from different groups were actually talking about the same thing. For example, on the question of whether the supply of religious artefacts for members of other faiths (prayer mats, incense and sacred texts) was adequate, 89 per cent of Anglican prison chaplains said 'yes', but only 25 per cent of Visiting Ministers from other faith communities agreed with them. Alternatively, only 12 per cent of Visiting Ministers could identify any multi-faith events in the prisons that they visited, whereas 33 per cent of chaplains reported that they had participated in such events.

The reason for wanting to compare the accounts given by different actors was not to check their validity or to construct a composite picture of reality. It was more a matter of wanting to appreciate the distinctiveness of the different perspectives and therefore the clash of the competing claims to truth. Prison chaplaincy is a politicised domain in some respects, and we wanted to grasp the significance of the tensions, conflicts and misunderstandings which make it such a challenging area in which to work (as well as an area of agreement and co-operation in some cases) in a religiously diverse society.

Qualitative and quantitative

One of the dilemmas facing social researchers is how to weigh up the relative merits of different methods for collecting information. We started with the intention of investing most of our time in predominantly qualitative research strategies, that is, interviews with heads of prison chaplaincy organisations and long periods of fieldwork at a small number of chaplaincy sites. This appeared to be a sensible strategy, but our opinion changed when we received greater co-operation than had been expected from staff in the PSC headquarters. Since they were willing to provide us with lists of all Anglican prison chaplains and of the Visiting Ministers of other faiths as well, the opportunity to sample opinion from a much larger and more diverse group of actors seemed too good to miss. Questionnaires were sent to virtually all Anglican clergy and Visiting Ministers active in prison chaplaincy in England. The details are shown in Table 1.1.

Open-ended questions, lots of them, were at the heart of the questionnaires. Pilot versions were tried out on people from all faith groups who were already associated with our research in the early Summer of 1995. In total, revised questionnaires were administered in the Summer of 1995 to 335 individuals, 173 of whom provided completed, usable returns. Reminders were issued on three occasions at intervals of two months, and

Table 1.1. *Response rates to questionnaires*

	Questionnaires distributed	Questionnaires returned	Response rate
Visiting Ministers in prisons	214	91	43%
Anglican chaplains in prisons	121	82	68%
Total	335	173	52%

additional attempts were made to improve the low response rate from Visiting Ministers. The overall response rate was 52 per cent. This is towards the lower end of the acceptable range, but the significantly lower rate for Visiting Ministers is disappointing. We used our contacts in the other faith communities, especially the leading representatives on our project's steering group, to try to stimulate a higher response rate from Visiting Ministers. These efforts were successful only to a small extent but at least they provided us with impressionistic and anecdotal information about the apparent reluctance of some Visiting Ministers to complete questionnaires. Lack of familiarity with the English language was the major problem among Hindus and Sikhs. Other problems were to do with the failure or inability of prison staff to deliver questionnaires to Visiting Ministers who visited only infrequently and the fact that it was not possible to replace some Visiting Ministers promptly when they ceased to serve at some establishments. The Prison Service Chaplaincy's list of Visiting Ministers was therefore out of date or inaccurate in some cases.

We did not abandon the other parts of our original strategy: we simply reduced their relative significance. And, of course, a certain amount of interviewing, observation and the analysis of official documents still needed to be done before the design of questionnaires could be finalised. But, instead of using information from the questionnaires as a check on our other impressions of prison chaplaincy sites we reversed the order of events and priorities, thereby establishing some generalisations from the questionnaires first and, only secondly, using observation to inspect these provisional generalisations.

There was also a political reason for deciding to favour extensive reliance on questionnaires. We knew that our study was going to be contentious in some circles. We also knew that very little research had ever been conducted on prison chaplaincy in England. In the circumstances, then, it seemed sensible to amass a wealth of data reflecting, we hoped, representative opinions so that it would be relatively difficult to dismiss our findings as 'soft' or partial. The phrase 'there is safety in numbers' takes on a very specific meaning in this context.

Analysis of questionnaire data

With so many open-ended questions on each questionnaire, we knew that it would be difficult to store the data in such a way that analysis would be practicable. Computerised methods of analysis recommended themselves in theory as an expedient for handling so much complex information. But most of the available software seemed designed either to cope with interview transcripts and continuous text by a code-and-retrieve method or to convert respondents' words into numbered codes for analysis in statistical packages. What we needed was a package for handling numerical and non-numerical data with equal facility.

'Idealist' is the package that we eventually selected for storing and aiding the analysis of questionnaire data. It functions as an all-purpose database package but it has the incomparable advantage of being able to store more or less unlimited amounts of text in any text field. We were therefore able to enter the full text of all answers to all questions into the database and then to review, retrieve or print any part, or combination of parts of, the text for analysis. The inputting was lengthy and tedious, but on balance the advantages outweighed the disadvantages. Anyway, it is unlikely that we could have coped with the answers to so many open-ended questions from so many respondents by any other method.

Interviews and observation

Semi-structured interviews were conducted with sixty chaplains, Visiting Ministers and co-ordinators of Visiting Ministers. We interviewed most of them during our visits to prisons, but some were interviewed on the telephone or in their places of work. The informants among Christian chaplains included twenty Anglicans, eleven Methodists, and twelve Roman Catholics. The Visiting Ministers and the three co-ordinators whom we interviewed included one Buddhist, three Hindus, one Jew, eight Muslims and four Sikhs.

In some cases, the purpose of the interviews was to reconnoitre unknown territory and, in other cases, to seek responses to the preliminary findings of the questionnaire surveys and to elicit broad reflections on the central issues of prison chaplaincy as seen from the informants' points of view. Questions about policy and future strategies were also in the schedules. Most of the interviews with chaplains and Visiting Ministers took place in prisons in response to our requests for permission to visit the establishments in order to talk to as many informants as possible. Anglican chaplains responded willingly and promptly to all but one of our requests for access to the prisons where they worked. The exception concerned an establishment for female inmates which had been at the centre of a major controversy at the time of our approach. In the event, we were able to interview one of the chaplains from this particular prison by telephone.

In view of the highly localised and variable character of prison chaplaincy, we felt it necessary to spend time *observing* the work of chaplains and Visiting Ministers and absorbing the atmosphere in which they work. We thought that it was important to ground and to check the opinions that we had collected about such things as exclusion, inclusion, power, authority, accountability and representation in the pattern of everyday social interactions among chaplains and other prison personnel. The physical setting and the quality of artefacts in prisons were also considered relevant to our understanding of how chaplaincy, as a social production, works or does not work.

By selecting the sites for observation in the light of initial findings from the questionnaires we were using 'case studies' as a way of checking our empirical discoveries and theoretical hunches. In other words, we chose fourteen particular sites for observation during one-day visits because they seemed likely to confirm or disconfirm what we thought we had already learned about chaplaincies. Most of our host chaplains arranged for us to visit various parts of their prisons, to talk to prison officers who worked closely with prisoners from 'other faith' backgrounds and to meet as many Visiting Ministers and other chaplaincy workers as were available on the day of our visits. Opportunities to discuss our research briefly with prisoners occurred in some establishments, but the main aim of our visits was to discover precisely how Anglican and other Christian chaplains facilitated the work of Visiting Ministers and how the latter responded to this facilitation.

The variety of establishments that we visited is indicated in table 1.2. Some establishments contained inmates of more than one security category. The labels that we attached to the prisons reflected our assessment of the highest level of security in operation at each site. None of them housed female inmates, but we interviewed chaplains from three women's establishments.

Again, the questionnaire findings focused our attention on certain features of social interaction and the physical setting of prison chaplaincy. In turn, our observations caused us to go back and re-inspect the questionnaire data in some respects. This alternation between evidence and inference never reached a natural conclusion. It achieved only provisional closure, and our thinking about the research data has continued to evolve as we have written about them.

Table 1.2. *Types of prisons visited*

High security	1
Medium security	8
Open	1
Psychiatric	1
Young Offenders Institution	3
Total	14

Structure of the book

The provision of religious and pastoral care to prisoners in England and Wales is governed by the Prison Act 1952, successive versions of the Prison Rules and administrative rulings. These instruments form a framework of regulations and customary practices which shape the types of permitted religious activity, the selection of people to foster religion and the place of chaplains and Visiting Ministers of other faiths in the organisational structure of prisons. Chapter 2 will analyse this framework and its implications for chaplains, Visiting Ministers and prisoners. There will also be an analysis of the changing patterns of prisoners' declarations of religious belonging, with special emphasis on the differential growth rates of the main 'other faiths'. Finally, the physical settings in which organised religious activities take place in prison will be discussed in detail because they are at the centre of processes of facilitation, brokerage, negotiation and contestation.

Having established the primacy of Church of England chaplains over the provision of religious and pastoral care in prisons we shall examine various aspects of chaplains' work in chapter 3. Their training, duties and changing structural position all dispose them to show respect for other faiths, but their views on how the practices of non-Christian religions should be resourced indicate some limits to their tolerance and even-handedness.

Switching to the Visiting Ministers of other faiths in chapter 4 we shall highlight the contrast between the specialist status that many of them have in their own communities and the dependence on Anglican chaplains which they are compelled to display in their prison work. Although there are obviously differences between the patterns of Visiting Ministers' religious and pastoral activities which reflect their differences in beliefs, practices and forms of authority, the Prison Service's regulations and administrative procedures have some standardising effects. Limitations on resources and facilities place further constraints on the prisoners' opportunities to practise religions other than Christianity.

When we discuss day-to-day relations between Church of England prison chaplains and Visiting Ministers of other faiths in chapter 5, a clearer picture will emerge of the perceived inequality of opportunities for prisoners of different faith communities to receive religious and pastoral care. Against a background of generally supportive attitudes on the part of chaplains and of gratitude on the part of Visiting Ministers, we shall describe the causes of mutual misunderstandings and suspicions. Our analysis will also show that fundamentally different conceptions of religious and pastoral care are at stake in some cases. These different ideas about the purposes of prison chaplaincy are reflected in differences of opinion about ways of improving the religious arrangements for prisoners belonging to other faiths.

Chapter 6 tackles the thorny issue of social inclusion and exclusion. It exposes the very limited extent to which Visiting Ministers are included in the social, administrative and operational aspects of chaplaincy 'teams'. Evidence of prison authorities' lack of sensitivity towards the cultural implications of other faiths is also assessed. But most of the chapter is concerned with the forms of brokerage practised by Anglican chaplains on behalf of other faiths and with the implications of this brokerage for the future of provision for other faiths in prison. Studies of relations between majority and minority communities have rarely taken the notion of brokerage seriously enough.

The point of comparing the arrangements for religious practice in English and American prisons in chapter 7 is to tease out the consequences of contrasting patterns of Church–State relations and of completely different systems for assuring equal respect and equal opportunities for all accepted religions. Our argument is that the US system has the advantage of being transparent and of being based on relatively clear-cut notions of prisoners' rights or entitlements but is also inflexible. By comparison, the English system is relatively opaque, *ad hoc* and dependent on unequal relations of patronage but is also flexible and more generous in terms of the space and time allowed for religious practices.

The conclusions in chapter 8 will tie the empirical findings back into the opening discussion of multiculturalism and equal opportunities but will also discuss the complexities facing a national church which, in conjunction with the state, presides over a system of chaplaincy in prisons which is struggling to adapt to the rapid growth of religious diversity among prisoners. The argument will stress that the challenges presented by non-Christian faiths call into question some of the taken-for-granted assumptions about relations between the state and the nation. This dimension is entirely missing from current debates about 'the state we're in' (Hutton 1995) but it is actually a crucial aspect of the forces of social integration and social exclusion.

2 Chaplaincy, chaplains, chapels and other faiths

The current arrangements for providing the inmates of prisons in England and Wales with pastoral and religious care have evolved from earlier types of prison regimes in which the Christian religion was dominant and Church of England clergy were the only chaplains. It is still true that Christianity is the dominant religious force in prisons, but two things have changed. The first is that religions other than Christianity, or 'other faiths', are now represented to varying degrees among the staff and inmates of most prisons, with the result that a variety of types of pastoral and religious care is available. The second change is that Church of England clergy now work not only alongside Roman Catholic and Free Church chaplains in increasingly inter-denominational schemes of co-operation but also alongside 'Visiting Ministers' representing other faiths. Both of these changes are a consequence of the growth of religious diversity in British society inside and outside prisons.

How is pastoral and religious care provided? What are the statutory, administrative and customary requirements affecting its delivery? What kind of personnel delivers this care? In what conditions do they work? And how many prisoners register as potential beneficiaries? This chapter will begin to answer these questions and will set the scene for the more fundamental question of whether all prisoners have an equal opportunity to receive pastoral and religious care which is appropriate to their religious identity. This question goes to the heart of concerns about the Church of England's role as a 'broker' for other faiths. In turn, the same question raises the issue of how an established church with strong links to the nation state can adapt to the growth of religious diversity in its territory.

The framework of prison chaplaincy

The origins of the term 'chaplain' are not entirely clear, but it probably derives from the Latin 'capella' meaning a cloak. Its modern meaning is said to come from the story that St Martin of Tours shared his cloak with a beggar one night in the fourth century. The cloak eventually became a religious relic and a talisman in battle. The priests who guarded the cloak became known as 'capellani' or 'chaplains' in English. If this story is correct, the root meaning of the term is clearly to do with religiously motivated care for those in need.

The history of chaplaincy in British prisons prior to the late eighteenth century legislation which authorised Justices to appoint and to pay chaplains in all their penal establishments is even more obscure than the etymology of 'chaplain'. There is no doubt, however, about the transformations wrought by John Howard's campaigns to reform prison regimes. He successfully advocated that chaplains should conduct religious services as well as welfare and pastoral duties. Experiments that took place in the early nineteenth century with prison regimes based on an entirely religious foundation led to a progressive enhancement of the chaplain's role to the point where

The great Victorian prisons were designed to have religion at their core. At the centre of most of them stands a Chapel, sometimes the size of a Cathedral, where all prisoners had perforce to come for Sunday worship . . . [T]he chapels remain, an enduring reminder of the original purpose of our prisons. They were designed, on a philosophical basis of Christianity and Utilitarianism, as factories of virtue . . . [O]fficers carried staves in one hand and bibles in the other. The chaplain was there to point the finger of accusation, to call to repentance, to work on the vulnerable as a technician of guilt. (Potter 1991)

Curiously, one of the historians of British penal policy considered that the 'original importance of the chaplain was that he was the one *neutral* force in an otherwise impersonal and repressive regime' (Grünhut 1948: 252). There was nothing neutral, however, about chaplains' views on the centrality of religion to successful prison regimes (McConville 1995; McGowen 1995).

The robust opinion of a writer who served a number of prison sentences at the turn of the nineteenth and twentieth centuries casts an entirely different light on the position of chaplains:

in 1879–80 and again in 1909–10 (but less so) I found little else but cant in the prison chapel, flavoured with a veneer of stale jokes and something which might pass muster for humour . . . I thought I was dealing with Christians on both occasions . . . I was mistaken on both occasions. I found they were censorious officials clad with a garb of innocence and the aroma of virtue. (Cook *c.* 1913)

So, opinions varied on the value of prison chaplains' work, but there can be no doubt about the power they wielded in the early modern prison.

The first major legislative reform of prison took place in 1823. It required chaplains, along with governors and medical officers, to visit cells frequently and to keep written records of their visits. A second reform, based on the Prison Ministers Act of 1863, permitted for the first time the appointment of ministers who were not Anglicans (in practice, only Roman Catholics, members of the Free Churches and Jews) but did not allow prisoners to register as 'nil religion' or as members of any other faith. After World War I, however, prisoners were allowed to apply for permission to be excused from compulsory attendance at chapel. (Compulsory chapel attendance for those who had not opted out was not abolished until 1976.) Many chaplains worked on a part-time basis in prisons in the inter-war period, combining their prison duties with responsibility for a parish. Only large establishments tended to have full-time chaplains with the status of civil servants. Even the vast majority of full-time chaplains did not have permanent, pensionable positions from the 1920s onwards but were appointed for a probationary year and then for a further six years with the possibility of a final extension to their contract of five years. Very few chaplains were recommended for service until the retirement age of sixty. In fact, only the Chaplain General, who was head of the Prison Service Chaplaincy (PSC), the Assistant Chaplain General and three other full-time chaplains held permanent posts in 1972. In line with the civil service's changing employment practices, however, this system of 'periodic' appointments was replaced in the mid-1970s with a system which permitted full-time chaplains to remain in post until normal retirement age unless they chose to leave the PSC earlier or were deemed unsuitable for continuing employment as prison chaplains.

Arrangements for the religious and pastoral care of prisoners from other faiths were local and mostly *ad hoc*, but at least there was a recognition of their special dietary requirements. For example, the dietary card issued to prisoners after World War II specified: 'If you are a Jew, a Mohammedan or a Hindu, the food which will be issued to you will include a substitute for those items which you are precluded from eating on religious grounds' (Fox 1952: 457).

The Prison Act, 1952 introduced much greater standardisation into all aspects of prison administration, including religion. It did not, however, change the conditions for prisoners' practice of religion. The established Church of England remained responsible for all chaplaincy arrangements, although in practice ecumenical co-operation with Roman Catholics and Methodists was beginning to occur. The Prison Act 1952, which is still the operative legislation in England and Wales,[1] made the following provisions for the practice of religion:

(a) The Act requires every prison to have a chaplain and every chaplain to be a 'clergyman of the Church of England'. Chaplains are to be appointed by the Secretary of State, although they must also be licensed by the local bishop.

(b) The religious 'denomination' to which each prisoner belongs must be recorded. Information about prisoners' religious registrations must be provided to any religious minister appointed to visit a prison.

(c) If the number of prisoners belonging to a 'religious denomination' other than the Church of England is high enough, relevant ministers may be appointed or allowed to visit them in prison. The Act forbids these ministers to visit prisoners who do not belong to their denomination, although the Home Office reminded Governors in January 1992[2] that a prisoner was no longer forced to re-register as a member of a different religion in order to meet a minister of that religion to discuss a possible change of registration.[3] Nevertheless, all prisoners, regardless of their religious registration, retain the right to receive the services of the Anglican chaplain.

The Prison Rules of 1964 further specify that prisoners may apply for permission to change their religious registration and that certain approved religious books should be available for the personal use of every prisoner. Echoing the kind of sentiments that were to guide later statements of the Prison Department's *raison d'être*, Standing Order 7A of 1989 (p.1) states:

The Prison Service respects the need for all prisoners to be free to practise their religion. It makes provision, therefore, for prisoners to participate in worship and other religious activities of a kind that may lead to personal growth, the fullest possible life in the prison setting and preparation for release into the community at the end of a sentence.

It also stipulates that appropriate chaplains and Visiting Ministers will be asked to submit reports on prisoners whose life sentences are being reviewed or who are being considered for release on licence. Finally, there is a recognition that 'prisoners are entitled to diet and dress which accord with the requirements of their religion as agreed between a relevant religious body and Prison Service Headquarters' (p.4).

Two aspects of the administrative framework for prison chaplaincy in England and Wales call for special comment.

(i) The first is that it is a statutory requirement for every prison establishment to have a chaplain who is a 'clergyman of the Church of England'. Administrative responsibility for chaplaincy now lies with the PSC, a department of the Prison Service within the Home Office, most of the principal officers of which are Anglican clergy. (The exceptions are the Principal Roman Catholic Chaplain, a Senior Roman Catholic Chaplain and the Superintendent Methodist Chaplain, who is paid by his own denomination.) The Chaplain General of the PSC, who holds the status of archdeacon in the Church of England, is Head of Chaplaincy Services and, as such, is fully integrated into the senior management structure of the Prison Service but ceased to be a member *ex officio* of the Prison Board many years ago. At the same time, he is personally commissioned by the archbishops of Canterbury, York and Wales to administer the PSC and he meets regularly with the Bishop to Prisons.

The linkage between the PSC and the General Synod of the Church of England is more complex. Following the report of a Commission established by the Church Assembly in 1957 'to enquire into the Church's ministration and use of the opportunities for evangelism in Her Majesty's prisons' (Church Assembly 1960), it was decided in 1961 to set up the Prison Chaplaincies Council (PCC) to liaise between the Home Office and the Church of England about 'spiritual ministration' in penal establishments, to advise the Church on penal issues, to foster the supply of prison chaplains, to co-operate with the Prison Department in providing training for chaplains and to assist the Church to support chaplains and prisoners during and after imprisonment. For reasons associated with the introduction of synodical government the PCC ceased to exist in 1976, and its functions were taken over by an Advisory Group of the Board for Social Responsibility.[4] The Chaplain General became a member *ex officio* of the General Synod and of the Board for Social Responsibility's Advisory Group on Criminal Justice Affairs, but discussion of prison chaplaincy virtually disappeared from the Board's Annual Reports in the 1980s. On the other hand, all dioceses are now encouraged to accept some responsibility for discussion of penal affairs through their Boards of Social Responsibility. The Chaplain General has also sought to establish a network of diocesan contacts as a way of keeping prison matters firmly in the minds of all clergy and laity.

(ii) The second point to emphasise is that Church of England chaplains tend to be regarded as having overall responsibility for chaplaincy arrangements and, therefore, for facilitating the pastoral care of prisoners and staff of *all* religious groups – not just Anglicans or even Christians. There is extensive co-operation between Anglican, Roman Catholic and Methodist chaplains, bordering on a non-denominational approach in some places. Indeed, Methodist and Catholic chaplains often stressed their interchangeability with their Anglican colleagues in all but strictly liturgical functions. They provided cover for each other's rest days, holidays and absences through illness. Some even found that they worked more closely than the Anglicans with Visiting Ministers simply because they happened to be on duty on the days when the Visiting Ministers were in their prisons. Nevertheless, 'Notes for the guidance of Visiting Ministers appointed under the Prison Act 1952' specify that 'the Church of England Chaplain is normally the liaison person' for Visiting Ministers. Moreover the job description for Church of England chaplains contains a reference to their responsibility for facilitating 'the observance of their faith by non-Christian inmates, seeking out suitable Visiting Ministers'. The Chief Inspector of HM Prisons emphasised this point in his report for 1994–95:

> 2.31 Religious practice in prison establishments, nominally under the administration of the Church of England Prison Chaplain, has for some time routinely encompassed the various Christian denominations, as well as the Jewish and number of other faiths. Although ecumenical in its outreach in recent years, the Prison Service Chaplaincy is now called upon to facilitate Muslims, Hindus, Bahai's, Buddhists, Sikhs and others to observe their religious traditions under the guidance of their own teachers and ministers. The Chaplaincy also, from time to time, has to deal with other non-mainstream religions.[5]

By comparison, responsibility for chaplaincy services in the Scottish Prison Service and the Prison Service of Northern Ireland is not predominantly in the hands of one church but is distributed among several. In fact, the lack of a co-ordinating agency for chaplains was identified as a problem in Scotland until two full-time chaplains were appointed for the first time in 1990. One was from the Church of Scotland and the other from the Roman Catholic Church. All other chaplains serving Scotland's nineteen prisons at that time were part-time appointees, most of whom combined their prison work with responsibilities for parishes in the locality of prisons. They represented the Church of Scotland, the Roman Catholic Church and the Episcopal Church of Scotland. A Joint Chaplaincy Board brought representatives of these churches together and added a further level of co-ordination. HM Chief Inspector of Prisons for Scotland reported in 1995 that he might be prepared to support the appointment of more full-time chaplains 'provided that links with the local community were maintained or strengthened'.[6]

Just as the Prison Service in England and Wales took time to adjust to the growing numbers of prisoners from the Caribbean, South Asia and East Africa in the 1960s and 1970s (Genders & Player 1989), so the recognition that Hindus, Muslims or Sikhs had specific religious requirements was also slow in coming. As late as 1979, for example, one influential chaplain was still calling for the Prison Department to collect and disseminate information about Asian religions in the same way as it had already done for Judaism (Russell 1979). The same author also warned chaplains about the danger of becoming the 'religion man', for 'In some ways the Prison Department . . . sees the Chaplain as conveniently discharging a role, something like a Head Waiter facilitating arrangements'. This had to be resisted because 'the Chaplain must nevertheless still stand for the Christian faith and avoid being some kind of theosophical ombudsman' (Russell 1979: 12).

As the number of 'other faith' registrations began to increase, the Chaplain General (CG) received more and more requests from Governors and chaplains for guidance about appropriate ways of meeting the religious needs of inmates who were not Christians. Representatives of other faith communities began pressing for greater sensitivity to the religious and cultural requirements of prisoners who did not come from Christian backgrounds. And there was some criticism of the fact that the Prison Service's draft race relations policy made no reference to religion. The first formalised response was to name one of the Assistant Chaplains General (ACG) as the CG's 'Chaplain Advisor for Ethnic and Minority Faiths' in 1982. Under his guidance, a small group of concerned chaplains started discussing their relations with other faiths and eventually produced a newsletter in July 1983.

One of the achievements of these pioneers in the PSC's attempts to consider the implications of the growing proportion of prisoners from other faiths in the prison population was to influence the wording of the Prison Service's Race Relations Statement (Prison Department Circular Instruction 56/1983). In fact, the ACG with responsibility for relations with other faiths became a member of the Prison Service Race Relations Group. Although the Race Relations Act of 1976 had not made it an offence to discriminate unlawfully on the grounds of religion, the new policy in prisons stipulated that 'All prisoners should be treated impartially and without discrimination on grounds of colour, race or religion'. Eventually about half of *Race Relations and Religion. A Pocketbook for Prison Staff* (nd) spelled out how staff should implement the principle that 'Members of non-Christian religions have the same right to practise their faith as Christians and they should be given the same opportunity to do so, whenever practicable in prison circumstances' (p.7). This Pocketbook is a distillation of the much larger and more comprehensive *Directory and Guide on Religious Practices in HM Prison Service*.

The *Directory and Guide* evolved between 1988 and 1993 into a comprehensive package of information about other faiths and the conditions in which they enjoy the right to practise their religion in prison. A revised edition appeared in 1996. It begins with a list of Circular Instructions and Memoranda relating to 'religious and other minorities' in the prison service; and it concludes with a general bibliography, names and addresses of relevant personnel and agencies, some notes on the appointment, induction and accommodation of Visiting Ministers, guidance for

staff escorting other faith inmates to weddings and funerals, and information about Vegans. The central section of the *Directory and Guide* describes the main features of Christianity, Buddhism, Hinduism, Islam,
Judaism and Sikhism plus six 'Religious Groups to which a growing
number of inmates profess membership', *viz.* Baha'i, Jainism, Jehovah's
Witnesses, the Church of Christ, Scientist, the Church of Jesus Christ of
Latter Day Saints and Seventh-day Adventism.

The entry for each faith tradition or group is structured in terms of (a)
theology or teachings (b) practices in the community (c) permitted observances and facilities in prison establishments (d) further reading, and
(e) resources and agencies. The amount of detail supplied about each
religion is varied, but attention is generally given to Holy Days, private
and public practice, sacred writings, diet, dress, ministry, social func-
tioning, and funerals and weddings. Early versions were produced largely in-house but, after complaints from leading representatives of some of
the faith communities in question, much of the information was revised
or augmented, amidst occasional tension and recrimination. Indeed, the
Chaplain General in 1993 described the package as 'a piece of work
which will never be finished, for there are always new religions represented in the list of those whose numbers appear in prison, and the work
needs constantly to be brought up-to-date'.[7] The second revised edition, which appeared in 1996, contains, for example, not only further
information about more faith traditions but also new information about
the special requirements of female prisoners who are members of other
faith communities. No doubt, the choice of a loose-leaf binder format
for the *Directory and Guide* is deliberate in view of the revision and
up-dating which will be constantly needed if the package is to serve its
purpose.

The late-1980s was a period in which formal and informal contacts
developed between Anglican chaplains, other Christian chaplains and
prominent representatives of other faiths, leading in part to the Chaplain
General's creation in 1992 of a Standing Consultation on Religion in
Prison, on which other faith communities were represented. It was also a
time when the rate at which Visiting Ministers were being appointed
accelerated sharply and when serious efforts were made to facilitate the
practice of their religions by other faith inmates. However, these efforts
did not always meet with the approval of those leading representatives of
some faith communities who wanted a major re-organisation of the legal
and administrative framework for prison chaplaincy. Their campaign for
a radical revision of the Prison Act entered its latest phase in March 1996
when they presented a discussion paper to the Secretary of State at the
Home Office in a meeting at the House of Commons. The paper's main

thrust was that 'the central role of one particular religious denomination in the prison system is unacceptable in a multi-faith society, and . . . that in the future when legislation is brought forward, it must ensure that all religions are treated equally'.[8] The paper proposes that an Advisory Council on Religion in Prisons should be created to replace the Standing Consultation on Religion in Prison and that the 'special privileges' conferred on the Church of England in relation to prison chaplaincy should be removed.

The refinement of Prison Service policy on race relations, the inclusion of religion in this policy, the creation of a special post in the PSC headquarters team for overseeing relations with other faiths, the collection and publication of detailed information about other faiths' beliefs and practices, the appointment of growing numbers of Visiting Ministers and the improvement of facilities for the practice of other faiths in prison have all taken place within a virtually unchanged framework of law, Prison Rules and administrative structure in the PSC. Even the evolution of the Prison Service to Agency status and the introduction of privately-run prisons and privatised services in many establishments have left the framework within which the PSC relates to other faiths virtually unchanged. Meanwhile, the proportion of prisoners registered as members of other faith groups continues to rise.

Although prison chaplaincy is not among the most contentious issues affecting prisons at present it has nevertheless been affected by the policy changes, administrative restructuring and political argument over prisons and criminal justice which have been such a salient feature of British political life in the past few decades (see King & Morgan 1980; Stern 1989; Mathiesen 1990; Matthews & Francis 1996). Moreover, prison chaplaincy is a complex, varied and difficult area in which many different groups have an interest. We have tried to disentangle the knot of conflicting interests represented by the Church of England and other faiths, recognising that this particular set of social relations, theological issues and political problems is only one aspect of a much wider range of questions about the governance of a religiously, culturally and ethnically diverse and divided society.

One final note about the context of prison chaplaincy is called for: the variety of penal establishments in England and Wales is wide. It includes Young Offenders Institutions, detention centres, women's prisons, remand prisons, local prisons, privately-run prisons, training prisons, dispersal prisons, open prisons, psychiatric prisons, and so on. In addition, the regimes in operation in all these different types of establishment reflect the variable security risk associated with prisoners who have committed, or are awaiting trial on suspicion of having committed, different

types of offences. Church of England chaplains, including our informants, serve in all these establishments. We tried to gather information
from chaplains working in all types of establishments except detention
centres. The reason for this exclusion is that the density of inmates from
other faiths is so great in these centres that the findings might have
distorted the picture which we obtained from other establishments.

Chaplains

There is at least as much variety among the people who serve as chaplains
as there is among prison establishments. Just as the term 'prison' covers a
bewilderingly diverse collection of institutions, so the term 'chaplain'
applies to people who all share something in common but who also go
about their work in very different ways. We shall consider their backgrounds in detail in later chapters, but it is important at this point simply
to establish the range of positions which they occupy in prison chaplaincies. Beginning with the chaplains and the other members of their Christian chaplaincy teams, we shall sketch their conditions of service and their
opportunities for interaction with members of other faiths. Then we shall
describe the position of Visiting Ministers who provide religious and
pastoral care to prisoners belonging to other faiths.

To set the scene for the 480 chaplains serving in prisons in England and
Wales in 1997 we need to emphasise that the mission of the PSC is
explicitly Christian. Chaplains are first and foremost religious personnel
who may, incidentally, do social work, personal counselling and advocacy
on behalf of prisoners, but their primary responsibility is clearly to deliver
religious and spiritual care in the Christian tradition(s). This applies to all
the Christian chaplains, nearly all of whom are from the Church of
England, the Roman Catholic Church and the Methodist Church. For
example, the purposes identified in the job description for Anglican
chaplains include 'To exercise a pastoral ministry to the whole establishment. To provide opportunities for worship, religious observance and
instruction. To make a *Christian* contribution to the management and
policies of the prison'.[9] The PSC's own brochure about careers in prison
chaplaincy contains the following quotation from a serving chaplain: 'The
Gospel seems so much more vital in prison because our theological
vocabulary of Justice, Guilt, Sin and Liberty has an immediate relevance.
The Bible comes out fresh.'[10] Moreover, chaplains are appointed as
representatives of their particular churches and, although much of their
work is done in a spirit of inter-denominational co-operation, they remain
clergy of these churches throughout their time in the Prison Service. And
although the PSC's brochure claims that 'In many establishments around

the country, the chaplaincy team extends to embrace the non-Christian religions' (p.13), the *Directory and Guide on Religious Practices in HM Prison Service* describes the 'Chaplaincy Team' as 'the Christian Chaplains working together' (p. 4). We shall be assessing this discrepancy between the 'inclusive' and 'exclusive' views of the PSC's status at many points in this book.

While most full-time Anglican chaplains spend many years in the PSC they can also be considered to be 'on secondment' from their churches for varying periods of time. Unless they reach retirement age as prison chaplains, then, many of these clergy will become available for other jobs in parishes or specialised ministries. They are therefore in the interesting position of being 'suspended' between their ecclesiastical organisation and their Government or private employers. In terms of their professional status, they are less like physicians working in health centres or hospitals, then, and more like 'company doctors' employed by private firms. They are salaried professionals for the duration of their contracts with the PSC and therefore to some extent peripheral to the ecclesiastical concerns of most other Anglican clergy. Their rates of remuneration are also higher than those of most parish-based clergy, but on the other hand prison chaplains exercise relatively less control over their place and conditions of work. They have to be prepared to move at short notice wherever the PSC requires them to work – a cause of grievance for some. This is not the case for chaplains in privately run prisons who are appointed by the establishments' Directors without passing through a Home Office Selection Group, although representatives of the PSC and the relevant dioceses serve on their selection panels. The PSC also provides professional supervision of chaplains in privately managed prisons and, according to the submission made by the Chaplain General's staff to a Church of England inquiry into private sector involvement in prisons, it welcomed the fact that chaplaincy provision in the first two privately managed prisons had been 'at least equal to that in the public sector' (Church of England 1996: 48).

Nevertheless, we received the clear impression that relations between the chaplain and the PSC were strained, to say the least, in one of the privately run prisons. This particular chaplain deliberately minimised the amount of contact with the PSC, considering it an imposition to have to submit to an annual inspection and report. It was alleged that, in return, the chaplaincy in this prison received no support from the PSC. In only one other establishment that we visited did we find evidence of such strong tension between the headquarters and local chaplains. The problem in this case centred on the policy of requiring chaplains to move, at short notice if necessary, to wherever their services were needed.

Table 2.1. *Prison chaplains, England and Wales, 1997*

	Full-time				Part-time				Total
	Male	Female	All	(%)	Male	Female	All	(%)	
Church of England	86	18	104	(79)	83	28	111	(32)	215
Roman Catholic Church	20	7	27	(20)	115	0	115	(33)	142
Free Churches	1	0	1	(1)	107	15	122	(35)	123
Total	107	25	132	(100)	305	43	348	(100)	480

Another implication of their position is that the number of chaplaincy posts is determined by the Prison Service rather than by their churches. The Chaplain General negotiates the precise complement of chaplains' posts with other senior managers in the Prison Service headquarters and is therefore constrained by the same kind of budgetary considerations as affect other heads of services in this Government agency. This is only one instance of the severe constraints under which PSC managers have to operate. Prison chaplains enjoy relatively little control over the material and organisational conditions in which they work, although some Visiting Ministers seem to regard chaplains as autonomous and powerful professionals.

The distribution of chaplains by gender, church and employment status is set out in table 2.1.

Full-time chaplains

Virtually all full-time prison chaplains are either from the Church of England or the Roman Catholic Church. There was only one full-time Methodist chaplain at the beginning of 1997, but a further three such appointments were planned for later in the same year. Three of these full-time Methodist chaplains were to be appointed in privately managed prisons. The 104 Anglicans, who constitute 79 per cent of all full-time prison chaplains, fall into two main categories. The majority of them pass through a Home Office selection procedure and are appointed to prisons when vacancies occur. They may begin as Deputy Chaplains in some establishments, but this is officially regarded as a probationary, training grade in which newly qualified chaplains are not expected to spend much longer than one year. Permanent positions are not always available, however, and some appointees have spent several years in the Deputy Chaplain grade. In any case, there is a formal programme of professional development activities for chaplains in the early phases of their career, although staff shortages and conditions of work do not always permit them to complete the programme on schedule. A few of those who remain in the PSC for most of their clerical career are appointed to the rank of Senior Chaplain in establishments with several other chaplains.

In addition to the category of full-time Anglican chaplains who enter chaplaincy through the Home Office selection procedure there is another category of people who come to chaplaincy by other routes. Most of them are officers in the Church Army, that is, trained evangelists who serve full-time as lay or ordained members of this uniformed society for practical evangelism. Other chaplains and assistant chaplains are priests or deacons who are supplied by dioceses to serve in the prisons of their locality or who are appointed, after consultation with the PSC, by the Directors of privately-run prisons.

The twenty-seven full-time Roman Catholic chaplains, who amount to roughly 20 per cent of all full-time prison chaplains, are found mainly in establishments where the number of Catholic prisoners is relatively high. They are selected, trained and appointed entirely by their own Church's authorities and they remain under the tutelage of their own bishop or the head of their order as well as that of the Principal Roman Catholic Chaplain in the PSC headquarters. Nineteen Roman Catholic full-time chaplains are priests; one is a religious brother; and six are women in religious orders.

Chaplains from all three churches believe that ecumenical co-operation and sharing characterise their working relationships. In the words of a Methodist co-ordinating chaplain in a prison where he actually works for more hours per week than his Anglican counterpart, 'Gone are the days when the Anglican chaplain reigned supreme'. Nevertheless, there was also a large measure of agreement among the Methodists and Catholics that it was still convenient for prison staff to regard the Anglican chaplain as the 'front line' person in the chaplaincy. A Catholic chaplain who was entirely satisfied with the friendly working relationships in the London prison where he served still had to admit that 'officially the Anglican is perceived as *the* chaplain'. And, although some Visiting Ministers had extensive contacts with Methodist and Catholic chaplains, there was still a tendency to refer any problems with other faith communities to full-time Anglican chaplains. This was not acceptable to all our informants from the other two churches, however. In the words of a Catholic chaplain, for example, 'Anglicans would like to box me in'. Rejecting their claim to act as 'the voice of the nation' he wanted to operate more independently. 'Chaplaincy team discourse', in his opinion, was only adopted when it was convenient. He also suspected that sharing responsibility for facilitating the visits of Visiting Ministers became a reality only when the Anglican chaplain did not wish to take the responsibility himself.

Part-time prison chaplains

The proportions of part-time chaplains provided by the three main churches are almost the same: 32 per cent are Anglicans; 33 per cent are Roman Catholics; and 35 per cent are from the Free Churches.

All but one of the 123 Free Church prison chaplains serve on a part-time basis for between seven and twelve hours per week. Only fifteen of them are women. Roughly 10 per cent are under 40 years of age; 30 per cent are between 40 and 50; and 60 per cent are over the age of 50. Most of them are Methodist ministers who are also responsible for one or more churches in the locality of the prison(s) where they serve.[11] Three Free Church chaplains are ministers in the United Reform Church and the Baptist Church but they are regarded, for the purposes of their prison ministry, as 'acting under the supervision of the Superintendent Methodist Chaplain'. In fact, the Methodist Church is charged by the Free Church Federal Council with the responsibility of acting as the 'lead denomination' in prison ministry. Although they look after the religious needs of the relatively small numbers of Free Church prisoners and of Church of Scotland prisoners in England and Wales as their first priority Free Church chaplains also share many of the duties of their full-time colleagues from other churches. Their work may involve, for example, visiting prisoners on residential wings regardless of their religious registration, conducting a monthly service in the prison chapel or standing in for Church of England chaplains when they take leave.

The 226 Church of England and Roman Catholic part-time prison chaplains are also likely to be parish priests who live or work in the vicinity of the prison(s) where they serve for one or more sessions ranging from 1.5 to 9.5 hours per week. They may also be the only chaplains in small establishments which do not warrant the appointment of a full-time chaplain. The precise number of sessions is determined by the Governor, taking account of the number of inmates in the establishment and the availability of other chaplains.

In fact, most Roman Catholic chaplains visit prisons on this sessional basis and, as a result, tend to act relatively independently from the other members of chaplaincy 'teams'. The Head of Programmes in one of the maximum security establishments we visited regarded part-time chaplains as less strongly committed to chaplaincy work than full-time Anglican chaplains. He recalled incidents at his present and previous prisons when Roman Catholic and Free Church chaplains had failed to co-operate with chaplaincy teams or had been lax about keeping good administrative records. He attributed these problems to the fact that some part-time chaplains are obliged to do prison work simply because their parishes include prison establishments: they do not always volunteer to serve as chaplains. This argument recurred with varying degrees of subtlety in conversations that we had with some, but by no means with all, other administrators and full-time chaplains. Even informants who valued highly the contributions made by part-time chaplains usually insisted that full-time chaplains were the essential framework within which part-timers could work. Nobody suggested that all chaplains should be part-time, although until the mid-1990s this was the situation in the Scottish Prison Service.

Part-time chaplains are well placed to forge relations between the chaplaincy team and churches in the vicinity of their prisons. The Anglican chaplains' job description specifies that they should 'represent the Church to the Prison and the Prison to the Church', so attempts are made to involve the members of local churches in schemes, for example, to take choral singing, amateur dramatics or religious services into establishments. Chaplains are also involved in talking to the surrounding congregations about life in their local prison and about penal issues in general. This is not a major aspect of most chaplains' work, but it can assume significant proportions in the case of open prisons from which inmates are allowed to visit local churches on a regular basis. By contrast, members of the chaplaincy team in a large Allocations Prison in the North of England told us that they had no relations with churches in its inner city locality. No church groups ever visited the prison. This was in sharp contrast to the situation in a maximum security prison in East Anglia where relations with local Free Church congregations seemed to be good.

Chaplaincy volunteers and 'teams'

In addition to the diversity of appointed chaplains, most prison chaplaincies also draw on the voluntary services of individuals who devote variable amounts of their time to prison work. They tend to be people who have retired from paid work or finished bringing up their children. They are active in churches and knowledgeable about their particular religion. Some of them have qualified as, for example, Lay Readers or Deacons. The tasks which they undertake in prison are as varied as their backgrounds. Some of them do clerical work in chaplaincy offices; some spend a lot of time visiting individual prisoners; some offer classes in education, good parenting or citizenship; and others share the statutory duties with full-time chaplains. In fact, they seem to do whatever needs doing at any given time. The time which they devote to their voluntary work in prisons varies from a few hours a week to several days a week. They often supply back-up services if the chaplains are absent.

Brief sketches of two particular volunteers who represented widely differing backgrounds and routes into chaplaincy work can serve as illustrations of the highly diverse ways in which chaplaincy teams operate. The first was a middle-aged woman who regarded her voluntary service in the chaplaincy of a large Victorian prison in the North as a natural application and extension of her training to become a Lay Reader in the Church of England. She visited the prison for several hours almost every day of the week and conducted discussion groups in the evenings. She was concerned about the difficulty experienced by

Muslim prisoners whose willingness to participate in her groups was allegedly being thwarted by prison officers' refusal to allow Muslims to attend meetings for Christians. Her aim was to create opportunities for sharing 'common ground' between prisoners of different faith traditions and thereby to play down the differences between them. At the same time she resisted the idea that the Visiting Imam should be invited to chaplaincy meetings. She felt that, since his commitment was exclusively to Muslim prisoners, it would be inappropriate for him to take part of the collective responsibility for the religious interests of all prisoners and staff in the establishment.

The second volunteer represented a strikingly different route into chaplaincy work. He was using his retirement from professional life to continue a lifelong commitment to Quaker ideals. Not only did he devote three full days each week to work in the chaplaincy of a privately run prison in the North but he was also active in voluntary aspects of the probation service. He was a genial and outgoing individual who clearly relished personal contact with prisoners. He particularly cherished the occasional moments of intimacy, warmth and humour when prisoners confided in him or asked him to do them strange favours. He beamed with delight as he recalled the occasions when he had been asked to read or write letters (on behalf of illiterate prisoners) containing gross obscenities or highly erotic suggestions. We could see that the warmth of his concern for prisoners was reflected in their relaxed responses to him as he accompanied us on a tour of part of the establishment. He was also favourably impressed by the caring attitudes of prison officers who some-times went out of their way to let him know informally that certain prisoners, especially Young Offenders, were experiencing personal diffi-culties. He also made a point of being equally available to prisoners from all faiths and none, confessing that he took more satisfaction from regis-tering an honest prisoner's religious affiliation as 'none' than from record-ing 'C of E, I suppose'.

Full-time, part-time and voluntary Christian workers in prison chap-laincy usually think of themselves as a *team*. Indeed, the term 'chaplaincy team' is widely used by chaplains and prison administrators. We found pride and satisfaction in the extent to which many of these teams operated successfully across denominational boundaries. So much so that when we asked one chaplain whether she had a team, she denied it but insisted that 'We *are* a team!'. Each of the members of her team (which did not include any Visiting Ministers of other faiths, incidentally) was virtually inter-changeable with the others, including the Roman Catholic part-time chaplain. The only task for which none of the others could substitute was conduct of the Mass, in his opinion. Team work was less evident in some other establishments, but we sensed that it usually represented an ideal or aspiration for most Senior Chaplains. One of the latter, working in a prison with a therapeutic regime, put this well when he said, 'We're becoming a team, very slowly'.

The high degree of cohesiveness and co-operation among the Christian chaplains in one particular establishment was repeatedly demonstrated during our visit. The chaplaincy offices were sometimes crowded and busy, with prison staff and volunteers reporting changes to the day's schedule and checking on the whereabouts or welfare of individual prisoners. The rota for various kinds of duties seemed highly complex and flexible, but the atmosphere was generally upbeat and positive. We heard few complaints or expressions of frustration. Above all, there was an evident willingness on the part of the chaplaincy staff to take on whatever tasks needed to be done at any given moment. Even responsibility for conducting reception interviews with incoming prisoners was shared among whoever happened to be available on the day in question, including the chaplaincy volunteers. The motto seemed to be 'Since I'm here I'll do it'. The chaplain confirmed this impression by explaining that formal meetings of the chaplaincy team had been abandoned because everyone was too busy. They saw each other frequently in the course of their duties; communication among them was good; and they trusted each other. That was the chaplain's justification for the lack of team meetings. Moreover, she had a direct line of communication to the head of the prison's administration and felt that she was able to get problems sorted out without the need for prior consultation with her chaplaincy colleagues in a formal way. The situation in the other establishments we visited was similar, with heavy emphasis on inter-denominational co-operation and ecumenical understanding. Free Church chaplains stressed the inter-changeability of Christian chaplains for most purposes. Yet, formal ecu-menical covenants were not common; and no chaplains spoke in favour of trying to make 'ecumenical appointments' of chaplains without regard to their denominational identity.

Although chaplaincy teams tend to operate in an informal and flexible fashion, it is interesting to note that formal agreements do exist between the Church of England, the Roman Catholic Church and the Methodist Church. A Concordat was first agreed in 1971 and subsequently refined in 1983. It recognises that all chaplains 'are colleagues with no relation-ship of superiority or inferiority' and 'are independent in their pastoral work' but that, for the sake of administrative convenience, Church of England chaplains will continue to act as representatives of chaplaincy teams in negotiations with local management – provided that the Angli-cans consult in advance with their other Christian colleagues. This is also the formula governing the basis on which the Chaplain General acts on behalf of the PSC:

> The Chaplain General stands at the head of the Prison Service Chaplaincy and in appropriate consultation with the senior representatives of the other churches concerned he is senior professional adviser to the Secretary of State and officials on all religious matters affecting Prison Department, except where the specific interests of the Roman Catholic Church are involved . . . He is representative spokesman, after appropriate consultation, on behalf of all prison chaplains . . . The Senior Roman Catholic Chaplain is entitled as of right to be consulted about other religious matters having a Roman Catholic perspective.[12]

It seems that 'administrative convenience' refers to the fact that prison Governors were confused by the decision to abolish relations of superiority and inferiority among chaplains because it threatened to deprive them of the long-established practice of regarding the Church of England chaplain as the single point of contact with chaplaincy in their establishments. In turn, chaplains feared that if Governors lacked a single point of contact with chaplaincies there was a danger that chaplaincy would be marginalised in the management structures arising from the re-organisation of the early 1980s based on the recommendations of the May Inquiry into the Prison Services of the United Kingdom. Making the Church of England chaplain *primus inter pares* was therefore an attempt to protect inter-denominational co-operation *and* the organisational integrity of chaplaincies at a time when many chaplains were worried about losing some of their authority and independence as a result of managerial re-organisation and the growth of other 'support' professions in the Prison Service.

Enthusiasm for inter-denominational co-operation was strong and widespread among Church of England and Free Church chaplains in our study. In fact, some regarded any form of denominational division as unhelpful, sometimes citing 'the scandal of particularism' or 'the scandal of separate churches' in support of their claims that ecumenism was indispensable to the operation of chaplaincy. Incidentally, some chaplains also used the same argument about the scandal of particularism as a reason for excluding Visiting Ministers from full membership of chaplaincy teams on the grounds that they lacked even-handed commitment to *all* prisoners and staff.

The principle of inter-denominational co-operation is clear; the practice less so. For, while Anglicans and Methodists certainly appear to work together without difficulty, we sensed a more distant relationship between them and the Roman Catholic chaplains in some establishments. For example, some Roman Catholic chaplains insisted on always conducting the chaplaincy reception interviews for in-coming prisoners of their church, whereas the other chaplains and chaplaincy volunteers were content to conduct reception interviews with prisoners of any church or faith. Similarly, informal interactions between all the chaplains appeared to be cordial in most places, but in some prisons it was rare for Anglicans or Methodists to be invited to enter the separate Roman Catholic chapel. This was explained by one Roman Catholic chaplain in terms of anxiety about losing his denominational identity and of a compensatory desire 'to keep his own prisoners to himself'. He thought that Roman Catholic chaplains 'struggled to find their place in establishments where the Church of England is the statutory authority' and became defensive as a result. This was echoed by the Anglican chaplain of a Young Offenders Institution who sensed some irritation on the part of Roman Catholic and Free Church chaplains with the primacy accorded to the Church of England in prisons. Nevertheless, in our view the strength and frequency of friction between part-time and full-time chaplains of all churches tended to be much lower than the tensions reported in many establishments between Christian chaplains and the Visiting Ministers of other faiths.

Visiting Ministers

The official view of the PSC is that Christian chaplains should ensure that all staff and inmates are able to practise their religion in prison and that this is the reason why chaplains should facilitate and co-ordinate religious and pastoral care for members of other faiths. This work of facilitation is complex and varied, as we shall show in Chapter Five. It is also contentious in some circles and will therefore require thorough analysis. But for present purposes we need only make clear that Christian chaplains undertake this facilitation on behalf of members of other faiths but that they expect Visiting Ministers to supply religious care and instruction to those prisoners and staff belonging to these faith traditions who request it.

Who, then, are Visiting Ministers? They are ministers of religion or other suitably qualified people who can offer religious, spiritual and pastoral care to the members of any religious tradition other than the Church of England, the Roman Catholic Church or the Free Churches. They include representatives of all the major world religions as well as of Christian churches, denominations, and sectarian movements except those in the PSC. None of them works full-time for the PSC, although a few devote much of their life as religious professionals to visiting prisoners. All of them are officially vetted and appointed by Home Office officials or by local prison Governors. Most of them receive fees for their services, and some are reimbursed for the travel expenses which they incur in visiting prisons. As individuals they are highly diverse in background, training and experience of chaplaincy work. Visiting Ministers are also varied in terms of the extent to which they are formally organised as collectivities. The history of Britain as a country with a significant diversity of faith communities is relatively short, and many of the Asian communities are still in the process of establishing their own institutions of civil society – not just for the tiny minority of their members who are in prison. Some faith communities have, in fact, established organisations specifically for the purpose of overseeing the work of their Visiting Ministers in prison. Others are less formally organised but nevertheless concerned about members of their faith who are in prison. The situation in some communities is that a few individuals have assumed responsibility for prison Visiting Ministers but that no formal organisation for this purpose exists.

The most formal organisation of Visiting Ministers exists among Buddhists. The Venerable Ajahn Khemadhammo, of the Wat Pah Santidhamma near Warwick, formed Angulimala, the Buddhist Prison Chaplaincy Organisation, in the mid-1980s after serving as a Visiting Minister for a number of years in many different establishments. About forty Buddhist Visiting Ministers, representing different traditions of Buddhism, currently visit about 200 prisoners who are registered as Buddhists. The Venerable Khemadhammo, two co-ordinators and a secretary/treasurer support the work of these Visiting Ministers and seek to ensure that all prisoners who show an interest in meeting with Buddhists are able to receive visits and relevant literature. Angulimala has also been responsible for creating 'Buddha groves' in four prisons. Each site contains a *rupa* or statue of a seated Buddha figure surrounded by a small garden. And, although the PSC regards Angulimala as the appropriate agency for nominating Buddhist Visiting Ministers, it receives no funding from the state.

Some other faith communities are involved in supporting Visiting Ministers but without creating a special organisation for that purpose. For example, the Jewish Visitation Committee of the United Synagogue in London and the Islamic Cultural Centre in London are both concerned with a wide range of issues affecting, respectively, Jews and Muslims in the UK but they also serve as points of contact between the Prison Service and their respective faith communities. Officials in these organisations keep a watching brief on the interests of prisoners and Visiting Ministers who belong to their communities. They are often consulted when a new or replacement Visiting Minister is being sought. They can also supply religious literature, religious artefacts, training courses and even special food on the occasions of religious festivals if establishments do not provide these resources themselves. Yet, again, there is no funding from the state for the services which they supply, although the PSC has recently offered to purchase a training course for Muslim Visiting Ministers from a Muslim organisation which specialises in adult education from an Islamic point of view.

The case of the Sikh communities is particularly interesting for what it reveals about the one-sided relationship between the Home Office and minority religious communities. Mr Indarjit Singh and a few associates have long acted as the Home Office's main point of contact and as a source of nominations for Visiting Ministers. The initiative originally came from the Home Office in the mid-1970s in the form of a request to the *Sikh Courier* newspaper, precursor of today's *Sikh Messenger*, for assistance and guidance on how best to meet the needs of Sikh prisoners. Mr Indarjit Singh agreed to act as the 'contact point' for answering questions about, for example, diet and festivals. Governors are instructed to consult him if questions arise about Sikh prisoners or Visiting Ministers, but he receives no funding or other support for the time-consuming work which he has been doing continuously for twenty years.[13] He is therefore in the position of being the official representative of Sikhs, at least in the eyes of the Home Office, but lack of resources prevents him from being able to collect all the necessary information about Visiting Ministers or to co-ordinate their training and appointment.

Estimates of the cost of running a small office to co-ordinate Sikh Visiting Ministers were supplied in the early 1990s in response to Home Office requests, but no action followed. In the absence of these basic organisational resources, Mr Indarjit Singh does not believe that the treatment of Sikh prisoners' religious needs is as good as that provided for Christians. A further handicap for Sikhs, as well as for some other religious minorities, is that prison Governors are unlikely to authorise payment of travel expenses to Visiting Ministers who have to make journeys of more than twenty or thirty miles to visit small numbers of inmates. Yet, very few Sikhs currently live in the relatively sparsely inhabited areas of the country where many prisons are located. In short, as far as facilities for meeting their religious needs are concerned, there is no equality of opportunity or treatment between Sikh and Christian prisoners.

Other faith prisoners

There were 130[14] prisons in England and Wales, holding 51,100 inmates, in March 1995. The proportion of inmates who were registered at that time as belonging to such 'other faiths' as Baha'ism, Buddhism, Hinduism, Jainism, Judaism, Islam, Sikhism and Zoroastrianism, varied between prison establishments from 0.4 per cent to 21.4 per cent according to the 82 chaplains from prisons in England who supplied us with information. Since then, the prison population has exceeded 60,000.

There is nothing new about finding prisoners who are not Christian in British prisons. Colonial exploits, warfare overseas and global trade brought people to this country from all over the world in the past few centuries, and some of them were imprisoned. It was originally left to the discretion of the Church of England chaplains, who used to function like Deputy Governors in some establishments, whether these 'other faith' prisoners received any pastoral or religious care. It was not until the second half of the nineteenth century that the law provided for pastoral services to be provided for prisoners who were not members of the Church of England. The Prison Act, 1952 and subsequent administrative measures finally made this 'facilitation' more formal and more standard.

Section 10 of the 1952 Act also formalised the position of Visiting Ministers. It permitted the Secretary of State to appoint ministers who did not belong to the Church of England to visit prisoners of their own denomination if their numbers in any establishment were high enough, although no prisoners were to be visited against their will. Appointed ministers were to receive lists of the prisoners who had 'declared themselves to belong to' their denominations, but they were forbidden to visit any other prisoners. In addition, Section 12(3) of the Prison Rules of 1964 permitted Governors to respond positively to prisoners' requests for regular visits by ministers of their own denomination if no such minister had been appointed. *Circular Instruction 51/89* further specified that 'The Governor and Chaplain will take the necessary steps for the appointment of such Visiting Ministers as may be required to meet the religious needs of prisoners and in accordance with Rule 12 of the Prison Rules 1964'. The inclusion of 'Chaplain' in this procedure is a pointer to many of the issues that will be discussed below.

The growing numbers of inmates from other faiths in British prisons in the 1970s and 1980s (following the large-scale immigration from the Caribbean, South Asia and East Africa which began in the 1950s) raised questions about the arrangements for meeting their religious needs. The Church of England, alongside other Christian churches, responded initially by trying to collect information about these prisoners' religious backgrounds and requirements. It took time to pool and to evaluate the highly variable and informal 'rules of thumb' that chaplains had already devised for helping other faith groups. Informal processes of negotiation and consultation at local and national levels eventually led, as we saw earlier, to the creation of the post of Chaplain Advisor for Ethnic and Minority Faiths and the production of the *Directory and Guide on Religious*

Table 2.2. *Annual census of religious registrations, prisoners in England and Wales, 1991–1997*

	1991	1992	1993	1994	1995	1996	1997	% of total in 1997	% change 1991–97
Main Christian[a]	32,991	33,532	30,334	31,858	30,300	34,452	36,498	62.92%	+11%
Other Christian[b]	644	682	668	719	651	486	527	0.9%	−18%
Main other Faiths:									
Buddhist	183	192	177	168	182	230	226		+24%
Hindu	151	135	161	157	162	201	198		+31%
Jewish	194	203	209	198	178	203	288		+48%
Muslim	1,959	2,095	2,106	2,513	2,745	3,340	3,693		+89%
Sikh	307	313	323	363	353	381	394		+28%
Sub-total	2,794	2,938	2,976	3,399	3,620	4,355	4,799	8.27%	+72%
Other Faiths:[c]	238	268	325	313	179	350	203	0.34%	−15%
Agnostic Atheist None	6,866	7,609	7,415	10,405	11,420	13,556	15,840	27.3%	+130%
Non-permitted Religions[d]	68	85	140	157	129	152	138	0.23%	+103%
Total	43,601	45,114	41,848	46,851	46,299	53,351	58,005	99.96%	+33%

Note: Adapted from 'Annual Religious Census', Prison Service Chaplaincy. The PSC's nomenclature and classification of religious groups are confusing and in some cases questionable. The probability of misregistration is high. We have rationalised the classification of several groups.
[a] Church of England; Methodist; Church of Scotland; Protestant; Pentecostal; Baptist; Roman Catholic; Non-Conformist.
[b] Calvinist; Celestial Church of God; Church in Wales; Church of Ireland; Congregationalist; Coptic; Episcopalian; Ethiopian Orthodox; Orthodox (Greek/Russian); Presbyterian; Quaker; Salvation Army; Seventh-day Adventist; United Reformed Church; Welsh Independent; Other Christian; Christadelphian; Jehovah's Witness; Christian Science.
[c] Baha'i, Druid, Jain, Mormon, Pagan, Parsi, Spiritualist, Taoist, others.
[d] Nation of Islam ('Black Muslim'); Rastafarian; Scientology.

Practices in HM Prison Service. Consideration of the cultural and religious beliefs and practices of other faith communities has subsequently influenced programmes for training chaplains and other prison staff in race relations and chaplaincy procedures.

According to the Prison Service Chaplaincy's own records, and to chaplains' informal assessments, the proportion of 'other faith' prisoners has been increasing for several decades. Complete series of official statistics were available to us only for the period 1991–97, and it must be emphasised that they are far from unproblematic. The most serious reservation about the data in table 2.2 is that they are drawn from the annual census of religious registrations based on information collected by chaplains and cannot be checked against any more objective sources of information. Not all chaplains make a return for every year on the census day; there is no way of knowing how reliable the chaplains' information is since it is based on evidence collected during wide-ranging reception interviews; and the census cannot cope easily with the many prisoners who are moving into, out of, and between prisons on the day on which it is conducted. An even more serious difficulty with trying to interpret the statistics is that there is no way of knowing how many individual prisoners are actually included over time. This is because the census does not reveal how many of the prisoners registered in, say, Year 1 were also counted in the total for Year 2 if their sentence straddled two census years, and so on. Unless an accurate record is kept of precisely which prisoners enter the prison system, which ones leave it, and which ones return, it is impossible to calculate how many *different* prisoners have passed through prisons over time. These problems may help to account for the shortfall of several thousands between the number of prisoners enumerated by chaplains and the official total of inmates in British prisons as well as for the curious downturn in some of the key statistics reported for 1993. Nevertheless, we have no reason to doubt that the *ratios* between the different categories of religious identity are roughly correct. It is these proportional changes in which we are most interested. Finally, we regret that the published statistics do not distinguish between male and female prisoners or between those born in the United Kingdom and those born overseas.

Despite the shortcomings of the data on religious (and non-religious) registrations it is important to try to set the discussion of chaplaincy against a background of the changes that are taking place in prisoners' self-reported religious identity. This is why we have chosen to present the statistics of religious registrations for the period 1991 to 1997 in full in table 2.2.

Several features are immediately clear from table 2.2. The first is that the number of prisoners enumerated in the religious census has increased sharply since 1995. The second is that the rate of increase in the number of registrations as 'no religion', 'agnostic' or 'atheist' outstrips all the other rates of change but, as we shall see later, it receives very little comment from the chaplains who completed our questionnaire survey. The third is that there are wide differences between 'other faith' communities in their rates of change, but, with the exception of Muslims, the numbers are still small compared with the categories of Christians.

In addition to these initial observations, it is also apparent that the number of 'other faith' registrations has been growing at a rate considerably in excess of that for the overall total of registrations. This does not mean, however, that the rate is increasing for each faith group at the same pace; there are major differences between their respective rates of change. The most significant point is that, as many chaplains are fully aware, Muslims constitute by a wide margin both the largest single category among the other faiths and, again by a wide margin, the fastest growing category. In fact, their numerical growth between 1991 and 1997 accounted for 86 per cent of the increase in the 'other faiths' category in that period. It means that discussion of growing religious diversity in the prison population is almost entirely about the disproportionate expansion of the Muslim category. In the light of data provided by FitzGerald & Marshall (1996), it seems likely that Muslim prisoners come mainly from Pakistani and Bangladeshi families and are predominantly young men, perhaps reflecting the age structure of South Asian communities in the United Kingdom. Moreover, as many as 65 per cent of Asian prisoners included in the National Prison Survey of 1991 had been born abroad.

The disproportionate growth of the 'other faith' registrations taken together finds an echo in the comments of many chaplains to the effect that they seem to be spending more and more of their time dealing with prisoners who are not Christian. These comments overwhelmingly reflect the increasing numbers of Muslim prisoners. Incidentally, not a single chaplain commented on the fact that the rapid increase in the number of prisoners who choose to register no religious identity does not appear to have lightened their workload or affected their conditions of work in any respect.

It is difficult to construct a reliable picture of the longer-term trends in prisoners' religious registrations, but we know from the text of a lecture delivered by the Chaplain General to the Howard League in June 1975 (Lloyd Rees 1975) that prisoners registered as members of the main Christian churches and denominations amounted to 94 per cent of 32,975 religious registrations recorded that year. Other Christian groups accounted for a further 0.7 per cent, and 'nil' registrations for 2.0 per cent. 3.3 per cent of prisoners were registered as members of other faiths. The main changes which took place between 1975 and 1997 are outlined in table 2.3.

In addition to the notes of caution that we sounded about the reliability of recent statistics on prisoners' religious registrations we have to point out that further difficulties arise from the fact that definitions of census categories are not necessarily the same in the two census years. Again, we believe that these difficulties do not entirely invalidate the main calculations of proportional changes in the numerical strength of the major faith groupings; but we undoubtedly need better statistics about all aspects of religious practice in prisons.

The most significant findings are:

(i)   The absolute numbers of prisoners in the main Christian churches have increased slightly since 1975, but their decline over twenty two years has been sharp as a proportion of the total of religious registrations, which has grown by about 30 per cent.

(ii) The proportion of 'other faiths' prisoners in the total of religious registrations has more than doubled, but most of the increase is clearly due to the steep rate of increase in numbers of Muslim prisoners.

(iii) By far the largest change is the thirteen-fold increase in the proportion of prisoners registering as Atheist, Agnostic or 'no religion'. What is not clear is how much of this change is due to real shifts in prisoners' beliefs and how much to chaplains' growing willingness to record 'no interest in religion' as such rather than as 'C of E'. The percentage of 'nil' registrations ranges from 0 to 54 per cent across all prisons.

We have no way of resolving the uncertainty about the meaning of the absolute and proportional increase in 'no religion' registrations, but, whatever it means, the steep rate of increase makes the growth of other faith registrations in recent years look even more impressive. For, as a proportion of prisoners who register *any* kind of religious interest, members of other faiths are considerably more significant than they are in the entire inmate population. In fact, they constituted just over 11 per cent of all prisoners who registered a religious affiliation in 1997. Many chaplains confirmed this point on the basis of their own professional experience, often adding that Muslim prisoners tended to be more serious than most Christian inmates about performing their religious observances.

Physical setting

The physical space in which prison chaplains and Visiting Ministers conduct religious services, ceremonies, meditation, discussion, counselling, 'chats' and advocacy varies in many different ways from prison

Table 2.3. *Religious registrations, 1975–1997, HM Prisons, England and Wales*

	1975	%	1997	%	% change 1975/97	Ratio of 1997 % to 1975 %
Main Christian	30,974	94.0	36,498	63.0	−31.0	0.67
Other Christian	240	0.7	527	0.9	+0.2	1.28
Main other faiths:						
Buddhist			226			
Hindu			198			
Jewish	273		288			
Muslim	529		3,693			
Sikh	310		394			
Sub-total	1,112	3.3	4,799	8.3	+5.0	2.51
Other faiths:	203	0.3				
Agnostic, Atheist None	649	2.0	15,840	27.3	+25.3	13.65
Non-permitted religions			138	0.2		
Total	32,975	100	58,005	100		

to prison and between faith groups. In fact, one of the most poignant indications of the changes which have taken place in prison chaplaincy since the 1950s is the re-distribution of space between Christian, secular and 'other faith' activities.

Whereas the Christian chapel used to be an impressive site at the very centre of many Victorian establishments it has shrivelled to the scale of a meeting room on the margins of more mainstream activities such as education, health care and sport in some places. Nowhere is this mutation clearer than in one of South London's largest prisons where the formerly Cathedral-like Protestant chapel has undergone a process of amputation. It has been reduced to about one third of its former size in order to provide for a gymnasium which, in turn, has been adapted to create space for a mosque. As a result, the Protestant chapel has a ceiling height and windows which are now out of all proportion to its floor area. Despite the soaring windows, natural light is weak because the gymnasium has blocked out most of the sun's rays. What was once the elegantly bow-shaped end of a large church has become an oddly distorted side wall of a small chapel. This particular example is not necessarily representative but it captures the essence of changes which have occurred in many large prison chapels.

Much more effective and aesthetically pleasing reductions in the scale of formerly massive chapels have been achieved in other establishments, sometimes involving the construction of a new and well-proportioned chapel in the roof space of its predecessor. Indeed, the refurbished chapel in one of the North West's largest Victorian prisons is a model of what can be achieved in restricted confines by skilful use of natural light and tasteful wooden furnishings. The design of this particular chapel, like that of many others, also enables the room to be easily re-arranged as a room for concerts or committee meetings. Again, the multi-purpose nature of the room, its easy transformation into a religiously-neutral space and its reduced scale all combine to symbolise the place of prison chaplaincy in the late twentieth century. It operates *alongside* other activities: not in ascendancy over them. One other notable feature of this establishment among many others is the existence of a quite separate Roman Catholic chapel. In fact, the Catholic chapel is located on a different floor of the chaplaincy wing and is a completely self-contained entity with its own entrance and office space. This degree of physical segregation symbolises the gulf which used to keep Catholic chaplains apart from their fellow Christian chaplains.

In keeping with recent architectural fashions and financial stringency, chapels in the prisons built in the past thirty years or so tend to be more utilitarian and 'domestic' in scale than their Victorian predecessors.

Seating is rarely provided for congregations of more than about 150. The style of furniture and fittings has to be neutral in terms of 'churchmanship' and denominational identity, for most modern prison chapels are expected to accommodate Anglicans, Free Church Protestants and Roman Catholics alike. Many of these newer chapels were also designed to be used occasionally for musical concerts, drama productions or committee meetings, so some of the religious fittings are movable. The shape of modern prison chapels, like their counterparts in hospitals, tends to be broadly oblong with a table or plain altar as the focal point in the middle of the long side of the room facing the entrance. Good use is made of natural light, and decoration is usually in muted but light colours. The quality of fitments, comfort and cleanliness in Christian chapels is higher than in any other parts of the prisons which we visited. The only strikingly distinctive aspect of prison chapels is that, unlike most churches, they lack all signs of children's interests or activities.

The contrast with the rooms used by members of other faiths when they meet with their Visiting Ministers is sometimes jarring. We shall analyse the availability of such rooms in a later chapter, but for the moment we simply wish to note that the quality of this accommodation varies between establishments but is usually inferior to that of the Christian chapels. The accommodation for other faiths takes many different forms. A few older establishments contain a purpose-built synagogue; and the number of mosques is certainly increasing. The quality of these 'dedicated' facilities comes close to that of the Christian facilities in terms of appropriate design, comfort and cleanliness. The vast majority of establishments cannot boast of such facilities, however. In fact, it is much more common for Visiting Ministers to meet with their prisoners in rooms which serve a variety of purposes ranging from education or therapeutic group-work to committee meetings. The chaplaincy may try to retain control over the rooms' use by other prison departments, but these arrangements are rarely regarded as adequate by Visiting Ministers.

The major advantage of the rooms available to most Visiting Ministers is that they lack fitments or symbols of any other religion and that their size is often conducive to an appropriate atmosphere for small group prayers, meditation or discussion. The major disadvantage is that these rooms tend to lack carpets or comfortable chairs and are sometimes left in a dirty condition, especially if previous occupants have been smoking in them. It is also unusual for Muslim prisoners to have access to ablution facilities in the vicinity of their meeting rooms. Only the most recently constructed prisons offer really clean and comfortable accommodation, often as part of a self-contained 'chaplaincy centre' containing a chapel, chaplaincy offices, multi-faith room(s), and ablution facilities.

Conclusion

Prison chaplains have made many different adaptations to their work practices in order to accommodate the growing number of prisoners from other faith backgrounds since the 1960s. It is a testimony to the chaplains' theology and their goodwill that so many changes have taken place with relatively few serious problems. By contrast, the statutory and administrative framework governing the PSC has undergone very few changes. Most of the adaptations associated with the provision of religious and pastoral care to other faiths have simply been 'bolted on' to long-standing structures and procedures. As we shall argue in the following chapters, however, the strains and tensions experienced by chaplains and Visiting Ministers alike are making it increasingly difficult for some prisons to meet the demands for appropriate religious care. Demands for equal respect for permitted religions and for equal opportunities to practise these religions are mounting. Some representatives of other faith communities are no longer prepared to be merely 'tolerated'. They reject the idea that provision should be made for other faiths by exception or concession. They insist on prisoners' rights to receive religious and pastoral care from suitably qualified people in appropriate settings. 'Christian prisoners aren't expected to pay for the chapel chairs, so why should Muslim prisoners be expected to buy their own prayer mats?' was how one disgruntled Visiting Minister couched his demand for equality of treatment and parity of esteem.

The Church of England remains the most representative religious organisation of the English nation. Indeed, the archbishop of Canterbury is sometimes called 'the nation's chaplain'. The Church has a parish system and an ethos which match its self-understanding as an institution available to serve all residents of the country. Since it also has many of the features of a 'state church', its dominant position in prison chaplaincy seems to be self-explanatory. But the growing proportion of prisoners in England and Wales who either refrain from registering as members of any religion or who belong to other faiths has called in question the appropriateness of chaplaincy arrangements which are still largely in the hands of Anglican chaplains. The next chapter will examine the selection and training of Anglican chaplains to discover how well prepared they are for dealing with the growing proportion of prisoners from other faiths.

3   Church of England prison chaplains

Church of England chaplains tend to hold most of the administrative responsibility for prison chaplaincy programmes. This is true at the level of the Prison Service Chaplaincy (PSC) headquarters in London, at the regional level as well as at the level of individual prison establishments. The reasons for the Anglican ascendancy have their roots in a complex mixture of history, statute, custom and expediency, as we explained in chapter 2. Even in cases where Church of England chaplains enthusiastically share the overall responsibility with fellow-chaplains from the Roman Catholic Church or the Methodist Church, other members of prison staff still tend to regard the Anglican as 'normally' or 'naturally' in charge of affairs. And, given that more than 80 per cent of all full-time chaplains are indeed Anglicans, and are therefore available more often than others, it is clear why they are usually expected to act as managers and representatives of chaplaincy when the need arises for someone to fill this role. This is a very important consideration, for the Prison Service places a premium on accountability in its distinctly hierarchical form of organisation.

   The questions which run through this chapter have to do with the extent to which the training and prior work experience of Church of England chaplains prepare them for the kind of managerial responsibility which most of them come to exercise and for the work which they do on behalf of, or in conjunction with, members of other faiths. Of course, other Christian chaplains also find themselves in positions of responsibility *vis-à-vis* inmates and Visiting Ministers from other faiths on occasion, but it is the Anglicans who do most of this work – particularly if it involves negotiation with prison managers. This is why our focus is so sharply and narrowly on the Church of England. Our argument will be that the working conditions of Anglican chaplains place them under an obligation to facilitate and to broker things on behalf of other faiths but that, in doing so, they reproduce relations of dependence or patronage to which the leaders of some faith communities take exception. What the chaplains regard as their even-handedness and tolerance is interpreted by some of their critics as exclusion and discrimination.

We shall examine the training and prior work experience of Anglican chaplains in the first place. Then we shall discuss the range of statutory and other duties which they usually perform, with special reference to the implications of these duties for members of other faiths. We shall also assess the position of Church of England chaplains in the organisational structure of English prisons, taking account of the changes which have occurred in recent years. Finally, we shall consider the part which Anglican chaplains play in helping to secure resources for other faiths in prison.

At many points we shall draw attention to the diversity of Anglican chaplains' opinions about virtually all aspects of their work in prisons, including their interaction with members of other faiths. It is important to recognise in advance that some chaplains who read our work may be dismayed or shocked by the opinions of some of their colleagues. There are a few deep divisions between Church of England chaplains, particularly about the appropriateness of various ways of meeting the religious and pastoral needs of prisoners belonging to other faiths. It is not our intention to aggravate these divisions or to stir up controversy, but we do believe that it is essential to take proper account of the sharp differences between chaplains on some sensitive issues. We also believe that we are under an obligation to 'tell it how it is', even if this means relaying comments and claims which will be regarded as offensive by some readers. For this reason we have not softened or sanitised any quotations. The sensitivity of issues surrounding chaplains' relations with other faith groups is an indication that the chaplains' role of facilitator and go-between is far from easy and is subject to widely differing interpretations.

The study of other faiths in chaplains' training

Most Church of England prison chaplains receive theological training as part of a university course and/or during ordination training, although others, such as Church Army officers acquire their professional knowledge through different channels. This training provides them with the kind of general understanding, background information, values and technical skills required for the performance of ministerial roles in parishes and other settings.

The Church does not provide much initial training for the highly specific role of prison chaplain. Given that many chaplains tend to serve in a wide variety of other posts before applying to become prison chaplains, the special opportunities and challenges presented by prison ministry form no part of *general* training for the priesthood, for the diaconate or for lay evangelism. The Prison Service Chaplaincy aims to provide appropriate and timely training for chaplains once they have been selected and appointed.

The study of the beliefs and practices of faiths other than the Christian was not a significant part of general ministerial training for the chaplains in our sample. In fact, only 19 per cent of respondents considered that this aspect of their preparation for ministry in general had been adequate or extensive. As figure 3.1 indicates, exactly two thirds of chaplains used words such as 'non-existent', 'minimal' or 'inadequate' to describe their study of other faiths. A further 15 per cent of respondents, without evaluating the quality of their study, simply mentioned that they had 'taken a course' or 'attended a few lectures'.

In the case of chaplains who have been in the prison service for many years, it is not surprising that their training involved little study of faiths which, at the time, had relatively few adherents in the United Kingdom. Nearly half of our chaplains explained that they had never worked, or been trained, in areas where the representatives of other faiths were numerous and that was why their study of religions other than Christianity had been so limited. Even some of the chaplains who had studied other faiths in courses on comparative religion or history of religions at university commented that this type of academic study had not prepared them adequately for day-to-day work with, for example, Buddhists, Hindus, Muslims or Sikhs. Nor was it common for chaplains to have served in ethnically mixed parishes before joining the Prison Service or to have been involved in inter-faith activities. By contrast, those who had worked as chaplains, missionaries or teachers in countries where Christians were a minority seemed more confident that this experience had helped to prepare them for dealing with staff and prisoners of other faiths in British prisons.

In short, training for the diaconate, lay evangelism or the Anglican priesthood provided relatively few opportunities for people who went on to become prison chaplains to gain a thorough understanding of other faith traditions. Despite the opportunities afforded by prison placement schemes for students on ordination and post-ordination courses these days, it seems as if familiarisation with other faith traditions does not receive high priority. But work experience in the mission field, education or social work equipped more than one third of our sample of chaplains with the kind of knowledge which would eventually be relevant to their work in prisons.

Turning now to the kind of study and training required specifically for prison chaplaincy, the picture is rather different. Chaplains seemed to be more positive about this aspect of their training than about their earlier theological studies. As figure 3.2 shows, nearly a third of the sample (31

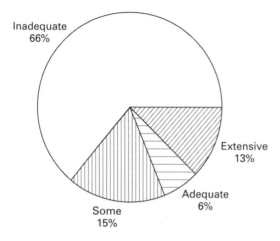

Fig. 3.1   How far was the study of faiths other than the Christian part of
your preparation for ministry in general?

per cent) indicated in various ways that this aspect of their preparation for
prison ministry had been suitable or adequate. But we need to stress that
four fifths of these particular responses referred to attendance at induction courses, in-service training and practical experience of working with
people of other faiths – not to initial training. It was common for chaplains to make favourable comments about in-service training and hands-
on experience when they sketched the kind of professional preparation
which seemed most appropriate to their work. On the other hand, four
out of ten respondents reported that studies of other faiths had played
very little or no part at all in their preparation for prison chaplaincy, while
others had attended a few lectures on the subject or done 'some' studies
on the subject. Only 7.5 per cent of respondents went so far as to describe
their study of other faiths as 'extensive', 'very good' or 'excellent'.

  It seems, then, that the academic study of other faiths does not constitute a major part of the preparation of chaplains for prison ministry but
that a combination of tailor-made courses and practical experience in
prisons is acknowledged as suitable training. The importance of 'learning
on the job' or 'learning by doing' also came through strongly in our
conversations with chaplains in prisons, as did the general theme that
chaplaincy work was craft-like in the sense of requiring dedication and
practical experience rather than theoretical knowledge or intellectual
brilliance. The purely academic or theoretical understanding of other
faith traditions was considered insufficient or inappropriate on its own. It
might provide a useful starting-point but it needed to be 'contextualised'

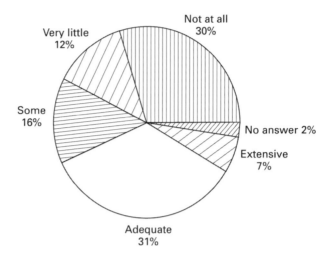

Fig. 3.2   How far was the study of faiths other than the Christian part of your preparation for prison miistry in particular?

in day-to-day prison life. The 'craft' could only be acquired by practical experience of dealing with members of other faith communities face-to-face while trying at the same time, of course, to cope with all the other demands made on chaplains in challenging circumstances.

Overall, close to two thirds of chaplains assessed their training to be adequate or excellent in the light of their current work. Even those who were less complimentary, nevertheless pointed out that the quality of training had improved significantly since they had first become chaplains. None claimed that the quality had deteriorated. Indeed, there was a strong sense that chaplaincy staff, including the leaders, had become more sensitive to the need for better information and deeper understanding of other faith traditions.

The mixed, but predominantly favourable, assessments of the quality of training for prison ministry in relation to other faiths were echoed in chaplains' suggestions for ways of improving their training. The range of ideas was rich and wide. Of course, there were a few who denied it was possible to devise any suitable form of training because, for example, 'you cannot train people to love their fellowmen' (D102),[1] while a larger number denied that there was any need to improve the training that was already available to chaplains. Only one person thought that it would be sufficient merely to raise awareness of other faiths, but two respondents were willing to accept 'anything' in place of the current provision. More specific suggestions included proposals that inter-faith training was required and that 'personal effort' was the way to improve training. The idea that better theological preparation was the way forward received support from only five of the sixty-eight respondents who outlined ideas for improved training. Perhaps more surprisingly, although practical experience of working with people of other faiths had been cited by a quarter of chaplains as their way of learning about religions other than Christianity, there was very little support for the view that training could be improved by incorporating more practical, on-the-job experience of dealing with other faiths. They had probably had enough of this experience, and only seven of them suggested that making personal visits to meetings and worship services of other faiths would improve their understanding significantly.

By contrast, as figure 3.3 shows, 40 per cent of chaplains proposed in-service courses as the best way of improving the training of prison chaplains to deal with members of other faiths. The individual responses specified that more detailed, in-depth, focused instruction on a broad range of faith groups and topics would be helpful. Some called for such courses to be offered, indeed required, at a very early stage of a prison chaplain's career; others wanted more frequent courses. There was also support for the idea that in-service courses should involve well-informed members of faith communities as teachers or consultants.

The popularity of in-service courses as a means of improving prison chaplains' understanding of other faiths is not at all surprising. It was clear from our informal discussions with chaplains in their own establishments that their conditions of work could be quite isolating – paradoxically so, given that prisons tend to be crowded places. Yet, it is this very sense of being continuously in close communication with large numbers of prisoners, from whom chaplains must also maintain some distance, which accentuates their 'difference' or 'apartness'. The camaraderie with fellow-chaplains is also double-edged. It is a source of comfort and support but it is also a reminder of how small and self-contained most chaplaincy teams are. Moreover, rates of mobility between establishments are not very high for chaplains, so the opportunities to meet different chaplains and to discuss common interests, gossip and problems are not very frequent. This does not mean that chaplains do not enjoy the regular gatherings at the level of regions or at their annual conferences, but these occasions do not provide the freedom to explore new ideas in a structured way. In-service training courses are therefore understandably popular with chaplains, but opportunities to participate in them are not as freely available as some would like them to be.

In fact, training courses ranked third among the resources that the chaplains identified as being currently provided by the Prison Service

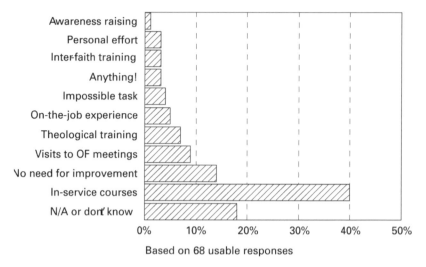

Based on 68 usable responses

Fig. 3.3   How might your training in the area of other faiths have been improved?

Chaplaincy to help them deal with prisoners of other faiths. Three quarters of our respondents were satisfied with their opportunities for *retraining* on other faith matters. In their day-to-day work, however, chaplains rely more than anything else on the *Directory and Guide on Religious Practices in HM Prison* Service. The second most frequently cited resource was advice from the PSC headquarters, with the name of the Revd John Hargreaves, who was Assistant Chaplain General with responsibility for 'other faith' matters until his retirement in June 1996, being mentioned in many cases. In fact, there was extensive overlap between reliance on *The Directory and Guide*, advice from headquarters and in-service training courses. The combination of these three things accounted for nearly all of the resources to which chaplains turned for help in their dealings with prisoners of other faiths. Other resources were identified as local faith communities, money for purchase of videos and training material, special rooms for the use of other faiths, and a reference library.

The *Directory and Guide* is provided as a matter of course for a range of staff in addition to chaplains in all establishments. If chaplains wish to be better informed about other faiths, they have to take the initiative and find the time to do so. This often involves exercising their imagination and making educated guesses. As a result, the range of sources from which chaplains sought guidance on other faith matters extended well beyond the PSC. By far the most frequently cited source of such guidance was personnel from relevant faith communities, including Visiting Ministers, inmates and leading national representatives. Less popular sources included Race Relations Management teams and prison staff. Only one quarter of our respondents reported involvement in multi-faith initiatives outside prison. In some cases, this was attributed to a dearth of 'other faith' practitioners in the locality, in others to a lack of time to cope with more pressing obligations. Only 10 per cent participated in 'race' relations or community relations groups; and a further 5 per cent were active in teaching, training and consultancy relating to other faiths.

The general picture that emerges of Church of England prison chaplains shows that their initial theological education, ordination training, post-ordination training and previous work experience typically did not dwell on the beliefs and practices of major faiths other than Christianity. Their preference for ways of improving chaplains' capacity to deal better with other faiths was for them to take more, intensive in-service training courses, preferably drawing on the expertise of suitable representatives of those faiths. This suggestion accords well with chaplains' stated preference for seeking guidance on 'other faith' matters from the *Directory and Guide* and from people in the relevant communities. It is also a form of training with which most chaplains would be familiar since it often involves preparatory reading, seminar-type discussion and in some cases a small project. The experience would therefore be similar to that of higher education or ordination training.

These findings need to be borne in mind when we consider the pattern of relationships between chaplains and Visiting Ministers in prisons. Although a small proportion of chaplains can draw on extensive theological knowledge and personal experience of some other faiths (mainly Islam, in fact) in their interactions with Visiting Ministers, the majority are in a different situation. They can draw on published guidance and on the advice of knowledgeable staff at headquarters but are not well versed in the beliefs and practices of other faiths. Nor did we detect much curiosity about these beliefs and practices in themselves. Chaplains seemed to think it was more important for them to be able to anticipate the kind of demands that other faith prisoners might make in the name of their culture or faith and to know what the approved response was.

Statutory and other duties

It is important, before considering how chaplains relate to Visiting Ministers and inmates of other faiths, to examine the range of things which chaplains regularly do for *all* prisoners. This will provide a framework in which we can then locate the aspects of their work which are specifically

to do with other faiths, but it was difficult for some chaplains to list the
kinds of things they did for all prisoners and to arrange these things in an
order of priority. In some cases this was because chaplains' duties were
too varied to be listed or that 'this is not relevant for me . . . I treat all
inmates and staff according to the need they have' (D091). We had not,
however, anticipated the response that 'this has varied from prison to
prison and my frustration is that one cannot do what either one did or one
would like to do' (D012). This comment was just the first of many signs
of unease which we detected among chaplains who felt that their work
had become more difficult and frustrating in recent years. Yet, despite the
complexity of day-to-day variations in the pattern of chaplains' work and
the difficulty of ranking their activities in order of perceived importance,
it is clear that worship and prayer are significantly more extensive than
any other activities. Counselling and problem-solving with individual
prisoners come next, with pastoral care and listening not far behind.
These first three areas of activity are significantly more important than,
for example, contact with prisoners' families, administration, reception of
new arrivals, visits to cells and wings, classes, report writing and 'statutory
duties'. Our findings about the salience of worship, counselling and
pastoral care in the workload of Anglican chaplains will provide a useful
point of reference when we come to consider in a later section what they
do specifically for Visiting Ministers and inmates of other faiths.

A comment about the reception of new arrivals and 'statutory duties' is
needed. The latter includes the former, as specified in the Prison Rules
1964:

Special duties of chaplains and prison ministers
   11. – (1) The chaplain or prison minister of a prison shall –
(a) interview every prisoner of his denomination individually soon after the
prisoner's reception into that prison and shortly before his release; and
(b) if no other arrangements are made, read the burial service at the funeral of any
prisoner of his denomination who dies in that prison.
(2) The chaplain shall visit daily all prisoners belonging to the Church of England
who are sick, under restraint or undergoing cellular confinement; and a prison
minister shall do the same, as far as he reasonably can, for prisoners of his own
denomination.
(3) If the prisoner is willing, the chaplain shall visit any prisoner not of the Church
of England who is sick, under restraint or undergoing cellular confinement, and is
not regularly visited by a minister of his own denomination.

Roman Catholic and Methodist chaplains, as well as chaplaincy volunteers, share many of the statutory duties with Anglican colleagues. This
arrangement is a matter of principle in some places and of expediency in
others. Although the Prison Rules 1964 also specify that each prison

minister shall perform the same 'special duties' (i.e. statutory duties) 'as far as he reasonably can for prisoners of his own denomination', we shall see in chapter 4 that in practice very few Visiting Ministers routinely perform these duties. Nor did we find evidence that many Christian chaplains encouraged Visiting Ministers to perform them. The exceptional cases were so unusual that chaplains commented on them at some length and, it must be stressed, welcomed them as a sign of improving relations between the Christian chaplains and Visiting Ministers. Thus, although all Visiting Ministers should receive a copy of *Notes for the Guidance of Visiting Ministers of Religion Appointed under the Prison Act 1952* when they are initially appointed and should therefore know that they are entitled to interview incoming prisoners belonging to their faith communities, opportunities to do so are rare for reasons to do mainly with the timing of their visits.

Our observation of chaplaincy reception interviews in a prison for Cat. B prisoners, many of whom were being prepared for release at the end of long sentences, showed that the procedure was mainly for the purpose of gathering and recording information but that some more subtle functions were also fulfilled at the same time. These particular interviews[2] took place in an atmosphere of informality bordering on bonhomie at times. The two prisoners were fully at their ease, occasionally bragging and bantering with the chaplain. The chaplain's style was, at different moments in the course of about an hour, jocular, solicitous and supportive. The only two notes of formality were, firstly, the fact that the chaplain occasionally consulted official documents and recorded information on printed forms and, secondly, the fact that the prisoners had been scheduled for the interview at a precise time of the day and that they had had to be accompanied from their residential wing to the art and craft room where the interview took place. This particular room was apparently the only accommodation available at the time. The background of unfinished paintings and the clutter of modelling clay, cardboard and paint brushes only added to the relaxed air of informality. We all sat at desks and exchanged conversation freely after the main part of the session had finished. Each prisoner left the room while the other was questioned about the details of his previous record, family relationships and so on.

The chaplain began by offering to supply information about the facilities for religious and pastoral care and to answer any questions. It was clear from the setting of the interviews that the chaplain was acting as a representative of the establishment and of the Prison Service, especially as he was prepared to discuss the nature of the local regime in comparison with that of other prisons where the incoming prisoners had spent time. Yet, he was also offering the prisoners a direct relationship with him and the chaplaincy. For, as well as recording or checking the record of their offences, sentences and history of time spent in custody, the chaplain questioned the prisoners about their views on religion and their involvement in chaplaincy activities in other establishments. He and the two prisoners swapped anecdotes about 'characters' and incidents in other prisons. It seemed as if a process of bonding was taking place between 'insiders' who accepted that they all understood and respected each other. After all, they shared the same religion and 'prison culture'. There was also an undercurrent of light-hearted conspiracy to mitigate the worst effects of the security regime by, for example, agreeing to try to find a way of persuading Prison Officers at the main gate to allow one of the prisoners to keep a musical instrument in his cell. This was, incidentally, just one trivial episode among others that we witnessed in various establishments when chaplains offered their services as prisoners' advocates. In some cases this occurred when they met accidentally in corridors, but in other cases prisoners approached chaplains deliberately for their help in resolving problems with, for example, fellow prisoners or Prison Officers. In fact, this informal type of advocacy loomed large in the work of chaplains, according to the Head of Programmes (Governor Grade 4) who was the chaplain's line manager in a Young Offenders Institution that we visited. He particularly valued the potential independence of chaplains as 'watchdogs' or 'whistle blowers'. He thought that chaplains played an especially important role in monitoring the risk of suicide, bullying and self-harm among young prisoners.

One of the prisoners whose chaplaincy reception interview we observed expressed firm interest in the chapel activities, but the other admitted that he preferred to play football rather than attend chapel fellowship meetings during his free time. This exchange gave the chaplain the opportunity to give copies of the chaplaincy leaflet to each prisoner and to explain in more detail how the chaplaincy operated. He mentioned, in passing, the availability of Visiting Ministers and he stressed how easy it was for prisoners to visit the chapel at any time when the chaplain or the chaplaincy orderly were present. The prisoners listened politely and said they were grateful for the information and the offer of help. Neither of them asked any questions, however, or requested the help of a volunteer Prison Visitor.

The concluding civilities were no less warm and informal than the rest of the reception interview. By this time the chaplain was addressing the prisoners by their first names and was, in effect, welcoming them into the establishment with his final 'Well, John, it's good to have you here with us'. He also encouraged them to take seriously, and to benefit from, the therapy that they were going to receive. Again, the tone of the communication was not only positive but also 'inclusive' in the sense that the chaplain, representing much more than simply the chaplaincy, was affirming that they were all in this together and that he was concerned to see that the establishment achieved its aim of rehabilitating them. He also repeated that his help could be enlisted if the prisoners encountered any problems. It was a reminder that the legitimacy of the establishment depended partly on having a chaplain who might be, to some extent, independent from the security officers or the therapeutic staff.

If we switch the focus to the things that Church of England chaplains do specifically for members of other faiths (rather than for *all* prisoners), it soon becomes clear that their contributions are extensive but different. To begin with, it usually falls to the Anglican chaplain(s) to make arrangements for inmates of other faiths to receive spiritual and religious care from appropriate ministers from their faith communities. This often means that chaplains have to locate, appoint and induct new Visiting Ministers, although the formal process also requires interviews, security checks, Governor's approval and, until recently, confirmation of appointment from PSC headquarters.[3]

Most chaplains reported that they had contacted prospective Visiting Ministers by means of more than one method. Making contact with local faith groups and consulting national organisations of other faith groups were the most frequently cited methods of obtaining Visiting Ministers. Other methods included requesting advice from neighbouring prison establishments and making independent, personal approaches to prospective Visiting Ministers. Two thirds of serving Visiting Ministers were appointed by means of one or more of these four strategies. Approaches to the PSC headquarters or the Home Office, self-nomination by would-be Visiting Ministers, and recommendation by the previous appointee, prison officers, Heads of Inmate Activities and inmates were much less common. There were only three cases in which chaplains had approached a Bishop's Adviser on Inter-faith Relations, a local Race Relations Council or a multi-faith group.

It is highly significant that chaplains' accounts of how they would go about seeking additional or replacement Visiting Ministers if the need arose emphasised the chaplains' willingness to consult with the PSC headquarters or the Assistant Chaplain General with special responsibility for relations with other faiths. Reasons for this shift towards more formal methods probably include chaplains' heightened sensitivity about the need for a methodical approach to relations with other faiths, the favourable impact on chaplains of the PSC's *Directory and Guide on Religious Practices in HM Prison Service* and the effect of increasing numbers of chaplains who had been exposed to recent PSC seminars and in-service training programmes. The personal qualities and expertise of the Revd John Hargreaves, the former ACG with special responsibility for relations with other faiths, had also drawn some chaplains into a closer relationship with the PSC headquarters staff.

In short, some significant changes have occurred in chaplains' thinking about methods of seeking new, additional or replacement Visiting Ministers. Selection of Visiting Ministers involved far more, however, than simply knowing where to find suitable candidates. It also involved looking for specific capacities in prospective Visiting Ministers. In view of the importance that chaplains attached to counselling, problem-solving and pastoral care in their own work, it is not surprising that chaplains attached greatest importance to general notions of pastoral care, personal ministry and spiritual support in their delineation of the Visiting Minister's typical role. Nearly half of their characterisations of this role fell into this category. The next most frequently cited aspects of the role concerned the conduct of worship, prayers and religious services (24 per cent) and religious teaching, instruction and study (14 per cent). The relative frequencies of these three main categories are interesting in themselves but, for our purposes, it is more significant that there was very heavy overlap between them. Chaplains typically described the Visiting Ministers' role in terms of, for example, 'pastoral care, teaching, lead worship, represent their faith community, encourage their lads in their faith, *and* work as part of a multi-faith team with respect for all' (D026, emphasis original) or 'to provide pastoral care and religious teaching and to see that inmates are able to observe prayer and worship requirements of their faith' (D122). These three main categories of pastoral care, teaching and worship account for 81 per cent of the components in chaplains' descriptions of Visiting Ministers' role. They also echo the functions which chaplains identified as their own. Indeed, some respondents chose to describe the Visiting Ministers' role *exclusively* in terms of its similarity with that of Christian chaplains. For example, 'to provide the equivalent pastoral, spiritual and liturgical care to that which I attempt to provide' (D057), 'broadly the same as full-time chaplains but without the management role' (D071) and 'same as any other chaplain' (D104).

We have taken time to examine chaplains' methods of seeking Visiting Ministers and their ideas about the kind of roles that Visiting Ministers should perform because the findings support the general argument that the prevailing model of prison chaplaincy is Christian. It is remarkable, for example, that not one of our sample of eighty-two chaplains commented on the possibility that different faith groups might have different concepts of 'pastoral', 'spiritual', 'religious' or 'teaching'. Nor was there any comment on the differences between Christianity and other faiths collectively. Only a handful of references were made to inmates' cultural requirements. This may imply that chaplains operate with a 'generic' notion of chaplaincy or pastoral and spiritual care which cuts across boundaries between faith traditions. Another possible interpretation is that chaplains do not have a very clear idea about the kinds of things which Visiting Ministers actually arrange for their prisoners. We came across the view in a number of prisons that Visiting Ministers arrived, 'did their own thing' and left without revealing much about their activities except the number of prisoners who participated. Indeed, very few chaplains indicated that they had asked Visiting Ministers about their activities. In these circumstances, it is quite likely that chaplains can only acquire a very general impression of Visiting Ministers' work in prisons. We shall see later that the range of Visiting Ministers' activities is actually much wider than is suggested by the chaplains' categorisations.

We found very little evidence to suggest that chaplains actively trained Visiting Ministers for their role, although many of the former claimed to have contributed towards the induction of new ministers into the service. In fact, about three quarters of chaplains said that they were involved in one or more phases of the process of training, inducting and giving advice to new Visiting Ministers. The degree of involvement ranged from 'nil' in a few cases to taking sole responsibility in about one fifth of cases. But there is a large discrepancy between the claims that chaplains made about the extent of their involvement in preparing Visiting Ministers for work in prison and the fact that only six per cent of Visiting Ministers reported receiving guidance and advice from chaplains. This is only one of several areas of chaplaincy life in which a gulf seems to separate the perceptions of chaplains and Visiting Ministers. It is as if the latter perceive everyday reality through completely different lenses. In the case of induction and advice, we suspect that some chaplains try to avoid the risk of appearing to be patronising towards Visiting Ministers and, as a result, give the impression that they are not interested in them. The 'preferred style' of many chaplains is to have 'friendly chats' with Visiting Ministers, often without warning or invitation, as a way of avoiding or politely disguising relations of authority. The Visiting Ministers' interpretation of this deliberately non-threatening style may, in fact, be quite the opposite of what chaplains hoped to achieve. They may feel that the lack of formality and the paucity of information about prison procedures betoken something very different from politeness. In their eyes, they may see themselves as excluded or marginalised, as we shall show in chapter 6.

In most cases, however, chaplains shared the responsibility for inducting new Visiting Ministers with other people and agencies in the establishment. A combination of chaplain, security staff and Governors accounted for nearly all of the training, inducting and advising of Visiting Ministers. One chaplain described the combined approach as: 'Informal training by chaplaincy; security training from staff; advice and oversight by Governor' (D048). A small number of chaplains also referred to training or induction courses offered either by an establishment or by the PSC. Nevertheless, there were some reservations about the availability of these courses. One chaplain noted a practical obstacle: 'Theoretically [Visiting Ministers] should undergo similar training to the rest of us, but as their visits are either irregular or very part-time it is difficult to do so' (D028). Another suggested that Visiting Ministers were reluctant to go on training courses; and a third noted that the courses were designed for Christian ministers. There was an echo of this last theme in the arguments of three chaplains that other faith groups should be responsible for training their own Visiting Ministers. Moreover, as we shall show in chapter 4, Visiting Ministers were aware of very few opportunities for training.

Although the appointment of Visiting Ministers is now the responsibility of Governors in each prison, Church of England chaplains still tend to be involved in the process of seeking prospective Visiting Ministers, assessing their suitability for chaplaincy work, establishing the kind of roles to be performed and ensuring that induction of new Visiting Ministers into the routines of chaplaincy takes place. It is an exaggeration to claim that Visiting Ministers are only allowed to work in prisons on the terms laid down by Christian chaplains, but there is no doubt that the PSC, as a Christian mission, finds that Visiting Ministers who conform with its expectations are the most acceptable. There is no pretence that chaplaincy is neutral towards all religions, but there is an implicit agreement that chaplains will tolerate and facilitate the practice of religions other than Christianity on condition that their practitioners conform with the general pattern of Christian chaplaincy. On the other hand, the PSC has not until very recently accepted any responsibility for training Visiting Ministers of other faiths. Space is created for other faiths in chaplaincy work, but Visiting Ministers do not have the same opportunities as Christian chaplains to be trained and to influence policies affecting religion in prisons.

Structural position and anomalies

The extent to which Anglican chaplains take responsibility for the induction of new Visiting Ministers is only one aspect of the so-called brokerage or facilitation which they perform on behalf of other faiths.[4] We shall examine in detail many other aspects of this facilitation later. But to begin with we shall consider how far chaplains thought that their role should include helping members of other faiths to feel that their religious traditions were respected in prison. This question gets at the very core of the principle of facilitation, namely, that there is an obligation on chaplains from the established church to ensure respect for religious traditions other than their own because their duty is to minister to *all* inmates and staff. After all, the title of their branch of the Prison Service is the *Prison Service* Chaplaincy: not the Prison Chaplaincy Service.

Our findings could hardly have been clearer. As many as 94 per cent of the sample of Anglican chaplains affirmed that their role included helping members of other faiths to feel that their religious tradition was respected in prison. In fact, only one respondent denied that this was part of his role, on the grounds that 'I was ordained to preach the Christian gospel!' (D060) (See Pound, Atherton & Davies 1989). Four other chaplains indicated that concern for other faith traditions was only a minor part of their duty and that it involved merely putting inmates in touch with appropriate Visiting Ministers.

The vast majority of chaplains considered themselves under an obligation to promote respect for other faith traditions, but their accounts of how they actually undertook the promotion reflected two different notions of 'obligation'. On the one hand, 46 per cent of chaplains described their support for other faith traditions as a *requirement* (in some cases 'legal') of their position; it was something that they 'made possible', 'facilitated' or 'enabled'. Most of these chaplains offered no comments on this aspect of their work. On the other hand, the remaining 48 per cent of our sample who affirmed their duty to promote respect for other faith traditions embraced it *with enthusiasm* or, at least, with a sense that it was among the most important aspects of their role. Thus, 'I think that this is an important function for us and it should be done with care and generosity' (D051) or 'This is a *very* important part of my role. I feel I must fight their corner' (D111, emphasis original).

Chaplains gave a wide variety of reasons for their enthusiasm for supporting other faith traditions in prison. In some cases, the reason was to do with ideas of equal rights for all prisoners; in others, the primary concern was that it was 'natural' for all prisoners to look to the chaplain for support; and still others argued along the lines that

no one else in the prison is likely to [support other faith traditions] with any sort of sensitivity. I have often been tempted to think that facilitating of other faiths should be put in the hands of the secular officers in the prison to avoid the sensitivities mentioned [earlier], but I know that this would be to the disadvantage of the other faiths, however much they may fail to see it. (D051)

We shall return to these issues in later discussions of brokerage.

Although chaplains overwhelmingly agreed that they should uphold respect for other faith traditions in prison, some of them nevertheless entered reservations or conditions which deserve consideration. These caveats are interesting to us because they signal the limits of the tolerance that many chaplains claimed to be a hallmark of Anglicanism (and, incidentally, one of the reasons why it was considered crucial for the Church of England to retain responsibility for prison chaplaincy in a religiously diverse society). It was emphasised that support for other faith traditions had to be balanced against, for example,

> conformity with prison rules ('I believe I am to facilitate within the rules, i.e., I am not likely to give a ceremonial dagger to a Sikh on request!' [D012)])
>
> the realisation that some religious groups would prove difficult ('very high in my priorities although Rastafarianism and other smaller cults prove difficult at times' [D007])
>
> the fact that 'minority demands take as much time and attention as provision for majority activity' (D016)
>
> the refusal to make compromises with the Christian faith, and the need for other faith leaders to take their own initiatives.

However, none of these caveats appeared to represent a serious retreat from the willingness of chaplains to promote respect for other faith traditions; they merely drew attention to the possible limits to which they were prepared to go.

What happens, however, if a prisoner who is not registered as a member of any other faith asks a chaplain about Buddhism, Hinduism, Judaism, Islam or Sikhism? How do chaplains respond to inquiries about, or expressions of interest in, other faiths? These questions bear on the issue of how chaplains translated their 'in principle' support for other faith traditions into practice (hypothetically, at least). Although the issue of 'inquirers' may appear on the surface of things to be innocuous or trivial it has considerable significance in prisons. This is partly because it is one of the areas in which Christian chaplains play a direct role in shaping the outcome of prisoners' expression of interest in religions other than Christianity. Chaplains do not make decisions entirely on their own about prisoners' requests to see a representative of a faith different from the ones in which they are registered but they can influence the likely outcome by being obstructive or constructive. Another reason why the issue of 'inquirers' into other faiths is contentious is that prison officers are sometimes reluctant to allow prisoners to attend a meeting of a religious group if they are not already categorised on the computer lists of inmates as being members of the group in question. In these cases, considerations of security or discipline outweigh those of sympathy for religious experimentation with other faiths.

Again, our findings about 'inquirers' accorded closely with those concerning attitudes towards respect for other faiths, with 90 per cent of chaplains sketching various ways of enabling prisoners to pursue an interest in a faith other than Christianity. The clearest pattern of action involved a combination of (a) listening sympathetically to inquiries about other faiths, (b) referring inquirers to Visiting Ministers, and (c) making relevant literature available. There were only two significant departures from (or refinements of) this pattern. The first involved above-average enthusiasm for interest in other faiths such as 'I respond enthusiastically and helpfully. Although I am a Christian I think it is very important for a person to take an interest in religion, even if it is one that I personally could not accept' (D065) or 'positively and encouragingly I hope! I personally feel I have more in common with those who are religious (whatever their religion) than with those who are atheists' (D067). It is interesting to compare this willingness to facilitate the possible movement of Christians towards other faiths with the reluctance expressed by one chaplain to facilitate a move in the opposite direction. Faced with a Sikh inmate who wanted to attend a class on the Christian faith, he wrote 'I felt it would be disloyal to encourage this!' (D122). Chaplains also expressed anxiety about being seen to 'poach' prisoners; they 'bend over backwards' to avoid appearing to proselytise. 'Patronising' is too strong as a description of this attitude, but 'paternalistic' is a fitting characterisation of many chaplains' assumption that they know what is in the prisoners' best interests as far as religion is concerned.

The second refinement of the way in which the majority of chaplains responded to 'inquirers' entailed referring inquirers to *inmates* of the faith in question. This is not as dismissive as it may appear to be at first glance. For we witnessed a number of occasions on which inmates, individually and in groups, were happy to take collective responsibility for their particular faith tradition. This sometimes involved taking charge of cleaning an area of the prison prior to holding a religious festival event or arranging the prayer mats prior to Friday prayers. This type of solidarity also extended to helping inquirers or new inmates to learn about group activities or shared beliefs. The circulation of religious literature among the members of some other faith groups was also effective as a means of drawing newcomers into the collectivity. In case these incidents create an all too rosy picture of religious harmony, we should quickly add that this strong sense of group identity and cohesion can also become a means of excluding outsiders or even rejecting members who are unwanted by the group. There is even evidence that a type of religious solidarity, bordering on that of a 'religious gang', is responsible for putting pressure on some inmates to join the gang against their wishes.

An interesting example of this came to light during a reception interview that we attended in a South Midlands prison. A young African-Caribbean prisoner who had been a chapel orderly in his previous prison explained to the Church of England chaplain who was conducting the interview that other African-Caribbean prisoners had repeatedly tried to persuade him to abandon Christianity and to become a Muslim. They argued that Islam was the only suitable religion for black people and that Christianity was for slaves. Such incidents of manipulativeness in the name of religion are, however, rare in England. We shall pick up this issue again in chapter 7 when conditions in US prisons will be discussed. The important point is that inmates who are active in some religious groups can effectively help fellow-inmates to learn about their religious activities and, in some cases, to become practising members. The fact that most Visiting Ministers were not in prisons very often probably makes chaplains more willing to refer 'religious inquirers' to fellow-inmates.

Although a few chaplains insisted that they would carefully assess the seriousness of an inmate's inquiry about another faith before deciding whether to refer the inquirer to a Visiting Minister, others took a much more intransigent line. There was frank cynicism about inquirers' questions 'which are not usually more than mere curiosity' (D072) as well as a sarcastic reluctance to accept that conversions to Islam could be genuine because 'no one wants to be other than a Muslim, and even then only for the diet. The official form [for re-registering as a Muslim] is a joke. Applications aren't refused' (D071).

Two chaplains said that they would actively discourage inquiries about other faiths. One would supply information and then discourage further interest; the other would ask inquirers about knowledge of 'biblical Christianity' as a way of filtering out insincere inquiries. The stated reason for this was that 'some wish to embrace a faith for dietary purposes only! Cocoa Mormons and curry Muslims' (D096). The belief that interest in other faiths was part of the manipulativeness attributed to many prisoners was shared by a number of other chaplains. For example, 'these are young offenders and sometimes they want to change religion for a variety of unjustifiable reasons, e.g. diet or hairstyle' (D021) and 'many prison enquiries are motivated by dietary aspirations!' (D076). Again, chaplains are in a position of power which allows them not only to express these critical assessments of other faiths but also to act on them by deterring would-be inquirers from pursuing an interest in a new religion.

Incidentally, chaplains differed widely in their understanding of how far the prison rules permitted inmates to pursue an interest in a religion other than the one in which they were registered. Some insisted that Visiting Ministers were still not allowed to visit inmates of a different religion, while others clearly believed that the old rules had been modified to permit this to take place. As we explained in chapter 2, administrative circulars from the PSC headquarters specify that genuine inquiries about other faiths (or Christianity) should be permitted. For example, the Chaplain General's *Newsletter* in the Spring of 1992 was categorical:

The Prison Rules say that a Visiting Minister 'shall not be permitted to visit any other prisoner' (i.e. anyone not registered in that religion). We have consistently taken the line that the Rule clearly prohibits such a minister visiting other prisoners against the prisoner's wishes, but that it does not apply when such a visit takes place by request. It is a defence against unwelcome proselytising. Nevertheless it has been alleged that the ruling is a contravention of European legislation.
As far as I can tell, any responsible request for a prisoner to follow up some new faith in which he or she is interested is usually honoured. Given goodwill all round, I do not believe that prisoners have been required first to change their religious registration before seeing a minister of another faith. (pp. 13–14)

Circulars to Governors have also been issued in similar terms, but not all chaplains and wing staff seem to be aware of these authoritative interpretations of statute or willing to act on them. For a variety of reasons, then, 'inquirers' are considered problematic. The response of Anglican chaplains is critical to the outcome of any prisoner's request to meet a representative of a religious group of which he or she is not already registered as a member. They perform this gate-keeper role routinely but unaccountably in most cases.

A further dimension of the Anglican facilitation of the practice of other faiths concerns chaplains' relations with prison staff whose religion is not Christianity. Prison staff of other faiths consult chaplains on different types of occasion, but most of them concern requests for information about religious requirements for inmates' diets, festivals, dress and time off work. In one case it was a 'Muslim Governor who wishes to ensure the observance of Islamic feasts' (D107). Other instances of consultation between chaplains and other faith staff centred on matters of personal life and religious faith. The remaining occasions were highly diverse: discussion of a project to build a Buddhist shrine, mediation with Visiting Ministers and inquiries about particular inmates. To our surprise, only one chaplain mentioned being consulted by prison staff of other faiths about training programmes. Moreover, more than half of our sample of chaplains had never had the experience of being consulted by members of staff who belonged to other faiths.

Does this picture of rather tenuous relations between chaplains and other faith staff change when we consider chaplains' contributions towards training prison staff about other faiths? In other words, does the Anglican brokerage on behalf of other faiths operate indirectly by means of the training that chaplains provide for prison staff? One quarter of our sample of chaplains had been responsible for training prison staff about other faiths. The descriptions which they gave of these activities suggested that they had been mostly brief, one-off, and rather informal sessions. It may also be significant that eight of the twenty examples of training occurred in the framework of Race Relations courses. It seems unlikely, then, that many chaplains are able to act as brokers for other faiths on a significant scale by contributing towards staff training. In fact, three quarters of our sample made no such contribution. This contrasts sharply with the situation in health care chaplaincy where Church of England chaplains are increasingly involved in training programmes designed to inform nursing and medical staff about other faiths' requirements (Beckford & Gilliat 1996). The advent of the Patient's Charter is widely credited with enhancing the consideration shown to patients' cultural and religious beliefs. In the absence of any such charter for prisoners, it seems that religious and cultural differences are categorised as 'racial' or 'ethnic' matters as far as the Prison Service is concerned. For example, Race Relations Liaison Officers have the responsibility in many prisons for ensuring that major religious festivals are organised; and the training course for these officers dwells on matters of religion and culture.

Perhaps the opportunities for facilitation are better when chaplains are working directly with prisoners rather than with staff, for it is clear that a very large proportion of chaplains regularly supplied pastoral care to other faith inmates. By far the largest category of care delivered by chaplains was in response to personal, domestic and health problems and bereavement. Two thirds of cases fell into this category. Several respondents commented on the fact that this type of pastoral care was no different from that offered to Christian inmates. Indeed, according to one chaplain, 'all inmates are treated the same; and we do not differentiate on the basis of faith' (D027). But a much more common response of chaplains was to listen sympathetically to inmates' problems before referring them to a Visiting Minister or to appropriate literature for advice and guidance in accordance with their particular faith tradition. For example, 'If a prisoner had a problem we would help if we could; if that problem was of a spiritual nature we would inform the Visiting Minister' (D062). But, in addition to dealing with personal, domestic and health problems chaplains also reported that other faith inmates had approached them for help on a wide range of subjects including legal problems, report writing, visitors, books and videos, diet, bullying, money and festivals.

Most chaplains appeared to have no difficulty in responding to requests for pastoral care from other faith inmates. Some clearly welcomed the opportunity. Others regarded it as an opportunity to deploy the various members of a chaplaincy team. The only notes of caution or reservation were sounded by chaplains who wanted to stress the unreliability of Visiting Ministers alleging, for example, that other faith inmates had been obliged to approach Anglican clergy only because their own Visiting Ministers had failed to visit the prison as agreed. Yet, these few sour notes were drowned by the majority's evident willingness to act on behalf of non-Christian prisoners either by giving pastoral care themselves or by referring prisoners to other authorities. The Church of England's broker-age function, in this particular sense, appeared to be operating well from the chaplains' point of view. This is not surprising in view of the fact that they constitute most of the full-time and part-time chaplains in the Prison Service. They are available much more often and for longer periods of time than are Visiting Ministers. They function in some ways like 'triage' nurses in hospital Accident and Emergency departments, making *prima facie* decisions about the urgency of cases and the kind of care that they require. No Visiting Ministers have the opportunity to perform these initial 'diagnoses' or assessments.

Another potential avenue for brokerage on behalf of other faiths is the relationship between chaplains and staff in the governor 4 or 5 grades, many of whom hold titles such as Head of Inmate Activities (HIA) and act as 'line managers' for chaplains. The discussions that chaplains had with these senior members of management about multi-faith issues were most often about diet, festivals, prayers times and holidays. Second in frequency were issues about the rooms and facilities available to other faith groups for worship or study. And third were issues concerning the appointment and payment of Visiting Ministers. The degree of overlap between these three types of issue was also strong, but eleven chaplains reported that multi-faith issues had never been raised at their meetings with governors. One of them explained that this was because 'under the new structure the Governor doesn't speak to the chaplain, and the HIA leaves me to get on with it as he knows I know my job' (D012). Others pointed out that religious issues usually occurred on the agenda of Race Relations Management Committee meetings. In fact, a number of chap-lains stressed the overlap between 'other faith' issues and 'race' issues.

Festivals and diets frequently came up for discussion between chap-lains and governors, and most chaplains regarded it as their responsibility to make arrangements for other faith prisoners to celebrate their festivals. This activity represented facilitation in its most practical mode. Only two out of eighty-two chaplains had no responsibilities for other faith festivals, but the overwhelming majority accepted the responsibility, and none of them seemed to resist it or complain about it. Nevertheless, the range of forms that their acceptance of the responsibility took was wide. A handful described their responsibility as 'full' or 'total'. A small number delegated some of their responsibility to, for example, Heads of Inmate Activities, while others confined their role to offering advice and even consultancy. The most common form of facilitation was a combination of supervision, co-ordination, facilitation, liaison, and communication. These activities brought chaplains into contact with many departments and personnel in prisons but especially with kitchens, security, workshops and Race Relations Liaison Officers. In other words, chaplains tended to see themselves as central, if not indispensable, to the successful organisation of religious festivals for other faith groups. Supporting Visiting Ministers in relation to festivals was also part of this activity, especially in the area of securing the necessary permissions and clearances from prison authorities.

All the chaplains' activities that we have considered so far centred on support for other faiths. The scope for facilitation or brokerage was extensive in every case, but it remains to be seen whether chaplains also take their supportive function further by co-operating in joint ventures with Visiting Ministers. In other words, does brokerage always entail an active role for the Anglicans and a relatively passive one for other faith ministers? Or is it possible for the relationship between chaplains and Visiting Ministers to be more evenly balanced in terms of agency and initiative?

Roughly one third of chaplains had either initiated or co-operated in ventures with Visiting Ministers. The range of ventures was wide, although eleven of the twenty-six cases concerned one-off meetings, study days or joint discussions. Six ventures were regular meetings of a general character for discussing any aspects of chaplaincy. Three of the ventures involved Anglican involvement in other faiths' religious festivals; and three more centred on race relations training. Ventures involving a campaign for multi-faith rooms, joint participation in a prayer for peace and the production and distribution of leaflets about all faiths in an establishment were also reported.

In sum, the range of joint ventures between Anglican chaplains and Visiting Ministers of other faiths is quite wide, but they are not very common, tend to take the form of discussions and rarely involve worship. There is a small overlap between these ventures and training activities. But was there any long-term effect? Two chaplains thought it was too early to assess the effect; and three definitely said 'no'. But the remainder all suggested, in different ways, that the joint initiative or venture had produced beneficial long-term effects. In some cases, levels of mutual understanding and inter-personal relations had apparently improved; in others, the effect could be seen in the creation of on-going structures and activities. There was also evidence that most staff and inmates responded positively to joint ventures, claiming, for example, that 'prisoners and staff like to know that fairness, justice and understanding are good' (D049) or 'there is a real awareness that we (Christian chaplains) mean them well and wish to help establish a proper relationship between prisoners and staff' (D085).

To return to the question of agency and brokerage, it seems to us that the scope for co-operation between chaplains and Visiting Ministers is extensive and that some co-operative ventures have already been success-ful. Yet, there is also evidence that the initiative still tended in most cases to lie with the Anglicans. For example, most of the chaplains indicated that it was they who had taken the initiative and had subsequently invited Visiting Ministers (and in some cases prisoners of their faith group as well) to participate. There was only one case in which Visiting Ministers appeared to have instigated a joint venture with chaplains. In fact, chap-lains tended to emphasise their own initiatives by claiming that '[Visiting Ministers] were asked for their views but we (the Anglicans) did *all* the work' (D026, emphasis original), '[Visiting Ministers] were encouraged to take the initiative and we offered support' (D076) or '[Visiting Minis-ters] were simply invited to take part in the proceedings' (D187). The conclusion is that, even when chaplains and Visiting Ministers run joint ventures, the leading role is usually played by the former. In this sense, co-operative events appear, perhaps paradoxically, to be a continuation of Anglican brokerage for other faiths. This is not surprising in view of the relatively small amount of time which most Visiting Ministers spend, are allowed to spend, or can afford to spend in prisons. They also tend to lack financial and administrative support for the work which they currently do – let alone new, co-operative ventures. And they do not find it as easy as do Church of England chaplains to get opportunities for meetings with governors to discuss their own ideas for joint initiatives.

The position of Anglican chaplains in prison chaplaincies is both robust and delicate. On the one hand, many of them have the advantage of being full-time members of staff with regular lines of access to gov-ernors, having control over budgets and 'inside' knowledge of prison procedures, influencing prisoners' inquiries about religion and requests for pastoral help, and being able to initiate joint ventures with Visiting Ministers if they wish. On the other hand, chaplains are conscious of the pressure on them to treat all prisoners equally and to avoid being seen to abuse their position by poaching prisoners from other faith groups. In any case, some of the issues concerning other faiths are officially categorised in the domain of 'race' relations; and chaplains have relatively few opportunities to train staff. In short, no other religious functionaries in prisons enjoy as much power, responsibility or influence as Anglican chaplains, but there are also serious constraints on their freedom to perform the roles of gatekeeper, facilitator or broker.

Facilitating resources for other faiths

We have argued that Anglican chaplains are usually instrumental, if not always successful, in finding and appointing Visiting Ministers, promoting respect for other faith religious traditions, raising issues relevant to other faiths in discussions with local management, arranging for religious festivals to be celebrated, and initiating joint ventures with Visiting Ministers. The question now is whether chaplains are in a position to play an equally facilitative role when it comes to the resourcing of the religious and pastoral care of non-Christian prisoners. If so, what does it imply for relations of authority and power between chaplains and Visiting Ministers?

Beginning with the most basic resources, namely, the accommodation in which Visiting Ministers meet with inmates of their faith, it is far from acceptable, let alone ideal, for members of some other faiths to have to hold their meetings in Christian chapels. Similarly, some Christians find it unacceptable that non-Christian worship has to take place in their holy places. The reality is that some prisons simply lack suitable rooms in which members of other faith groups can meet. As it happens, only 17 per cent of chaplains reported that other faith groups met in chapels in their establishments. The relatively low usage of chapels partly reflects the fact that not all establishments have a chapel. It may also signify that some Visiting Ministers choose not to hold meetings in places of Christian worship even when they have the opportunity to do so. In any event, it would be a mistake to infer from our findings that other faith groups are necessarily excluded from over 80 per cent of prison chapels. In fact, 61 per cent of our sample of chaplains and 68 per cent of our sample of Visiting Ministers reported that other faith groups in their establishments had access to multi-faith rooms, i.e. rooms reserved, at least partially, for the use of other faith groups. Some of the rooms are dedicated to a particular faith group; others are shared by several different groups. Allowing for the fact that a few of the chaplains in our sample came from the same prisons, the likelihood is still that more than half of establishments contain a room for the use of other faith groups. Of course, these facilities may not be fully acceptable to the groups concerned, as our sample of Visiting Ministers made plain to us and as we shall show in the next chapter. The pressure for more or better facilities for other faith groups remains strong in some establishments. Nevertheless, the point is that the majority of other faith groups are not obliged to hold meetings in Christian chapels.

Incidentally, other faith groups which did not meet in chapels and which did not have access to multi-faith rooms or their own dedicated places of worship conducted their meetings in a wide variety of places. They included, in declining order of frequency, chaplains' offices, general purpose meeting rooms, education classrooms, individual cells, visits rooms and libraries. Many prisons built since about 1980 contain multi-faith rooms, but the provision of suitable accommodation for other faiths in many older prisons is still inadequate. HM Chief Inspector of Prisons has often commented on this inadequacy in his annual reports.

The question of what happens in those places where other faith groups are obliged to use chapels is directly relevant to our investigation of the brokerage exercised by Anglican chaplains. Chaplains tended to be tolerant towards the other faith groups which were obliged to use Christian chapels for their meetings. Sharing chapel premises was not considered to be a major problem by chaplains, although the evidence that we collected from Visiting Ministers indicated that the lack of special rooms for the use of other faith groups constituted a very serious problem from their point of view. Very few problems indeed were reported by chaplains, however. There was one complaint that 'Muslim prisoners abused the chapel. Stole the candles and left the chapel in a dreadful mess' (D013); and another chaplain grumbled about the difficulty of arranging escorts for other faith prisoners who met in a chapel.

Turning now to establishments where there were multi-faith rooms, the extent to which other faith groups were consulted about the use of 'their' facilities was a major indicator of how Church of England chaplains exercised their facilitative role. The extent to which chaplains exercised any control over the use of this accommodation was particularly important. We found that sixteen of the fifty chaplains who worked in establishments with special rooms for other faiths consulted Visiting Ministers about their use. Nevertheless, it was also clear that, in many cases, the chaplains held control of the rooms and only consulted Visiting Ministers about such things as room bookings or cleaning. Indeed, one chaplain pointed out that it was he, not the other faith group or Visiting Ministers, who decided how the special room should be used. More typical of the tone of chaplains' statements were the claims that other faiths 'are always shown the room and asked about their requirements' (D073) and that consultation took place 'any time they wish to discuss care and cleanliness etc.' (D027).

Some chaplains had never consulted Visiting Ministers about the use of other faith rooms. One revealing reason was that 'we try to keep the room exclusively for use by other faith groups, so there is generally no need for consultation' (D062), while another chaplain argued that, since he was responsible for the room, 'Visiting Ministers can, and do, consult the chaplain regarding its use' (D065). This was not what we meant by 'consultation', but it clearly conveys the sense of 'patronage' that many Anglican chaplains exercised over facilities provided for the use of other faith groups. They tended to see themselves in a position of stewardship as far as these facilities were concerned. Visiting Ministers of other faiths were like tenants who were permitted to use the facilities on occasion but who had very little influence over their configuration or use. On the other hand, there was also a suggestion that things were different in establishments with separate mosques or synagogues.

There was further indirect evidence of chaplains' brokerage for other faiths in the way that chaplains discussed plans for changing existing religious facilities for members of other faiths. The majority of establishments in which our sample of chaplains worked had no plans for change, although some of them had recently made new provision for other faith groups. But one third of chaplains reported various plans for change, most of which involved creating and extending multi-faith rooms or mosques. For example, 'We plan to move the chaplaincy completely in the next 6 months – and will designate one room as "mosque" – and have an additional "other faiths" room with library' (D076). In none of these cases did chaplains make any reference to consultation with other faith groups or Visiting Ministers. The language which they used clearly implied that they considered it was their responsibility to plan for the future of chaplaincy – including provision for other faiths. Phrases such as '*I* would like an outdoor shrine (Buddhist) as a meditation area' (D036, emphasis added) indicate the extent to which some Anglican chaplains were willing to argue for the interests of other faiths – but they are also evidence of the fact that the custom and practice of chaplaincy enabled chaplains to exercise discretion, authority and power over other faith groups. The Church of England chaplain is 'the voice of chaplaincy' in more ways than one.

Opposition to proposed change was also reported in one establishment which had two chapels, one of which was Roman Catholic. 'The Governor with the full support of the Prison Service Chaplaincy would like to have a combined chapel and special room for other faiths. The Roman Catholic chaplain has stood firmly against this to date' (D063). This is an important reminder that relations between the Church of England and other faiths are undoubtedly affected by the presence of Roman Catholic, Methodist and other Christian ministers.

In short, the brokerage that Anglican chaplains exercise on behalf of other faith groups extends to the accommodation which is provided specifically for the use of these groups in many establishments. Church of England chaplains were responsible in many cases for negotiating with prison management for multi-faith rooms in the first place. They also continue to have a role to play in cases where facilities for other faiths are shared with other prison departments, for chaplains (unlike most Visiting Ministers) are available to serve on committees where space in prisons is competed for and defended if necessary. In cases where the rooms are shared among different faith groups and/or where the rooms serve other purposes as well, chaplains hold themselves responsible for organising room bookings and for ensuring that the premises are kept clean and tidy. Another consideration is that no group should leave symbols in the room which might offend other groups' religious or cultural sensitivities. Chaplains therefore have to act as broker *and* 'buffer' between different other faith communities on occasions. This is yet another aspect of the importance which attaches to the simple fact that chaplains are the only members of the chaplaincy staff who are more or less continuously on duty or available on call. The 'housekeeping' jobs tend therefore to be left to them. Adjudicating complaints and disputes between different faith communities is one of these domestic tasks and is often cited by chaplains as evidence of their even-handed attitude towards other faiths.

As for other aspects of resourcing, the role of Anglican chaplains as brokers for other faiths is less apparent but no less important. For example, chaplains are involved in the process of ordering religious texts and artefacts for other faith prisoners. The supply of texts and artefacts was described as adequate by 89 per cent of chaplains, but as we shall see in the next chapter, Visiting Ministers took a very different view of the situation, often complaining about the slowness of the process or the alleged reluctance of some chaplains to submit orders on behalf of other faith groups. Chaplains were less confident about their success in helping to supply items for the use of individual members of other faiths, but some still claimed to have negotiated the supply of religious books, videos, images, prayer mats, scarves, caps, mats, beads, candles and incense and to have made newspapers and/or magazines published by other faith communities available to inmates through the library or the chaplaincy.

When it comes to providing Visiting Ministers with access to chaplaincy offices, their records and their noticeboards, the picture is more variable. As far as chaplains could tell, there seemed to be few problems with access to noticeboards and not many more difficulties with access to offices. Indeed, we made a point of assessing the visibility of notices,

posters, calendars, maps and pictures associated with other faith traditions or cultures. SHAP calendars were the most frequent sign of an
awareness of multi-faith issues, but chaplaincy noticeboards, both in
offices and on prison wings, carried relatively little evidence of activities
for members of other faith communities. However, this did not appear to
be a major problem for 55 per cent of Visiting Ministers. Some nevertheless regarded it as symbolic of their marginal status in prisons and as one
of the many irritations which were insignificant in themselves but which
added up to a serious and long-running injustice. Visiting Ministers
tended to be even less concerned about their access to chaplaincy offices
because their visits were usually brief and devoted almost entirely to
meetings with prisoners. In any case, they could plainly see that office
facilities for chaplains were inadequate in many establishments. Most
Visiting Ministers merely needed somewhere to collect messages and
mail and to talk to chaplaincy staff.

The question of Visiting Ministers' access to chaplaincy records about
inmates was more significant for them and for Church of England chaplains. Half of the Visiting Ministers and nearly one third of chaplains
considered that the former's access to records was inadequate. Indeed,
twelve per cent of our Visiting Ministers were unaware that such records
existed. Chaplains offered very few reasons for this, although one clue
was provided by a chaplain who wrote that 'chaplaincy records not
normally open but information available on request. Security/confiden-
tial information could be a problem' (D074). It is an open question
whether Visiting Ministers could perform their statutory duties without,
at least on occasion, having access to the records which chaplaincies hold
about inmates. One also wonders whether Visiting Ministers are alerted
to the risk which some of their charges run of attempting suicide or
self-harm. Suicide awareness receives a mention in their induction process at some establishments, but it is unclear how much information they
receive about the risks associated with particular individuals in their faith
communities. Conversely, no Visiting Ministers informed us that they
were consulted about the state of mind of any prisoners thought to be at
risk of suicide, self-harm or any other threatening condition. One would
expect that spiritual advisers, religious teachers or pastoral carers would
normally be mobilised or alerted in these circumstances, but this seems to
be another area in which the Church of England chaplains act on behalf of
other faiths – or, at least, are presumed by prison authorities to do so. The
question of whether it is adequate and/or reasonable to expect Anglican
chaplains to continue to act on behalf of other faith prisoners in this way
lies close to the centre of our interest in official responses to the growing
numbers of non-Christian inmates in England and Wales.

We had no way of probing more deeply into this issue, but it seems to highlight a boundary between what chaplains deem it necessary for Visiting Ministers to know about their inmates and what they consider to be the preserve of the Christian chaplaincy team only. Information, as a resource, is unevenly distributed between chaplains and Visiting Ministers. The boundary between them may mark the limit to which many chaplains are prepared to take the practice of facilitation.

It should not be forgotten, however, that chaplains are far from autonomous. They are subject to a variety of limitations on what they can achieve on behalf of other faiths even when their inclination is to be as helpful as possible. To take the example of a large Northern prison where we learned about the enforced limits of facilitation, the physical arrangement of wings and chapels made movement of prisoners between them particularly difficult. The tiered wings, radiating from a central hub, looked almost elegant in their symmetry. With its impressive wrought ironwork, gleaming paint and soaring glass roofs this establishment could have been mistaken for a scale model of a Victorian prison. At times, there was surprisingly little noise or movement. At other times, the tramp of prisoners' feet on the iron stairs and the staccato shouts of prison officers turned the echoing spaces into a huge, clattering machine. This architectural embodiment of the principles governing security and surveillance was also a major obstacle to the efficient movement of selected prisoners into the wing which had been adapted for use as the chaplaincy centre. In fact, this physical structure of wings was the main reason for the chaplain's complaint about the difficulty of ensuring that Muslim prisoners, for example, could be accompanied to prayers. They were scattered through several different wings; their entitlement to attend prayers varied with their recent good or bad conduct; and the Imam refused to collect them from the wings himself (despite carrying the necessary keys). But the most resistant obstacle was the alleged reluctance of prison security officers to comply with requests to facilitate the movement of Muslims to the chaplaincy centre.

There seemed to be something of a power struggle going on between the chaplaincy and the security staff in this prison, with the latter having the upper hand most of the time. Chaplaincy staff had no authority to do more than request the assistance of security officers; but the latter could choose how far and how promptly to respond to those requests. As in most prisons, security considerations took precedence over others. The result was that chaplains were sometimes unable to facilitate the attendance of all eligible prisoners at prayers or other religious meetings; but they felt that this situation was effectively beyond their control. In this particular case, the chaplain was also frustrated by the unwillingness of prison officers to allow prisoners who were registered as members of one religion to attend, as inquirers, meetings for other religious groups. He personally had no objection to 'inquirers' attending meetings of religious groups of which they were not formally members, but believed that prison officers on the wings were reluctant to show flexibility. Computer print-outs of prisoners' religious registrations were supposedly used as justification for refusing to permit 'inquirers' to find out about religious groups before they had formally changed their registration. The situation in a maximum security Young Offenders Institution was similar but more complicated because the chapel 'red band' orderly was a Muslim prisoner. The chaplain clearly enjoyed describing the bewilderment of the Prison Officers who simply could not understand how a Muslim could be allowed to attend Christian religious services.

The Anglican chaplaincy staff in the Northern prison we have just described were not only frustrated by the difficulty of getting Muslim prisoners to their prayer meetings but were also annoyed by what they saw as the Imam's habit of bypassing them in his attempts to conduct negotiations directly with the governing Governor. This was experienced as another form of constraint on the chaplains' freedom of action. For example, it was alleged that the Imam resented having to ask the chaplains to intercede on behalf of the Muslim prisoners in their requests for halal meat and for special food to be brought into the prison on religious festivals. The senior chaplain was equally resentful that, as he saw it, the Imam had 'gone behind his back' in order to talk directly to governors. He definitely considered himself to be 'caught in the middle' between obstructive prison officers and a manipulative Visiting Minister. Hardly surprisingly, it was not the practice in this prison to invite Visiting Ministers to any chaplaincy meetings or to social gatherings. We encountered a variant on this situation in another, very different type of establishment where the chaplain made no secret of his annoyance with the governor for authorising the erection of a Buddha rupa in the face of the chaplain's disapproval. It seemed to us that it was unusual for governors to intervene quite so directly in chaplaincy affairs and that chaplains resented any such 'intrusion' or 'interference' in their work. This again emphasises the fact that there are real constraints on chaplains' freedom of manoeuvre and that pressure for better treatment of other faiths and various religious minorities can highlight the limits of Anglican facilitation.

Conclusion

Neither the academic study of other faiths nor the experience of living and working in proximity to members of other faith communities is prominent in the background of most Church of England prison chaplains. Much of their knowledge of Buddhism, Hinduism, Judaism, Islam and Sikhism is usually acquired in the course of their daily work with prisoners from these faith traditions or as a result of in-service training. In fact, chaplains spend a lot of time enabling members of other faith groups to perform their religious observances. Chaplains are also willing to foster respect for other faiths in prison, although their involvement in training prison staff about other faiths and participating in multi-faith initiatives is not extensive. Facilitating resources for other faith groups is a further demand on chaplains' time, energy and goodwill.

Yet, there are very few signs that the PSC has raised the profile of its work with other faiths or that it is planning to make more investments in the training of chaplains to work better with prisoners and/or Visiting Ministers. The Chaplain General did not regard relations with other faiths as a high priority on his agenda in 1996: he described himself as 'content with things as they are'.[5] At the same time the leading representatives of Buddhist, Muslim and Sikh Visiting Ministers were dissatisfied with the PSC's responses to their demands for change. In fact, they were losing patience with a system which appeared to exclude them from opportunities to influence policy or practice. In the words of Lord Avebury (1996: 7), a long-standing advocate of a major overhaul of the PSC, 'Whilst the intermittent consultations held by the Chaplain-General, since they were inaugurated in 1992, are "better than nothing", they have not provided other faiths with satisfactory means of redress'. This complaint exemplifies the 'paradoxes of multiculturalism' (Ålund & Schierup 1992) in which state-initiated processes of consultation allegedly cover up for an official reluctance or failure to deal with the real grievances of ethnic or religious minorities.

Chaplains act as the gatekeepers of chaplaincy. It is they who strongly influence the selection of Visiting Ministers and their access to facilities. But they face a dilemma which arises from the fact that the number of prisoners registered as members of other faiths, mainly Islam, is increasing, while the number of 'registered Christians' is at best static. Since chaplaincy budgets are like a zero-sum game, the allocation of resources to some groups entails a reduction for others. Chaplains are required to minister to all, but it is becoming more difficult for them to reconcile their principled support for other faith groups with the need to make savings in their other activities. In these circumstances, it is hard to see how members of other faiths could enjoy equality of opportunity to practise their religions. The structure of the PSC and its position in the Prison Service favour Christian groups and constitute other faiths as exceptions which call for, at best, tolerance and concessionary treatment. There is no place for other faiths as equal partners in prison chaplaincy. Indeed, we shall show in chapter 5 that some Church of England chaplains doubt whether non-Christian faiths are hospitable to the universalism and even-handedness which are claimed as the hallmark of Anglicanism and as the *sine qua non* of prison chaplaincy in a religiously diverse society.

The price which other faith communities pay for the facilitation provided by Church of England chaplains is their own lack of autonomy or self-management. Visiting Ministers in particular are heavily dependent on the goodwill and efficiency of chaplains for their access to prisons, the conditions in which they conduct their religious and pastoral work and the resources with which they accomplish it. The framework of law, administrative arrangements and financial stringency combine to make it virtually impossible for Visiting Ministers to take greater control over their prison work.

It seems to us that some of the difficulties which leaders of some other faith communities experience in their attempts to augment or sustain the work of Visiting Ministers flow from a fundamental anomaly in the PSC's relations with other faiths. On the one hand, Church of England chaplains appear to be in control of virtually everything to which Visiting Ministers need to have access. On the other hand, chaplains are far from autonomous or omnipotent but are actually struggling to retain professional power in a system which has marginalised them to some extent and in which the proportion of prisoners taking an active part in religious activities has declined sharply. The mismatch between the Church of England chaplains' continuing power to mediate or facilitate relatively unproblematic facilities for other faith communities and their declining capacity to meet the growing demands emanating from other faiths is at the root of many misunderstandings and tensions. In other words, the position of the facilitator has become more difficult as the demands for facilitation have grown but the supply of resources has failed to keep pace. The next chapter will analyse some of the implications of this situation for Visiting Ministers of other faiths.

4 Visiting Ministers of other faiths

Neither the Prison Act 1952 nor the Prison Rules 1964 accords to prisoners in England and Wales the *right* to practise any religion while in custody. This is an odd situation and may be at odds with European legislation (Loucks 1994). It is certainly different from the provisions of much more recent legislation for Scotland where statute now recognises that 'Every prisoner shall be allowed to observe the requirements of his religious and moral beliefs' subject to various conditions.[1] The thrust of the law in England and Wales is towards establishing the framework within which ministers of religion may visit prisoners and perform various religious tasks. Nevertheless, it is widely *assumed* that prisoners do have the right to practise their religion; and the Prison Service aspires to uphold the rights of all prisoners to equality of opportunity to practise their religion. For example, 'Members of non-Christian religions have the same right to practise their faith as Christians and they should be given the same opportunity to do so, whenever practicable in prison circumstances'.[2] It is worth commenting in passing on the fact that this quotation seems to take for granted that Christian prisoners have the right to practise their faith. There may also be an underlying implication that non-Christian prisoners have the right to practise their faith only because the Christians already have the same right. Otherwise, it would have been simpler to state that *all* prisoners had the right to practise their faith. Leaving these matters of semantics aside, the final clause in the quotation is crucial to an understanding of the arrangements made for prisoners from, for example, Buddhist, Hindu, Jewish, Muslim and Sikh communities in English prisons.

The aim of this chapter is to examine the social background of Visiting Ministers and their patterns of work in prison chaplaincy. In the opening section we shall pay special attention to their qualifications, prior experience and ways of becoming Visiting Ministers. The second section will analyse their work with prisoners in each of the major faith traditions. Finally, we shall consider the material conditions in which Visiting Ministers do their religious and pastoral work and the problems of resourcing.

89

Throughout, we shall be considering the question of how far the social background and conditions of work in prisons enable Visiting Ministers to provide a standard of religious and pastoral care which is comparable with that provided by Christian chaplains. In other words, do the current arrangements for Visiting Ministers show that the faiths which they represent receive equal respect in prisons? And does the system administered by the Prison Service Chaplaincy (PSC) give prisoners from all the permitted religions the same opportunities to receive appropriate religious and pastoral care?

Who are the Visiting Ministers?

Staff at the PSC headquarters maintain a computerised list of Visiting Ministers of other faiths known to be ministering to inmates of their faith in prisons. The list is based on information supplied mainly by Christian chaplains at each establishment. Periodic reviews of the list take place, but it is currently out of date in some respects. This is not at all surprising, since the relationships that many Visiting Ministers have with their local chaplains are not close or continuous. Moreover, now that Visiting Ministers are appointed by governors at the level of individual prison establishments, it is much more difficult for centralised records to be compiled and kept up to date.

Other factors which make it difficult to keep the list up to date include the infrequency with which some Visiting Ministers visit establishments, the relatively high turn-over rate of prisoners (which means that there may be no need for a visit in the absence of relevant prisoners from time to time), the fact that some Visiting Ministers visit a number of establishments but do not necessarily spend long in any of them, the fact that most Visiting Ministers are part-time appointees and therefore more likely than whole-time chaplains to serve only for short periods of time, and the problems of communication which arise when English is not the Visiting Ministers' first or second language.

We tried to contact all the Visiting Ministers whose names appeared on the headquarters list. In addition, we contacted Visiting Ministers who were named by Anglican chaplains on their completed questionnaires. Even so, it would be an exaggeration to say that we were able to assemble a fully accurate and reliable list. Our list is nonetheless more comprehensive than any other.

In total, we tried to contact 214 Visiting Ministers. As table 4.1 shows, the response rates and the number of usable responses received vary widely between faith communities. The relatively low response from

Table 4.1. *Responses to the questionnaire survey of Visiting Ministers to prisons in England and Wales*

	Questionnaires			
	Distributed	Returned	Response rate	% of sample
Buddhists	37	32	86%	35
Hindus	28	7	25%	8
Jews	18	12	67%	13
Muslims	74	22	30%	24
Sikhs	57	18	32%	20
Total	214	91	43%	100

some faiths probably reflects communication difficulties and a high turn-over rate among Visiting Ministers.

We tried, through the good offices of some leading representatives of the Hindu, Muslim and Sikh communities, to find out why the response rate was relatively low for their Visiting Ministers. Language problems seemed to be the main deterrent. The questionnaires were formal, long and complicated. In the circumstances, we are fortunate to have received such a positive response from people who, almost by definition, are busy and preoccupied with the daunting responsibility of maintaining regular contact with prisoners in a system which provides little or no administrative support for Visiting Ministers.

We could identify (by their titles) only ten women on the PSC list of Visiting Ministers. There were six Buddhists, no Hindus, one Jew, two Muslims, no Sikhs and one Baha'i. Three of the Buddhists visit more than one establishment, but it is not unusual for establishments for female prisoners to have a chaplain or Visiting Ministers who are men. In the event, the nine women who completed our questionnaires are a disproportionately large part of the total of female Visiting Ministers. Six of our female respondents are Buddhists, one is Jewish, and two are Muslims.

The gender of Visiting Ministers has a direct bearing on several aspects of the relations between the Church of England and other faiths. Firstly, some faith traditions are not accustomed to regard women as appropriate suppliers of religious or pastoral care in a formal sense. In these circumstances, Church of England chaplains sometimes find themselves in the difficult position of trying to persuade the local leaders of a community to overcome their reluctance and nominate a female Visiting Minister for female prisoners. This is one of those areas where facilitation shades off into an activity more akin to inducement or pre-empting. Chaplains in this position do far more than simply make it possible for Visiting Ministers to visit prisoners: they go one stage further and actually stimulate the partici-pation of other faith communities in prison chaplaincy.

Secondly, some male Visiting Ministers are reluctant to visit female prisoners on their own. The prisoners complain that they are thereby deprived of their right to receive pastoral visits. Again, it is common for Church of England chaplains to be drawn into the discussion in the hope that they can negotiate a satisfactory resolution of the problem. But we heard of at least one case where a governor pre-empted the chaplain by taking the initiative to find a married Visiting Minister who was willing to visit female prisoners in the company of his wife. An interesting complica-tion in this case was that some of the prisoners were women who wished to receive instruction from an Imam with a view to conversion to Islam so that they could share the religion of their male partners outside the prison. This was a case in which non-Muslim prisoners tried to put pressure on a Muslim Visiting Minister to conform with their cultural ways instead of his own. The Christian and Western character of prison chaplaincy in England sometimes exposes Visiting Ministers to influences and press-ures which are alien and threatening to them.

Thirdly, some female Visiting Ministers complain that their personal safety is unnecessarily put at risk if they have to visit prisoners in remote parts of a prison without an escort. This situation is aggravated if a security alert occurs during their visit and they find themselves isolated for lengthy periods of time and unable to contact anyone outside the prison. There seems to be an expectation that conscientious Church of England chaplains would find a way of preventing this type of situation from arising.

Finally, gender has a bearing on relations between the Church of England and other faiths in cases where female chaplains object to the fact that Muslim Visiting Ministers do not treat them on a par with male colleagues. For example, a female Anglican chaplain is offended because the visiting Imam refuses to shake her hand when he greets her. He shakes hands with the male chaplains but not with women in the chaplaincy office, and this is offensive to her because it implies that he is not recognising her professional equality with her male colleagues. This is why she would accept that an Imam could be appointed as a full-time chaplain but not as a Senior Chaplain in charge of a chaplaincy team. In fact, she would be happier with a religiously neutral administrator than with a male Muslim in charge of chaplaincy. This is an unusual case because it is an Anglican who is claiming that her religion does not receive equal respect from a representative of an other faith.

Since the number of female prisoners who belong to other faith com-munities is small, however, and since few female Visiting Ministers visit male prisoners belonging to other faiths, relations between the Church of England and other faiths are not often complicated by gender differences. On the other hand, when gender-related difficulties do occur they seem to aggravate tensions which are more widespread and more deeply rooted in chaplaincies.

Given the uneven geographical distribution of the members of other faiths in England and Wales, it is not surprising that most Visiting Ministers come predominantly from urban locations. Even establishments located in remote rural places tend to receive Visiting Ministers who live in towns or cities. Indeed, the difficulty of finding people who are prepared to travel long distances to visit prisoners of their own faith who are held in remote places is high on the list of problems that other faiths present to Anglican chaplains. But this is only one aspect of the problem. It is complicated by the reluctance of some Church of England chaplains to support the appointment of Visiting Ministers whose travel expenses might absorb too much of the chaplaincy budget. Similarly, some governors impose their own limits on the distances for which they are willing to reimburse Visiting Ministers' travel expenses. This has led some Visiting Ministers to complain that these restrictions are unreasonable, especially in relatively thinly populated rural areas of, for example, East Anglia or South West England.

Our reason for wanting to know the age of Visiting Ministers was that we wanted to test a hypothesis that it was customary for the members of some faith communities to take on this role after retiring from employment. Table 4.2 indicates that there is some truth in this but that the pattern is far from uniform across the communities. In fact, the pattern is not simply a function of old age; for in some communities it can also be a function of relative youth. As we shall explain below, type of employment is just as important as age.

The number of respondents in some categories is too small to bear the weight of much analysis, but several points can be established about our sample. First, Buddhist Visiting Ministers are predominantly in their 40s and 50s. Second, most of the Jewish Visiting Ministers are over the age of 50. Third, there are proportionally more Visiting Ministers under the age of 30 among the Muslims than in any other faith community.

The last observation may reflect the relatively young age profile of the Muslim communities in the United Kingdom but it is also a function of the position occupied by Imams among Visiting Ministers. Seven of the thirteen Muslims under the age of forty who serve as Visiting Ministers are also Imams; an eighth is currently a student. These relatively young men manage to combine their duties in mosques or Muslim organisations with visiting Muslim prisoners on a part-time (but extensive) basis. One of

Table 4.2. *Visiting Ministers, by age and faith community*

	Under 30	30–39	40–49	50–59	60–65	66 and over	Total
Buddhist	1	2	19	6	0	4	32
Hindu	0	1	1	2	0	3	7
Jewish	1	0	1	5	2	3	12
Muslim	2	11	2	5	0	2	22
Sikh	0	0	7	5	3	3	18
Total	4	14	30	23	5	15	91

them finds time to work as a part-time taxi driver as well. One of the Imams visits prisoners in six different establishments, while another visits four.

The Muslim communities are not unique in this respect: eight of the eighteen Sikh Visiting Ministers are also full-time Granthis or priests. One of them visits prisoners in four establishments, one visits five establishments, and one visits ten establishments. Being a Visiting Minister must constitute a major part of their professional life. Similarly, three of the seven Hindu Visiting Ministers were, until recently, priests in Temples. One of them visits five establishments. A similar pattern is true for the Jewish Visiting Ministers. No fewer than seven of them are Rabbis (one retired), and a further one is now retired from a full-time position as Welfare and Community worker employed by the United Synagogue. The youngest of them visits five establishments, and one of the oldest finds time to visit prisoners in nine establishments.

Many Visiting Ministers are religious professionals in the sense that they possess the qualifications usually expected of members of their communities who have completed special training in religious matters and whose livelihood is based at least partly on their performance of religious tasks. Of course, the nature of their training and of their religious roles varies widely from community to community. Nevertheless, 27 per cent of them described their position in their communities in these terms, with a further 28 per cent indicating that they served as lay leaders in religious organisations. Only 15 per cent reported that they played little or no role in their faith communities.

In short, religious professionals in all other faith communities except the Buddhist are disproportionately represented among the Visiting Ministers in our sample.[3] A number of Church of England chaplains confirmed that this was not an aberration of our particular sample but was true for other Visiting Ministers known to them, yet few chaplains commented on the high proportion of Imams, Granthis, Priests and Rabbis among Visiting Ministers. Chaplains were willing to discuss the personal qualities of Visiting Ministers at length, but there seemed to be some reluctance to recognise them as religious professionals. By contrast, many chaplains wrote freely about what they saw as the divisions and factions among the Visiting Ministers of other faiths, sometimes arguing that factionalism disqualified them from being entirely acceptable as full members of chaplaincy teams. Yet, our evidence about the extent of diversity in traditions or 'schools' represented by the Visiting Ministers in our sample does not suggest that factionalism is common or material to the work of Visiting Ministers. Table 4.3 summarises the terms used by our respondents to describe the tradition or 'school' to which they belonged.

The overall picture is clearly not one of implacable tension between factions. There is a tendency for one particular tradition to be dominant among each of the groups of Buddhist, Jewish and Muslim Visiting Ministers, while no clear pattern emerges among the Hindus. The question of theological 'schools' among Sikhs is virtually irrelevant anyway.

Moreover, when we asked Visiting Ministers how they dealt with prisoners from a different group within their own religious tradition, their responses underlined the importance that they attached to bridging any differences that existed. Almost one quarter either denied that there was a problem about factional differences or reported that they had never encountered the phenomenon. The strategies that the other Visiting Ministers adopted for dealing with differences fell into four categories, although there was also a small amount of overlap between them. Exactly one third of our Visiting Ministers said that they followed the principle of treating all members of their faith group alike, often stressing the equality of all believers. In the words of two Sikhs 'I deal with all prisoners on merit of their being, and treat all prisoners equally' (B185) and 'In the name of God and my religion everybody is equal and has to be treated the same as regards his colour, creed and background. The Sikh religion does not allow to differentiate a person from others. All human beings are equal' (B195).[4]

The second largest category (23 per cent of respondents) stressed the need to be sensitive to differences and to adapt to them sympathetically where possible. This involved showing respect for different traditions and, for example, providing appropriate literature. The need for keeping an 'open mind' was uppermost in some of these responses. Responses in the third, and much smaller, category (8 per cent of respondents) centred on attempts to find common ground between 'mainstream' and 'minority' traditions. This took such forms as 'I am positive and concentrate on basics. I only talk about things upon which we all agree' (B027) or 'Ch'an

Table 4.3. *Number of Visiting Ministers, by faith community and tradition or 'school'*

Faith	'School'
Buddhist	Theravada 18; Zen 4; WBO[a] 4; None 3; Eclectic 1; Tibetan 1; Ch'an 1
Hindu	None 3; Vedic 2; BKWSU[b] 1; Shaiva 1
Jewish	Orthodox 11; Reform 1
Muslim	Sunni 15; None 5; Hanafi 2
Sikh	None 15; Gurmat 2; 'Modern' 1

Note: [a] Western Buddhist Order
[b] BK World Spiritual University

Buddhist ministers have to study *all* aspects of Buddhism . . . The many schools of Buddhism have the same teachings at their base' (B182, emphasis original). One Visiting Minister emphasised the benefits of deliberately keeping the followers of different spiritual traditions in the same group so that they could learn from each other.

Finally, a small group of six Visiting Ministers, acknowledging that differences between 'schools' could be problematic, reported that they either referred inmates belonging to minority 'factions' to suitable authorities or took advice from relevant authorities about how they should respond personally. For example, 'In Islam, the differences between the four traditions/schools are not that different from the day-to-day needs of a Muslim, but if they wanted to talk to someone who had knowledge of their school of thought, I would arrange for someone from the Islamic Academy to visit with me' (B189).

In the light of the above findings, we suspect that insofar as chaplains perceive a problem of factionalism among other faiths in prisons it is more likely to be the result of differences between prisoners than between Visiting Ministers.[5] The latter, with the exception of Buddhists, rarely have opportunities to meet each other, so disagreements are rare. Indeed, not a single Visiting Minister reported any tension with other Visiting Ministers, although many respondents took the opportunity to list their points of friction with Anglican chaplains. But the prisoners of some faith groups are sufficiently numerous and diverse in some establishments to form religious factions. Problems can arise when a faction of prisoners is not in sympathy with their Visiting Minister's approach to their religion.[6]

Several chaplains regarded friction between prisoners and 'their' Visiting Ministers as one of the most challenging aspects of their facilitative role. They found themselves caught in the crossfire without a really clear understanding of the problems, let alone solutions. The risk of jeopardising relations with an entire faith community or at least with one of its factions was a major constraint on the chaplains' freedom of manoeuvre. Negotiations to ensure a peaceful replacement of one Visiting Minister by another could last for months. For example, these difficulties were uppermost in the mind of the chaplain at one establishment who dearly wanted to replace a long-serving Imam who was allegedly 'too pushy' and unpopular with Muslim inmates because he refused to visit them on their residential wings. But the chaplain was also well aware that the Imam was adept at bypassing him and talking directly to the governor in order to get his own way. There were even fears that any attempt to oust the Imam would provoke a hostile response from his mosque. On the other hand, the chaplain knew that the leaders of a different mosque in the same city were enthusiastic about substituting one of their own number for the serving Imam. This was a classic instance of the Church of England chaplain's difficulties in trying to facilitate religious care for prisoners whose faith community was divided. At the time of writing, the chaplain had made no attempt to bring in a different Imam. In short, factional divisions in some faith communities can give rise to problems for chaplains in their role as gatekeepers, but such problems are not common.

In terms of their current or pre-retirement occupations, the Visiting Ministers in our sample are probably not representative of their faith communities. As we have already observed, the proportion of religious professionals among them is considerably higher than it is in the communities of Hindus, Muslims and Sikhs at large. Secondly, the number of manual workers is disproportionately low. In fact, none of the Hindu or Jewish Visiting Ministers falls into this category of occupation; and the work of only one of the Muslims (a process worker) could be categorised in this way. The Sikhs include a machine operator and a London Underground ticket collector, and there is a cleaner of carpets and windows among the Buddhists. The occupations of virtually all the other Visiting Ministers could be categorised as 'white collar'.

The occupational profile of Buddhist Visiting Ministers requires a separate analysis in order to bring out the contrasts with the other faiths. First, only two of the thirty-two respondents are religious professionals (monks), and a third works full-time in a Buddhist centre. Second, it is common for Buddhists to list more than one occupation, as in the case of a Visiting Minister who described herself as 'tour hostess/potter/welfare work with WVS ("Jack of all Trades")' or another who described the work that she does for a living as 'aromatherapist/massage therapist and tutor (self-employed)'. Third, the number of people who are at least partly self-employed is higher among Buddhists than any other category of Visiting Minister. Fourth, there is evidence to suggest that even those who included 'gardener' or 'carpenter' among their occupations are actually people with skills which are usually much more highly rewarded but who have chosen to undertake some manual work for religious or spiritual reasons.

The single most important characteristic of Buddhist Visiting Ministers is the fact that, with the exception of five people employed in business and one exclusively manual worker, the other occupational activities all fall into the categories of the arts, teaching, helping and healing. None of them works in a profit-seeking enterprise; and very few of them work in large organisations. This is a very distinctive occupational profile which is closer to that of the Society of Friends or the supporters of CND than to the members of other faith communities (Byrne 1988).

There are several well established ways of being considered for appointment as a Visiting Minister. Most of the Buddhists and a small number from other faiths, amounting to 37 per cent of the total sample, became Visiting Ministers mainly through the agency of a chaplaincy organisation or some other formal organisation at the national level. Angulimala, the Buddhist Prison Chaplaincy Organisation[7] and the United Synagogue are the most active and effective agencies for recruiting, nominating and preparing would-be Visiting Ministers.

The second most common way of becoming a Visiting Minister is to be selected for nomination by a local or regional grouping of a faith community's members. Of respondents who supplied information on this point, 20 per cent reported that they had been approached and persuaded by leaders of their own community to make themselves available for visiting prisoners.

A slightly less common route into Visiting Ministry is to be invited by a chaplain or member of a prison's staff. This was the experience of 13 per cent of our respondents. Some approaches were personal, as in the case of a Visiting Minister who was 'coopted by the chaplain' or another who reported that the chaplain 'came to my house and asked me to help him in the matter of Muslim inmates'. Finally, only 3 per cent of our sample seemed to take the personal initiative to offer themselves, without invitation, as Visiting Ministers. And a further 4 per cent began as temporary replacements for incumbents who had died or were ill.

Our respondents gave no hints of dissatisfaction with the procedures for being nominated, vetted and appointed by officials at the Home Office or, since 1996, at individual prisons. It is worth noting, however, that one of them was initially rejected but later accepted without explanation and that a few others had to wait for varying lengths of time before receiving an assignment – in one case for four years. On the other hand, the leaders of some other faith groups with a special interest in prison chaplaincy have become increasingly critical of the appointing procedures since the early 1990s. Now that nominations are mainly processed at the level of each prison establishment, the scope for variations in procedure and for idiosyncratic decisions has grown. Coupled with the pressure on governors and chaplains to contain or cut back expenditure, the switch to local decision-making about the appointment of Visiting Ministers has allegedly created new and serious problems. We discussed on p. 93 the greater readiness of governors to impose a limit on the travel expenses for which prisons would be liable. Other limitations are being imposed on the maximum number of hours which some Visiting Ministers are allowed to spend in prisons and on the minimum number of prisoners required to justify a Visiting Minister's journey. The result is greater uncertainty and less transparency in the appointing procedures, according to the critics of the move towards local administration of Visiting Ministers' contracts.

The shift towards local administration began in the Summer of 1995 shortly after most chaplains had completed our questionnaires, so we have very little information about their opinions on the new procedures. But we collected scattered evidence suggesting that some of them already had misgivings about the payment of Visiting Ministers, especially those who could draw keys at the main gate and gain entrance to the prison even when it contained no inmates from their community at the time. Travel expenses and fees could therefore be claimed for little or no work. We shall return to the issue of chaplains' criticisms of Visiting Ministers later.

As far as Visiting Ministers' dates of appointment and length of service are concerned, the range stretches from 1970 until 1995. Five out of the eight longest serving Visiting Ministers who supplied information about their date of appointment are Jewish. Buddhists and Sikhs did not begin to be appointed frequently until the mid-1980s; the first Hindu in our sample was appointed in 1988. The modal or most frequent length of service among our sample is currently five years, with very few serving for longer than eight years. The arithmetic mean is 6.67 years. It is not easy to reconcile these findings with the suggestions made by some chaplains that the turn-over rate among Visiting Ministers is high enough to cause them problems, although we must concede that our data do not reveal how many appointments in different prisons each of our Visiting Ministers has had. We do know, however, that some Visiting Ministers choose, or are obliged, to move from one prison to another – sometimes for infringing the regulations and sometimes in protest against the way chaplaincy was organised.

If the Prison Service is to show equal respect to all permitted religions, one might expect that it would offer, or require, a training programme for Visiting Ministers. Not until 1996, in fact, did it offer the first such course. Nevertheless, many Visiting Ministers had already benefited from professional preparation before beginning their work in prisons. The types of experience or training that Visiting Ministers had received fall into the four main categories of figure 4.1.

Nearly half of our sample of Visiting Ministers reported benefiting from a wide range of experiences associated with their prior involvement in religious groups. Some, for example, had been trained as religious teachers or counsellors. A quarter of respondents, the second largest category, denied that they had received any training for the tasks of a Visiting Minister. The third largest category of responses refers to the preparatory and on-going training provided by some chaplaincy organisations, in particular Angulimala. Fourthly, the experience derived from various forms of employment in social work or social welfare was described by ten per cent of respondents as relevant preparation for being a Visiting Minister. In addition, a few of them regarded their experience of prison visiting as an appropriate form of training.

These findings support our earlier claim that most Visiting Ministers are well integrated into their faith communities, with 38 per cent of them receiving general, non-specific help and support from members of their religious groups. In addition, nearly one third of respondents specified that they had received specific forms of support from chaplaincy organisations such as Angulimala or the Visitation Committee of the United Synagogue. A few also benefited from receiving material objects and services, such as the loan of a car for prison visits or the gift of religious literature, that were felt to be supportive of their work in prisons. The relative paucity of material support is of great concern to the coordinators of Visiting Ministers in some other faith communities. It signifies that, in combination with the lack of state resources for their prison chaplaincy organisations, the capacity of other faith communities to sustain or expand the services of Visiting Ministers is very limited. Some of their leading representatives believe that it is unjust for the PSC to expect other faith communities to finance their Visiting Ministers while the state meets most of the costs of providing chaplaincy services for Christian prisoners. We shall return to consider this contention at greater length in chapter 8 where we shall analyse the argument, which is popular among chaplains, that resources should be distributed in proportion to the number of prisoners belonging to each faith community.

As for Visiting Ministers' perception of the opportunities for training provided by the Prison Service Chaplaincy, a very large proportion were unaware that any such opportunities existed. Fully 84 per cent of respondents who commented on this point said that no opportunities were provided, and we met only one Visiting Minister who had taken a Prison

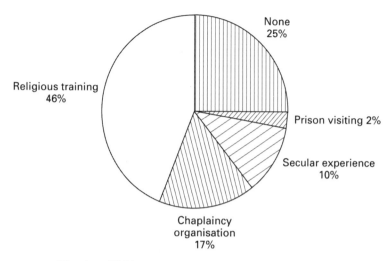

Fig. 4.1   Visiting Ministers, by type of prior experience or training

Service course – in race relations management. Ten per cent had participated in formal or informal induction courses about such things as security, suicide awareness and personal safety; and a further 6 per cent reported that chaplains had offered guidance and advice. The clear picture that emerges from these findings, then, is that Visiting Ministers appear to have received considerably more of their preparation from sources outside the PSC than from inside it. And, although the leaders of some other faith chaplaincy organisations have volunteered to set up training for their Visiting Ministers or for members of prison staff if the PSC provided basic resources, this kind of offer has not yet been accepted. It will be important to bear this in mind when we consider the social relationships that prevail in prisons between Visiting Ministers and Church of England chaplains.

Visiting patterns

Despite the fact that one third of Visiting Ministers are religious professionals, few of them are in a position to devote themselves full-time to visiting inmates of prisons. Nevertheless, the exceptions are worthy of note. One visits ten different establishments; two visit nine establishments; two visit six; and six visit five. It is not surprising that five of these eleven Visiting Ministers are religious professionals. Three of the others are retired, one is a student, and one a manual worker. The occupation of

the eleventh is unknown. It is worth adding that the eleven Visiting
Ministers who visit five or more establishments include three Buddhists,
three Jews, two Muslims and three Sikhs.

The majority of our respondents visit more than one establishment,
and this has implications for the kind of relationships that they develop
with the Christian chaplains. Relations between chaplains and Visiting
Ministers are also affected by the frequency with which Visiting Ministers
visit prisons. Weekly visits are the most frequent, but visits at intervals of
between once a week and once a month are also common. Three quarters
of all visits fall into these two categories. There are no significant differences between the faith groups in terms of the frequency with which their
Visiting Ministers go into prisons. As we shall see later, however, this does
not mean that all groups are equally satisfied with the current arrangements for their visits. Nor does it imply that the Visiting Ministers of
different faith groups make the same kind of use of their visits to prisons.

In fact, the uses to which Visiting Ministers put their visits to inmates
are varied and mixed. That is, the proportions of their visits which are (a)
regular, routine, (b) in response to prisoners' requests, (c) in response to
chaplains' requests, or (d) other reveal a complicated pattern. The salient
facts are that 40 per cent of visits are usually routine; 5 per cent are usually
in response to requests from prisoners; and only 2 per cent are usually in
response to requests from chaplains. In other words, although Visiting
Ministers are necessarily dependent on Anglican chaplains for many
aspects of their work in prisons, most of their visits are part of routine
arrangements which require relatively little assistance from chaplains
once they have been set up. In fact, about a quarter of Visiting Ministers
make nothing but scheduled visits to prisons: their visits have no connection with requests from inmates or chaplains. By contrast, only four
Visiting Ministers (three Buddhists and one Muslim) reported that *all*
their visits were exclusively in response to requests from inmates.

Although Visiting Ministers have to organise their activities carefully
they do not necessarily perform their tasks in the manner of their own
choosing. Each establishment has a set of rules and informal understandings about the ways in which other faith prisoners are to receive the
services of their Visiting Ministers. Their typical patterns of work are
heavily influenced by prevailing rules and procedures – which vary from
prison to prison. This process begins with the ways in which they get to
know that there are prisoners of their faith group in the establishment and
that one or more prisoners have requested visits from them.

Even the registration of prisoners' religious identity can be problematic
from the point of view of Visiting Ministers. Chaplains normally conduct
reception interviews in which they ask prisoners about their religious

registration, and this has led some sceptics to claim that the chaplain is in a strong position to influence prisoners and thereby to influence the 'official' statistics of prisoners' religious identity. It follows, according to this thinking, that the Anglican chaplain is capable of determining the extent to which Visiting Ministers' services will be required.[8] Indeed, some Visiting Ministers complain that they are not allowed to visit prisoners as often as they think necessary or desirable. But very few Visiting Ministers are invited or available to conduct reception interviews with new or in-coming prisoners from their own faith community. One of the reasons for this is that the interviews are often scheduled too early in the morning to allow Visiting Ministers to reach the prison in time. Another reason is that advance information about the religious affiliation of new arrivals is either not available or not passed on to Visiting Ministers, with the result that they never know when to expect a new member of their faith group. We know of only one Visiting Minister who regularly conducts reception interviews.

Yet, only 16 per cent of the 75 Visiting Ministers who commented on registration procedures reported that the religious identity of any of the prisoners in their faith group had been wrongly registered more than once or twice. A further 24 per cent reported that wrong registrations had occurred occasionally. In some cases, prisoners gave wrong or misleading information about themselves by mistake or out of ignorance about religion. There were also suggestions that some prisoners knowingly falsified their religious identity in order to avoid anticipated discrimination[9] or to gain advantages. Nevertheless, cases in which Visiting Ministers did not hold prisoners responsible for misregistration were well documented. For example, a number of Buddhists complained that 'registered Buddhists often find they are registered as Church of England on moving prison. Some put "Buddhist" down but get registered as "C of E". Anyone wishing to change to "Buddhist" finds it very difficult; even when having filled all necessary forms they rarely get re-registered. It is not worth trying really' (B010); 'I often have to personally register them on the computer. They are not registered accurately at [a central London prison]' (B029); and '[wrong registration] used to be a very common event prior to the Anglican chaplain taking part in the induction of new prisoners. The standard practice for all other prison staff is to register all prisoners as Church of England unless a strong protest is made by the prisoner' (B149).

Information about the number of prisoners belonging to their faith groups is essential for Visiting Ministers who need to plan their visits accordingly. Although few prisoners actually request visits from Visiting Ministers, the latter need to know for how many prisoners to prepare. They also like to know whether prisoners have been released or transferred to other prisons. Some Visiting Ministers identified combinations of 'prison authorities', prison officers, a chaplaincy organisation, prisoners or prisoners' relatives as the sole sources of information about inmates. The remaining 83 per cent of responses referred to Anglican chaplains or staff in the chaplaincy office as the people who conveyed this information, sometimes in conjunction with the Education Officer, prison officers and Governors. This reinforces the point that Visiting Ministers are heavily dependent on the goodwill, conscientiousness or efficiency of chaplains in this respect.

The response of Visiting Ministers from different faith groups to their dependence on the Church of England chaplains is highly variable. About half of our sample had nothing to say about the prevailing methods of informing them that prisoners had asked them to visit, but only 23 per cent said that they were definitely satisfied with the current situation. This group includes disproportionately large numbers of Sikhs and small numbers of other faiths. Meanwhile, one third of them made no secret of their dissatisfaction. Buddhists were overrepresented, and the other faiths underrepresented, in this group.

The reasons given for Visiting Ministers' dissatisfaction tended to centre on the alleged unreliability, inefficiency or sheer failure of the system of communication between Visiting Ministers and chaplains. Other concerns were expressed about the chaplains' unco-operativeness and the variable nature of their responses.

Visiting Ministers' suggestions for improving ways of informing them about prisoners were varied, although a clear majority favoured more efficient machinery for administering the compilation and distribution of inmate lists. The most comprehensive proposal specified that 'an efficient secretary, computer-literate, with a computer, without sectarian or religious bias with a clear responsibility for managing matters religious – visits, etc. – is the answer' (B146). Other Visiting Ministers proposed better co-operation with chaplains, more opportunities to publicise their services in prison, earlier contact with new inmates and more reliance on the inmates' own 'grapevine'.

Some Visiting Ministers find out about inmates of their own faith by consulting each establishment's computerised list of inmates. Of course, the lists do not indicate whether any particular prisoners have actually requested a visit from their Visiting Minister. But at least the knowledge that one or more inmates are registered as members of their faith group can help Visiting Ministers to take appropriate action. Nevertheless, we discovered that only 45 per cent of our sample of Visiting Ministers received these lists regularly for all the prisons that they visited. And, although a further 21 per cent receive lists from some prisons, one third of respondents never received them from any prisons at all. Two thirds of Buddhist Visiting Ministers denied receiving lists, but the other faith groups did not appear to be disproportionately disadvantaged in this respect.

Governors were officially instructed in April 1996[10] to ensure that Visiting Ministers received written notification on a weekly basis of the inmates who were registered as members of their religion in each of the establishments that they visited. We discovered that only twelve prisons had actually provided lists of inmates to the Visiting Ministers of one faith community two months after the issue of the instruction to governors. Many other prisons contain inmates of this particular faith, but they do not appear to be complying fully with the Prison Service's instruction.

Obtaining information about prisoners is only the first stage in the process whereby Visiting Ministers make arrangements for their visits. If they know that prisoners have requested a visit, or if a routine visit is arranged, they still need to gain access to the establishment and to 'their' prisoners. The normal practice seems to be for the chaplaincy to inform staff at the gate that visits by named Visiting Ministers are scheduled at certain times. The identity of the Visiting Ministers is checked on arrival, and, on occasion, searches are conducted of their clothing, personal effects and anything which they intend to bring into the prison in conjunction with their religious or pastoral tasks. These security procedures are the cause of resentment on the part of some Visiting Ministers who claim that they are singled out for special treatment and that, in any case, Christian chaplains are exempt from some of these checks.[11] Feelings run particularly high when the special food that some Visiting Ministers take into prison on festival or holiday occasions is subjected to apparently insensitive security checks. And there is still anger in one other faith community about the fact that one of its Visiting Ministers was detained by prison officers with a dog on suspicion of carrying drugs into the prison. The experience shocked the Visiting Minister so deeply that he was unable to visit again for several months. There have also been problems with the reluctance of some Sikh Visiting Ministers to surrender their ceremonial daggers on entry to the prison. These problems have led at least one establishment to publish a policy which clarifies the limits of acceptable practice as far as taking ceremonial daggers and special food into the hospital is concerned.

Gaining access to 'their' prisoners involves more for Visiting Ministers than being admitted at the prison gate. Arrangements must be made for them to move safely through the prison to the place(s) where they will meet with the prisoners – either individually or in groups. The level of security in the establishment seems to be the main determinant of the kind of arrangements which are made. In many places, Visiting Ministers are issued with keys on arrival and are allowed to move around freely within the prison; but in others it is necessary for them to make precise plans in advance and to be escorted from one location to another.

Of our sample of Visiting Ministers, 42 per cent were not issued with keys at any prison; 30 per cent had keys at some establishments; and 29 per cent had keys at all the prisons that they visited. There were no significant differences between the 'other faith' groups in relation to the issuing of keys, but some Visiting Ministers voiced suspicion of inequality of treatment. For example, 'I received keys one month after starting. I had to personally protest to Security and see a Governor before receiving them. New Christian ministers have keys waiting for them on their first day' (B199).

Almost three quarters of Visiting Ministers were satisfied with the kind of access that they had to prisoners, although there were some misgivings about the extent of reliance on Church of England chaplains and restrictions on time and places for meetings. In addition, 8 per cent of our respondents described their access to prisoners as adequate but qualified their expressions of satisfaction with 'can be inconvenient', 'not always', 'could be better' or 'only limited'. When these arrangements fail to operate satisfactorily (for example, prisoners are not where they are supposed to be; prisoners arrive late for a meeting; the meeting room is inaccessible to some prisoners), there is a temptation for Visiting Ministers to blame the chaplain, although the problems often arise from staffing levels or security conditions over which chaplains have no power. As we shall argue later, however, the goodwill of prison officers is also suspect in the eyes of some Visiting Ministers.

The sixteen Visiting Ministers who described their access to prisoners as inadequate included one Sikh, nine Muslims and six Buddhists. Their criticisms ranged from 'have had a lot of trouble. Access depends on the availability of the Anglican chaplain, which has been unreliable' (B014) to 'when I have been denied access I wasn't aware of it for several months and only found out by chance' (B012).

The difficulties which Visiting Ministers sometimes experience in trying to meet with their prisoners stem in part from the timing of their visits and the fact that other activities may clash with them. A large minority of Visiting Ministers maintained that there was interference with their work from other prison activities such as family visits, meal times and sports. The consequences were a waste of their own time or inadequate time for ministering to the inmates. This was captured in detail by a Buddhist Visiting Minister who complained that,

visits, sports etc. happen when the prisoners can be easily moved. So it is also the time when you can hold a meeting or see inmates. These often clash. There are quite narrow time slots when you can visit. E.g. I have to go away for 1.5 hours while inmates are having a meal and are locked up before being available, if I want to see someone who has a visit in the afternoon and is only available in the evening. (B043)

On the other hand, other Visiting Ministers acknowledged that these problems were probably unavoidable and were aggravated in some establishments by special security arrangements. We also heard complaints from chaplains that Christian activities were not immune from timetable clashes with secular activities.

We expected that the high turnover rate of the population of some prisons would cause problems to Visiting Ministers, but again it was only a minority who listed a range of difficulties associated with high turnover rates. They included lack of time to establish good relationships with prisoners or to complete courses of religious instruction, the inability to monitor prisoners' spiritual development, and the loss of books and other items on loan to prisoners who were released or transferred at short notice. There was also concern for the disruption experienced by prisoners, as in the claim that a high turnover rate 'presents problems to *them* – they feel insecure and bereft if someone close is suddenly transferred' (B041, emphasis original).

None of the issues raised so far about Visiting Ministers' access to prisons and prisoners has been specific to any particular faith community, but other issues stem directly from activities which are distinctive of some, but not of all, communities. This is why we asked Visiting Ministers to specify the kinds of things that they regularly did for prisoners of their faith and to indicate the proportion of their time spent on them. The lists include a wide variety of functions with differing degrees of importance attached to them. The mass of detailed information is less important than the underlying patterns which are discernible.

(i)   Firstly, a significant part of the work of Visiting Ministers is done outside prisons. For example, they spend time writing reports on their inmates, liaising by correspondence with authorities, reporting back to their communities, trying to find suitable literature to loan to prisoners, pursuing prisoners' grievances, collecting video and audio tapes for loan to prisoners, and arranging for prisoners to visit places of worship outside their prisons.

(ii) Secondly, Visiting Ministers of every faith tend to attach greatest importance to matters of worship, belief and personal guidance. The more practical matters to do with inmates' diets, living conditions, and legal representation usually assume a lower priority in the Visiting Ministers' assessments of the things which they do for prisoners. Anglican chaplains display a similar set of priorities.

(iii) Thirdly, the terms 'teaching', 'discussion' and 'counselling' occur in the Visiting Ministers' own written responses but they tend to have different meanings in different communities. These common labels conceal considerable variety of practice and emphasis. In addition to the underlying similarities between the activities of Visiting Ministers from different faith communities there are also differences which reflect distinctive beliefs, values and practices.

The *Buddhist Visiting Ministers'* responses followed a clear pattern. Counselling, guidance and listening to prisoners' problems were identified as their most important functions in prison. Teaching, study and instruction were the second most important functions, while meditation and devotion occupied the third place. Offering practical assistance to prisoners by lending them books or mediating between them and the prison authorities was the least commonly reported function of Visiting Ministers. Another distinctive feature of the Buddhist responses is that their range was largely restricted to four basic categories; there seemed to be very few activities outside this core.

The pattern for *Hindu Visiting Ministers* gave a high priority to the recital of prayers and to the reading of sacred texts. Listening to prisoners' problems and discussing their personal circumstances came next in the order of priority.

The pattern for *Jewish Visiting Ministers* resembles that of some other faith groups insofar as the functions of greatest importance centre on counselling and religious services. But a distinctive feature which runs through the other functions for Jews is a concern with prisoners' families, either in terms of their welfare or in terms of relations with prisoners. The notions of 'mediation' and 'contact' were emphasised by some respondents much more heavily than in any other faith group. Two other notable features of the Jewish pattern are apparent. The first is the fact that Jewish Visiting Ministers listed proportionally more functions than did members of other faith groups. This implies a wider range of activities and, perhaps, a greater degree of personal choice on the part of these Visiting Ministers about their methods of dealing with prisoners. The second is that Jewish Visiting Ministers reported more frequently than others that they liaised with prison authorities and lawyers.

The distinctiveness of the *Muslim Visiting Ministers'* pattern of reported functions lies partly in the priority given to the recital of prayers and to religious teaching, which is entirely in keeping with Muslim practices in the wider society outside prisons. Muslim Visiting Ministers' activities are also distinctive for the attention given to writing reports, teaching inmates to read and providing religious artefacts such as prayer timetables.

Finally, the functions reported by *Sikh Visiting Ministers* have much in common with those of other faith communities but they are also distinctive in three main respects. Firstly, the range of activities is particularly wide and not easily categorised under a small number of headings. Secondly, communication of Sikh history and culture, along with the Punjabi language, occupies a prominent position in the work of Visiting Ministers. Thirdly, the term 'counselling' appeared only once in the responses from Sikh Visiting Ministers, whereas respondents from other faith communities used the term much more freely. Similarly, the term 'guidance' does not appear at all. By contrast, there is more attention in the Sikh responses to practical matters of welfare, language and rehabilitation than in some other communities.

This information about the uses to which Visiting Ministers put their time when visiting prisoners provides an insight into their religious and cultural priorities. But it must be remembered that Visiting Ministers are not entirely free to choose their activities: they are constrained by the time available, their physical surroundings, the availability of artefacts and the dictates of prison security. This is why we shall return to the question of Visiting Ministers' priorities in chapter 6 in order to explore their suggestions for how the Prison Service could *ideally* meet prisoners' religious and pastoral needs. Given ideal conditions, defined in their own terms, many Visiting Ministers would prioritise their work differently.

Visiting Ministers of each faith group tend to interpret their role in distinctively patterned ways, and the range of things that they do for prisoners of their own faith is wide. There are also personal variations in how their role is carried out. The arrangements for reimbursing their travel expenses and paying their fees seem to be equally varied. For example, four of them did not expect any form of payment. There were two reasons for this: three preferred to work voluntarily at their own expense; and one had payments made directly to a charity. These cases have been excluded from the following analysis. Roughly 90 per cent of Visiting Ministers had their expenses and/or fees reimbursed by the prisons that they visited, but there were wide differences in the length of time that they had to wait.

Visiting Ministers' opinions on their fees or expenses were highly diverse but were not closely correlated with differences between faith communities. Nearly half of the respondents offered no opinion on the matter, thereby suggesting that the current arrangements are probably acceptable to them. But a variety of negative opinions was shared by about one third, some of whom believed that the level of payment or reimbursement was too low; others were critical of the delays in making payments; and still others complained about confusion over taxation, administrative errors and the failure to pay for work carried out at home. Three respondents were surprised to learn from our questionnaire that it was even possible to receive payment or expenses!

It may be significant that when Visiting Ministers outlined 'better alternatives to the current arrangements for the work that [they] do in prison', only one of them touched on levels of fees or expenses. Her claim was that 'we should be paid at a professional level since I have to take time off work' (B029). In addition, two other suggested improvements involved increasing the number of hours which Visiting Ministers were allowed to spend in prisons, but without specifically mentioning the financial implications. Moreover, fees and expenses were not mentioned by a single Visiting Minister when they were asked to list the main issues that they regularly raise with Anglican chaplains or governors. In short, the issue of fees and expenses is not high on the list of Visiting Ministers' concerns about the work that they do in prisons, although many of them believe that there is scope for improvements in their administration. Many of the other problems which they confront are more challenging.

The conditions in which Visiting Ministers work

Just as Visiting Ministers have to conform with prison timetables and other conditions which cause difficulty to some of them, so the facilities available to them in prison also impose restrictions on how they perform their religious and pastoral roles. In view of the overriding concern with security in many establishments, this is not surprising. Matters are made even more complicated by the diversity of faiths which Visiting Ministers and prisoners represent and by the differences between faith groups in terms of their ways of defining and implementing religious and pastoral care.

The numbers of 'multi-faith' rooms or separate rooms for particular faith groups have been increasing slowly in recent years. In fact, a quarter of our sample of 91 Visiting Ministers reported that new, additional or improved religious facilities had been provided for prisoners of their own faith. Incidentally, it would be naïve to think that these changes met with universal or unqualified approval. We have evidence to show that some Visiting Ministers were resentful of the changes which benefited faith groups other than their own. There was also criticism of some of the new facilities. For example, 'They have given the Muslims a bigger and better room. But they have just partitioned off a toilet which we used to use. But we cannot use it now' (B087).

As far as existing facilities are concerned, fifty-three Visiting Ministers or 68 per cent of those who provided information on this point indicated that at least one of the establishments which they visited had a special room for the use of members of religions other than Christianity. In most cases the matter was reported without qualification, but eight respondents added reservations of various kinds. For example, the room was available only to Muslims, was not available to Buddhists, or was the wrong size.

Overall, 80 per cent of our respondents who commented on the multi-faith rooms available to them seemed to find them adequate, although some entered reservations about, for example, size, availability at festival times, smell and their 'Spartan' character. Only eleven Visiting Ministers (three Buddhist, one Hindu, two Jewish, three Muslim and two Sikh) described the rooms as inadequate. Their reasons for criticising the special rooms ranged from being uncomfortable to being shared with other faiths. Fairly typical of their criticisms was the complaint of a Muslim Visiting Minister that 'Muslims require a clean and quiet place for worship. This room is sometimes used for education, chapel visits, etc. People smoke in it' (B199).

Slightly more than one third of Visiting Ministers reported that they had never made use of a multi-faith room (either because their prison[s] lacked one or because the room was unsuitable/not available). The frequency with which the remaining fifty-eight respondents used multi-faith rooms varied widely, with weekly visits being the most common. Muslims and Sikhs were the only Visiting Ministers to use multi-faith rooms on a daily basis in some places. As for the number of inmates who attend meetings in multi-faith rooms, relatively few Visiting Ministers supplied relevant information, but their responses suggest that numbers range from the extremes of one to forty. Only Muslims constitute groups in excess of fifteen. It is unlikely, however, that the arithmetic mean would be higher than ten across all faith groups.

The final point to be made about the place of multi-faith rooms in prisons is that, as we showed in chapter 3, most Visiting Ministers are not consulted about them. Only nine of our sample had been consulted, thereby illustrating the extent to which Church of England chaplains act on behalf of other faith communities even when the latter's Visiting Ministers work in the same prisons. This is another reason why some Visiting Ministers feel that they are marginal to chaplaincy and that their faith communities do not receive the same degree of respect as Christianity.

Visiting Ministers are not alone in complaining about the accommodation for members of other faiths. The question of separate and suitable accommodation for use by members of other faiths has been one of the recurrent issues raised by HM Chief Inspector of Prisons in his annual reports since 1988. A selection of his observations on this issue will help to explain why some Visiting Ministers regard the question of accommodation for their meetings with prisoners as most important:

1988 'The needs of minority faiths were carefully observed, with the help of visiting Rabbis, Imams and other ministers, but some establishments still had not made proper provision for rooms for religious observance.' (p. 22)

1989 'The Chaplaincy teams were gradually getting to grips with the needs of minority faiths but too little provision was made for them and we found it unacceptable that two Moslem inmates at Low Newton had to go on Rule 43 (own protection) simply to be in a position to exercise their religious observance and ritual cleansing.' (p.24)

1990–1991
'The needs of Christian inmates were well catered for in most establishments... Regrettably the facilities for those of non-Christian faiths still vary considerably. Muslims are poorly served in most establishments.' (p. 32)

1992–1993
'We continue to call for each establishment to have an area in which prisoners from other faiths can worship together in reasonable comfort. These areas should be carpeted and have access to running water.' (p. 26)

1994–1995
'While there appears to be no shortage of willingness to help and set aside areas for multi-faith use, we have not always been impressed by the results. Deerbolt YOI and Blakenhurst Prison provided examples of the best multi-faith provision. But these were far outnumbered by establishments whose awareness and promises had not been translated into action . . . We believe that adequate facilities should be provided without delay for the use of non-Christian religions in prison.' (pp. 18–19)

As we indicated in chapter 3, relatively few Visiting Ministers make use of Christian chapels; and most Church of England chaplains have little difficulty with this usage. Similarly, the Visiting Ministers who have to conduct their meetings in prison chapels encountered relatively few problems, but one respondent objected, for example, to the presence of statues, 'idols' and pictures. A more common problem was the lack of privacy. Prisoners and staff allegedly had a habit of wandering uninvited into chapels either to find other people or to play the piano and relax. It was also difficult in some establishments (for security reasons) to assemble all the appropriate prisoners from different wings in the chapel. Finally, a Muslim Visiting Minister found it irksome that there were no suitable ablution facilities in the chapel's vicinity. All of this supports the observation that 'The lack of suitable or dedicated accommodation for non-Christian forms of worship often became a serious cause of complaints' in the five prisons studied exhaustively by King and McDermott (1995: 178).

Special rooms reserved (or primarily intended) for the use of prisoners other than Christians are only the most visible facilities available to Visiting Ministers. Our research tried to find out what other facilities and resources were provided. As we reported in chapter 3, 89 per cent of chaplains considered the supply of religious artefacts and religious texts to be adequate, but 65 per cent of our sample of Visiting Ministers explicitly contradicted this assessment. Some referred specifically to the lack of, for example, statues, prayer mats, incense, images or books; others merely denied that any artefacts were available. Eleven respondents stressed that they furnished artefacts themselves because prison authorities did not provide them. One Sikh seemed surprised that things could be different: 'NON-Muslims and NON-Christian prisoners and priests will NOT normally expect or demand anything of the kind. They belong to countries where STATE or AUTHORITY has nothing to do with religion' (B127, emphasis in original), perhaps missing the point that the British state has very close connections with two particular churches of one particular religion.

Some Visiting Ministers linked the practice of taking their own artefacts into prison with them to the lack of storage space in the establishment. Others reported that they had given up trying to keep artefacts in prison because they had been stolen or spoiled too many times. Storage facilities were no good unless they were thoroughly secure. There were many echoes of these concerns about accommodation, artefacts and secure storage areas in Visiting Ministers' accounts of how the religious and cultural needs of their prisoners could *ideally* be met in prison. A closely related concern of some Jewish, Hindu, Muslim and Sikh Visiting Ministers was that prisoners of each of their faith groups should have the exclusive use of kitchen facilities which would be entirely free from 'contamination' by people of other faiths. In fact, many statements of ideal conditions in prison embodied safeguards for communal and ritual purity.

A minor theme which runs through Visiting Ministers' comments on the adequacy of artefacts and storage facilities is the desirability of being able to organise their activities independently from Church of England chaplains. This applies, for example, to the frustration felt by Visiting

Ministers who have to rely on chaplains to order 'approved' religious literature on their behalf or who have to ask chaplains to look after religious artefacts until their next visit. Even Visiting Ministers who told us that, from most points of view, they had no complaints about Church of England chaplains sometimes added that they would nevertheless prefer to be able to operate independently of them.

Even basic information about the availability of Visiting Ministers is communicated to prisoners mainly through the agency of chaplains or leaflets produced by them – if such information is conveyed at all. Many Visiting Ministers were not aware that any such information was in circulation. Nearly half of them denied that the chaplaincy supplied any information at all to prisoners belonging to their faith groups. Almost the same proportion of Visiting Ministers reported that prisoners received books and/or leaflets from the chaplaincy.

All of the leaflets which we collected from the prisons we visited made at least some reference to facilities for other faiths, but there was a wide variety of styles. The least informative leaflet simply noted that facilities were available for non-Christian inmates. The most informative was prepared exclusively for Muslim inmates, naming the Imam, specifying the day and time of his visit, and quoting from the Qur'an. Visiting Ministers all agreed that the practice of naming them in chaplaincy information was or would be welcome. None was opposed to, or critical of, the idea. Some also stressed the advisability of printing the leaflets in the prisoners' own community languages, as is already done in some establishments.

Finally, many Visiting Ministers considered it unjust that they had to compensate for the Prison Service's failure to supply religious materials for use by members of other faiths. Of Visiting Ministers listed, 90 per cent listed various kinds of written or recorded materials which they supplied to prisoners either as gifts or as loans. But only 45 per cent of them reported that prison authorities supplied the religious materials which they needed.

In short, it is impossible to isolate one specific cause of the feeling, which is widespread but far from universal among Visiting Ministers, that they are not treated fairly. Rather, there is a range of separate issues, each of which contributes towards the general perception that equal respect and equal opportunities are not accorded to other faiths. Some of these issues may seem trivial in themselves, especially when set against all the other serious problems besetting the entire prison system in England and Wales, but it is the accumulation of issues which lends them significance in the long-term.

Conclusion

Despite the evident differences between other faith communities in terms of the type of religious and pastoral care which their Visiting Ministers deliver, there are structural features of prison chaplaincy which create challenges and opportunities that are common to Buddhists, Hindus, Muslims and Sikhs. The most significant feature of prison chaplaincy in England and Wales is the indispensability of Church of England chaplains to virtually every aspect of Visiting Ministers' work. Chaplains are currently inseparable from the processes of locating and inducting the Ministers. The access which Visiting Ministers have to prisons and prisoners is facilitated by chaplains. And the resourcing of Visiting Ministers' activities depends heavily on the chaplains' support.

The dependence of Visiting Ministers on the goodwill and conscientiousness of Church of England chaplains, as well as on other members of Christian chaplaincy teams, is all the more marked because the state does not financially assist other faith communities with resources to support and co-ordinate Visiting Ministers' work. These communities vary in terms of the funds which they can afford to make available for prison chaplaincy, but none of them receives any direct contribution from the public purse towards the costs of training or administering their own Visiting Ministers. All of this is in marked contrast to the official and direct financing of Christian chaplains who are then expected to channel some resources towards Visiting Ministers.

The Church of England has made, and continues to make, many contributions towards the provision of religious and pastoral care for prisoners who come from other faith traditions. The fact that Anglican chaplains enjoy relatively high standing in the Prison Service has probably worked to the advantage of other faith communities in so far as chaplains have been in a strong position to negotiate access, accommodation and resources on their behalf. Indeed, most Visiting Ministers are grateful for the generous help that they regularly receive from Christian chaplains who, it is widely acknowledged, operate with very tight budgets and management constraints in the Prison Service. Nevertheless, the results of all this facilitation are disappointing for some Visiting Ministers and for the co-ordinators of some prison chaplaincy organisations who tend to attribute the problems experienced by Visiting Ministers less to individual chaplains and more to the chaplaincy 'system' in which chaplains have very little scope for manoeuvre. The next chapter will consider the effects of facilitation and of its mixed results on everyday relations between chaplains and Visiting Ministers in this system.

5   'Facilitation' or 'dependence'? Relations between chaplains and Visiting Ministers

Equal respect among all faith communities is not a static or abstract matter of values and attitudes. It is an active matter of social relationships and interactions. Having considered the social backgrounds and qualifications of Church of England prison chaplains and of Visiting Ministers we shall now analyse their day-to-day interactions, emphasising that their different positions in the organisational structure of prisons shape the way in which the two sets of chaplaincy workers deal with each other. A socio-logic is at work in chaplaincies, and sociological forces shape the mutual relations between chaplains and Visiting Ministers. Personal opinions, attitudes and dispositions need to be situated in their social context.

We shall begin by analysing the patterns of routine interactions between Church of England chaplains and Visiting Ministers. The interrelationship is more often constructive than destructive, but the sources of both harmony and friction need to be explained. Special attention will be paid in the second section to the imbalance of authority between chaplains and Visiting Ministers as well as to ideas about the future of other faiths' involvement in prison chaplaincy. The third section will consider Visiting Ministers' opinions about the role of Anglican chaplains, the organisational structure of chaplaincies and the conditions for improving the religious and pastoral care of prisoners from other faiths. The perceived advantages and disadvantages of the current arrangements for chaplaincy will be considered in the fourth section. And the concluding section will analyse Visiting Ministers' ideas about the value of prison chaplaincy for individual inmates and about the contribution that it could make to the empowerment of their faith communities.

Day-to-day relations between chaplains and Visiting Ministers

As we noted in chapter 4, Visiting Ministers are heavily dependent on Anglican chaplains to notify them that members of their faith group require religious or pastoral services. Most chaplains agree that they have a responsibility to act as the intermediary in this sense between other faith inmates and their Visiting Ministers. What we need to discuss further at this point is how they carry out this role and how the Visiting Ministers respond to it. In other words, the focus of our study shifts from the principle of 'facilitation' to its practice – often in conditions of imperfect knowledge, weak communications and over-stretched resources.

Chaplains usually have to inform Visiting Ministers by telephone that prisoners have requested a visit from them. Two thirds of our sample of chaplains found Visiting Ministers' responses to requests for a visit perfectly acceptable, and there was some praise for those who made special efforts to visit inmates at short notice when emergencies occurred. Chaplains also recognised the difficulties which faced Visiting Ministers who had to juggle the demands of employment or domestic responsibilities with their visits to inmates. In addition it was pointed out that some Visiting Ministers had to travel long distances to reach the prison(s) where inmates were expecting them. By contrast, about a quarter of chaplains described Visiting Ministers' responses as variable. For example: 'Muslim – pretty good; Sikh – good intention, but rather hopeless; Hindu – rather not visit' (D013) and 'Sikhs/Jews – by return; others vary from nil to "poor response"' (D107). This kind of terse categorisation was not uncommon among those chaplains who adopted a patronising attitude towards Visiting Ministers.

The criticisms of Visiting Ministers ranged from the observation that 'Imam can be a bit slow' (D018) to the more fundamental claim that Muslims responded 'usually with reluctance' (D067). Echoes of these claims about the alleged slowness or reluctance of Visiting Ministers to meet their inmates reverberated through some chaplains' comments on other aspects of chaplaincy for other faith communities. These chaplains were certainly a small minority, but they made their critical points forcefully. The Visiting Ministers' views of the procedures for informing them about prisoners' requests for visits were also mixed, with one third of our sample expressing clear dissatisfaction.

Allegations that chaplains failed to notify Visiting Ministers about the presence of inmates of their particular faiths were widespread. For example, a Buddhist cited the chaplain's 'failure to let me know about a prisoner – his illness, attempted suicide, parole or F75 report and his presence in the gaol. In other words, [the chaplain's] arrogance, incompetence and ignorance' (B146). Another complaint turned on the claim that chaplains tended to deal with parole and other reports for other faith inmates 'because people can't be bothered to contact me' (B012). The most articulate summary of these problems came from a Muslim who wrote,

> Because I am not a full-time chaplain, for every event or need I have to see the Anglican chaplains. For example, I have to ask every time I see them for the list of Muslims to be available on the days I go to that particular prison. For them to inform me of the needs of the inmates who want to see me. Sometimes, the inmates tell me they had to fill in 3 or 4 forms to see me, whereas I have only received one or sometimes heard from other inmates that they wanted to see me. (B110)

The variability in chaplains' responsiveness to Visiting Ministers was also an issue in some cases. For example: 'On a daily basis I have not found many major problems as a Buddhist chaplain, but I am always aware that the way I am treated varies from chaplain (Anglican) to chaplain and that on the two occasions where I have strongly disagreed they have used the power their position gives them to enforce their point of view. It is not a question of who is right, simply that the positions are so imbalanced' (B012).

Another area of difficult communication and interaction is proselytism. Just under a third of chaplains complained that some Visiting Ministers abused their access to a literally 'captive audience' in order to spread their religious ideas to people who do not belong to their particular faith group, possibly with a view to converting and recruiting them. Proselytism is a highly sensitive and contentious issue in prisons, not least because of the difficulties of getting agreement on precisely what it means in practical terms. The boundary between 'normal' witnessing to one's religious faith and proselytising is far from clear; it is very much a matter of opinion and perspective. None the less, the Prison Act 1952 (Section 10 [5]) specifies that a Visiting Minister 'shall not be permitted to visit any other prisoners' than those 'who have declared themselves to belong to his denomination'. We explained in chapter 2 that this condition has officially been relaxed in recent years, thereby ironically increasing the risk of accusations of proselytism.

Of our sample of chaplains, 70 per cent declared that proselytism was very rare in their establishments. Most respondents simply stated that this was the situation, but a few went further and asserted that proselytism was not permitted. Some even exclaimed, 'I will not allow space for it!!' (D076) and 'I *actively* discourage it . . . *I will not have* faiths criticising other faiths' (D036, emphasis original). These remarks may seem trivial in themselves but they accurately convey the proprietorial tone which characterises some chaplains' statements about 'their' prisons. They are also consonant with chaplains' views about what members of other faiths are 'permitted' to do in chaplaincy activities. There is no doubt that Church of England chaplains are the guardians of chaplaincies.

On the other hand, 30 per cent of chaplains reported that proselytism did take place. In addition to those who merely recorded this as a fact, others identified the 'culprits'. Seven chaplains identified Jehovah's Witnesses, Pentecostalists or Assemblies of God ministers; two identified Buddhists; and seven identified Muslims. There were three notable elaborations of the claims that Muslims had proselytised. According to one chaplain, a visiting Imam had made special efforts to reach black inmates.[1] A second report claimed that 'much of the Imam's work was anti-Christian' (D031). And a third observed that the proselytism was 'usually between inmates' (D096). We shall return to these special considerations about chaplains' views of Muslim Visiting Ministers and inmates in a later section.

The chaplains' preferred method of dealing with proselytism was to try to discourage the activity by offering 'tactful' or 'diplomatic' advice to Visiting Ministers and by counselling inmates who had sought to change their religious registration. A second response involved reminding Visiting Ministers of the relevant clauses of the Prison Act 1952 and of prison rules prohibiting proselytism. The third most frequent response was a 'softly, softly' approach; it took the form of merely observing what was happening and of not showing anxiety about it. The final category of responses was the most decisive. The tone of these chaplains' remarks made it clear that proselytism was 'stamped on whenever we hear about it. A big foot!' (D026). These particular respondents had complained to Governors and taken steps to exclude offending Visiting Ministers from the establishment.

To put proselytism in its perspective, however, slightly fewer than one third of our sample of chaplains had encountered it. The majority of them responded to it in a variety of measured ways, and it did not appear to be an issue which frequently caused chaplains to question the integrity of Visiting Ministers, although it did reveal a set of assumptions about the rights of chaplains to monitor and, if necessary, to police the activities of Visiting Ministers.

On the other hand, some of the chaplains seemed to take it for granted that their own evangelism among, for example, prisoners registered as 'nil' religion or lapsed Christians did not constitute proselytism. As one chaplain stated quite explicitly, 'we proselytise – but mainly among nominal Church of England and "nil religion"' (D121). Some of them responded to prisoners who were considering re-registering as members of other faiths by openly evangelical methods. For example, 'the response is to be bold in presenting the Gospel and then let men decide for themselves' (D096) or 'with the Christian Gospel' (D081), perhaps substantiating the claim that an evangelical revival is currently taking place in British prisons (Apichella 1996).

There was also unease among Visiting Ministers about the background assumption in prison chaplaincy that, since Christianity was the statistical norm among prisoners and since the Church of England was responsible for the PSC, it was permissible (if not expected) for chaplains to 'missionise' openly. By contrast, Visiting Ministers were forbidden to proselytise. This was one of the grounds on which some of the latter were prepared to mount a challenge against the perceived unfairness of the present arrangements. Indeed, none of the chaplains in our sample seemed disposed to allow other faiths the same opportunity to missionise, and one of our Methodist informants admitted that a double standard operated in prisons: Christian missions were permitted, but proselytism by Visiting Ministers was forbidden.

Some Visiting Ministers accused Christian chaplains of trying to convert 'their' prisoners to Christianity. As a Buddhist put it, 'In my limited experience they seem rather "suspicious" that the inmate is being encouraged to "convert" away from the church. Also some inmates have been told that meditation, e.g., "lets in the devil" and have warned them off' (B150). The tone of a Muslim's claim was more robust: 'When Christian inmates wish to convert to Islam they are persuaded against conversion by the chaplaincy' (B120). Another Visiting Minister objected to the spread of 'evangelical posters' around the prison (B007), but it was the perceived unfairness of current practices which annoyed a Buddhist: 'We are not allowed to proselytise, and wouldn't want to. Christians can, and openly do so' (B166). Finally, an interesting variant on these accusations concerned alleged 'over-avuncularity' on the part of a chaplain who wanted to warn a Buddhist Visiting Minister against accepting change-of-religion applications without scrutinising them carefully.

In sum, chaplains and Visiting Ministers agreed that proselytism was not a frequent occurrence, but their respective explanations of how it happens and who is mainly responsible for it are quite different. Each group tends to blame the other, no doubt indicating different assumptions about their notions of what is 'normal' in mission. We sensed some resentment among Visiting Ministers about the Church of England chaplains' self-appointed role as police, prosecutor, judge and jury of accusations of proselytism. But these difficulties must be kept in perspective:

while they are intensely annoying to the people concerned they are not representative of the generally co-operative relations that prevail much of the time between Visiting Ministers and chaplains. They do reveal, however, the structural imbalance in power and authority between chaplains and Visiting Ministers.

The frequency of informal interaction between chaplains and Visiting Ministers also throws light on the nature of their mutual relations. Table 5.1 shows that 14 per cent of chaplains never met informally with Visiting Ministers in their establishments. In only one case was this because no minister had been formally appointed to the prison in question. All the other respondents reported having had between one and 'too numerous' Visiting Ministers in their establishments. None of them offered any comments on this lack of interaction, but nine out of these ten chaplains had never held formal meetings with their Visiting Ministers either; the tenth had met Visiting Ministers once a year. It remains possible, of course, that other members of their chaplaincy teams were in touch with Visiting Ministers but, even so, the lack of informal social contact is striking. The overall pattern of informal meetings is therefore mixed but definitely not intense.

Our visit to one of London's largest nineteenth-century prisons was arranged so that we could meet most of the Visiting Ministers in the course of their weekly visits. Spending more than four hours almost continuously in the main chaplaincy office, we had the opportunity to observe plenty of informal interaction among chaplains, 'red band' chapel orderlies, volunteers and Visiting Ministers. The oblong office in one of the oldest parts of the prison was large enough to accommodate several desks and tables around the walls. The part-time volunteer in charge of the telephone and various other secretarial functions occupied one corner of the room, but other personnel seemed to make do with whatever furniture they could find. There was also a small table with equipment for making hot drinks. All the furniture was sturdy but worn. None of the electronic equipment to be found in most modern offices was visible. Only the spiritual texts on display would have been out of place in the staff room of an old-fashioned secondary school. This was the busy hub of chaplaincy operations and a place where chaplains and Visiting Ministers could relax briefly before or after meetings with prisoners. The coming and going was hectic at times; and the telephone often interrupted quieter periods. It was virtually impossible to hold private conversations in these surroundings, but this was where most of the informal meetings between chaplains and Visiting Ministers took place. Leaving aside the days when chaplains are on leave, it would actually be difficult for chaplains to fail to meet Visiting Ministers at least

Table 5.1. *Frequency of chaplains' informal*
meetings with Visiting Ministers

	N	%
From time to time	22	31
Weekly	8	11
Fortnightly	2	3
Monthly	6	8
Quarterly	1	1
As requested	19	26
Rarely	4	6
Never	10	14
Total	72	100

briefly during their visits, but the physical arrangements of the chaplaincy office and the density of 'traffic' passing through it would probably preclude anything more than casual conversation and the transmission of messages.

Yet, this was the place where, for example, a newly appointed Visiting Minister had come to pick up information from his predecessor about how to arrange and conduct his visits. The exchange took place with both men standing in the middle of a crowded office while other people came and went around them. Nobody suggested a more appropriate venue for this potentially important exchange of last-minute information. Shortly afterwards the Senior Chaplain told a different Visiting Minister that the location of his weekly meeting with prisoners would have to be changed for the following two weeks so that members of another faith community could clean it and use it for their annual festival. Again, this conversation took place informally, if not casually, in the midst of all the other activity in the chaplaincy office. It seemed as if no written notification or request had been issued to the Visiting Minister and that the chaplain had already taken responsibility for ensuring that prisoners would be collected and delivered to the re-arranged venue on the appropriate dates. We witnessed similar encounters in other prisons where the physical surroundings seemed to preclude proper discussion or private conversation with Visiting Ministers and where the pressure of work on chaplains (to say nothing of unpredictable security contingencies) seemed to impose a 'just-in-time' style of management. Equally, few Visiting Ministers have the time to engage in serious discussions with chaplains during their brief visits to prisons. In fact, it would be difficult to imagine a setting less conducive than a prison chaplaincy to sensitive negotiations or reflective discussions between different faith communities. We met many people who regretted the lack of opportunities for chaplains and Visiting Ministers to explore their mutual interests in a relaxed atmosphere.

The pattern of *formal* meetings between chaplains and Visiting Ministers was different, as can be seen from table 5.2. In particular, the percentage of chaplains who never met formally with Visiting Ministers was much higher at 64 per cent. The modal frequency of the meetings that did take place was between three and six months, with the next most frequent category being annual meetings.

These findings corresponded roughly with the information that Visiting Ministers gave us about the frequency of their meetings with chaplains. In fact, this was one of the very few matters of which chaplains and Visiting Ministers shared very similar perceptions and interpretations. It was also supported to some extent by our experience of visiting sites of prison chaplaincy. Our conversations with chaplaincy staff suggested that in some places Visiting Ministers were rarely seen or only briefly glimpsed and that chaplains were too busy to convene formal meetings. Chaplains and Visiting Ministers 'bumped into each other' on occasion, and this was apparently accepted by some Governors as normal. There was also confusion in one or two establishments about the frequency and timing of some Visiting Ministers' visits. By contrast, chaplains in other prisons were clearly on good personal terms with their Visiting Ministers and were thoroughly familiar with their pastoral activities. Most of these chaplains had taken the trouble to inform Visiting Ministers about our visits in advance in the hope that they could come and meet us.

The topics for discussion at these formal meetings between chaplains and Visiting Ministers were just as revealing about relations between chaplains and Visiting Ministers as was their frequency. Six issues clearly stood out in terms of their frequency from the bewildering variety of other issues that chaplains reported discussing with Visiting Ministers:

> diet
> practical problems of running meetings for other faiths
> festivals
> facilities for worship and meetings
> Visiting Ministers' access to prisoners
> resources and equipment.

Less frequently cited issues included:

> security
> cases of individual inmates
> prison plans
> Visiting Ministers' pay and expenses
> reviews of ministry.

Table 5.2. *Frequency of chaplains' formal meetings with Visiting Ministers*

	N	%
From time to time	2	3
Monthly	3	4
Between 1 and 3 months	3	4
Between 4 and 6 months	11	16
Annually	5	7
Never	46	66
Total	70	100

None of these findings is unexpected, but some of the differences of perception between chaplains and Visiting Ministers, omissions or infrequently listed topics call for comment. Complaints, for example, were mentioned by only one chaplain as a topic for discussion, whereas Visiting Ministers indicated that they regularly took complaints to chaplains. Matters to do with training were also listed by only two chaplains, thereby reinforcing our claim in chapter 3 that Anglican facilitation stops short of systematic preparation of Visiting Ministers for prison chaplaincy work. Thirdly, inter-faith and multi-faith matters appeared in the lists of not more than two chaplains, confirming our view that, for whatever reasons, prison chaplaincy did not appear to be a particularly favourable environment for joint activities between different faith groups.

The fact that the most frequent topics of discussion between chaplains and Visiting Ministers concerned mainly practical matters of prison routine indicates that there are few opportunities for joint discussions between chaplains and Visiting Ministers about the 'principles' underlying chaplaincy. Indeed, many chaplains pointed out, explicitly or more subtly, that they were hard-pressed and under-resourced as far as their work with *Christian* prisoners was concerned and that it was therefore unreasonable to expect them to devote much time or thought to 'big questions' about their relations with other faiths. This point became even clearer in chaplains' accounts of the challenges or problems that Visiting Ministers presented to them, especially when chaplains' authority was at stake.

Authority relations

Chaplains had remarkably few 'in principle' problems with Visiting Ministers. In fact, nearly one third of chaplains reported 'no problem' with Visiting Ministers. But 22 per cent of the reported problems had to do with breaches of prison rules in general and of security routines in particular. In other words, relations of authority and obedience were at issue. For example, one chaplain accused Visiting Ministers of displaying 'a cavalier approach to security regulations' (D071); and another complaint was about a former Imam who 'had a great disregard for the prison rules – and despite several talks brought food into the Moslem prayer time. He also took keys out of the prison' (D076). A third category of problems concerned the difficulties of arranging suitable times and frequencies for visits to other faith inmates. Chaplains often acknowledged that Visiting Ministers had relatively little control over their times of availability since many of them held full-time jobs. But further problems were still laid firmly at the door of Visiting Ministers who, according to chaplains, were unreliable and insufficiently committed to visiting their prisoners.

Other issues regarded by chaplains as problematic included factional disputes within other faith groups, fraud, harassment, poor grasp of English and the difficulty of validating Visiting Ministers' authenticity. Only two chaplains blamed problems on people other than Visiting Ministers. They both cited cases in which prison staff had been insensitive to Visiting Ministers, including the incident reported in chapter 3 in which an Imam had been 'subjected to a search which involved a dog and a handler. The Imam was upset as he felt defiled and unable to lead prayers' (D082).

If a comparison is made between the issues that were identified as problematic to chaplains and Visiting Ministers, respectively, it is immediately clear that Visiting Ministers were much more likely than chaplains to report having problems with the structure of social relations in chaplaincies. Questions of authority, power, discretion, sensitivity and accountability were on the minds of Visiting Ministers (especially Buddhist and some Muslim) but not on chaplains' minds.

Although the things that chaplains considered problematic or challenging were virtually all to do with day-to-day interactions with Visiting Ministers, chaplains considered some faith groups more difficult than others. 58 per cent of the situations identified by chaplains as problematic or challenging concerned Muslims. This figure is 19 percentage points lower than the proportion of inmates registered as Muslims among all other faith prisoners in England and Wales in 1995. The sheer number of claims that Muslims presented challenges to Anglican chaplains was not therefore the most significant aspect of this finding. The reasons that chaplains gave for claiming that Muslims were challenging were more interesting and highly distinctive, although the numerical preponderance of Muslims among other faith inmates was clearly associated with the case's distinctiveness. Much more important in the opinion of chaplains, however, were the allegations of assertive or 'militant' conduct, intolerance, internal divisiveness, weakness of Imams, ease of 'conversion',[2] 'political pressure and propaganda from the Islamic Cultural Centre', reluctance of Imams to visit female prisoners, and political aggressiveness. This partial listing of chaplains' claims about the challenging aspects of Islam is quite different from the claims made about other faith groups. A typical generalisation was that 'Muslims are *always* the ones who cause the challenges. There are more of them and they have a new-found confidence' (D071, emphasis original). A much less typical observation was that, 'Muslim Visiting Ministers can be influenced by a strong sense of marginalisation and perceptions of intolerance and disrespect. The prison culture can present like this to Christian ministers too, but they aren't automatically racially/culturally separated out!' (D031). Muslims undoubtedly represented the largest and most distinctive problem for chaplains, and it often involved a perceived challenge to their authority.

Sikhs were the second most frequently cited cause of challenges to chaplains, but there were only eight citations; and the reasons for the challenges were quite different from those associated with Muslims. They included allegations that it was difficult to appoint Sikh Visiting Ministers and to persuade them to travel to the prison, that the insistence on carrying daggers or wearing turbans was irksome, that some Visiting Ministers were awkward about the level of fees and expenses, and that (like some Hindus) there was reluctance to minister to convicted prisoners.

By comparison, the challenges presented by Buddhism and Buddhists seemed to be more fundamental in character. For example, there was a theological challenge on the grounds that Buddhism's emphasis on harmony with one's environment and circumstances might inculcate fatalism. Several chaplains remarked on the politicised and confrontational attitude of some Visiting Ministers towards the organisation of chaplaincy: 'The Buddhist group represents more challenges than any other. The reason is the line taken by Buddhists over the last few years and trying to disestablish the Christian chaplaincy . . . This problem is further exacerbated by the preferential treatment given to Buddhists' (D051). And one chaplain claimed that a Buddhist leader 'seemingly refused to accept restrictions on proselytisation' (D094).

The very small number of citations of challenges from Jews referred to the difficulty of persuading Visiting Ministers to visit prisoners outside times of festivals and of getting the festivals organised. The two challenges from Hindus concerned the difficulty of appointing a Visiting Minister and the alleged reluctance to minister to convicted prisoners.

Although chaplains often insist that they treat all prisoners alike, regardless of their religion, their perceptions of the challenges presented by Visiting Ministers vary significantly with the faith groups. This is important because it helps to make sense of the concerns expressed by some chaplains that the efforts being made to accommodate Muslim requirements are in danger of creating envy and a sense of unfairness among other groups, especially the 'Christian majority'. There is also an underlying implication that Muslim Visiting Ministers, many of whom are experienced Imams, are reluctant to be seen acknowledging the influence and authority that chaplains, who are fellow religious professionals, have over them. This may be why some Imams prefer to deal directly with governors rather than with chaplains.

Despite the prickliness of their relations with Visiting Ministers in some cases, about half of our sample of chaplains denied that they had tried to exercise influence over Visiting Ministers. Several argued along the lines that 'I do not think it would have any influence as "other faiths" keep to themselves when coming into the prison and have little dialogue with us' (D050). The frequency of responses like this matched quite well the pattern of chaplains' other statements about their relatively tenuous relations with Visiting Ministers. By contrast, 18 per cent of chaplains accepted that they had directly affected Visiting Ministers' pastoral style. The existence of a chaplaincy team had allegedly been a factor in one case in so far as 'The chaplaincy team's standard of work and accountability has become a benchmark for other faiths' ministers' (D013). Another claimed that 'Visiting Ministers often adopt the "house style" of ministry and use the space created by the full-time chaplains' (D076). The most ambitious and possibly contentious statement was that Visiting Ministers 'learn by seeing our depth of pastoral care and action – not common in their "spiritual" ministries' (D072). Another claim was that influence had been exerted on Visiting Ministers through the cultivation of mutual respect between faith groups. A handful of other chaplains gave specific examples of the kind of influence which they had tried to exert on Visiting Ministers. They included encouragement to visit prisoners more often, to emphasise teaching and prayer in their visits and to take advantage of the opportunities and facilities accorded to Christian chaplains. In view of all these claims about the influence of chaplains, it is interesting to note that eight out of ten Visiting Ministers reported that they did not feel under any pressure to conform with Anglican styles of chaplaincy.

Nevertheless, when chaplains assessed the challenges facing other faith communities in prison chaplaincy about one fifth of them cited the necessity for Visiting Ministers to be sufficiently interested in prisoners and motivated to help them pastorally. There were claims, for example, that 'Some [Visiting Ministers] really do not wish to be involved with the prisoners or are selective (as to race etc.)' (D013), that Visiting Ministers 'often don't seem to see the necessity of very deep involvement' (D022) and simply that Visiting Ministers 'don't want to do it!' (D127). In a similar vein, 11 per cent of chaplains complained that some Visiting Ministers failed to appreciate the importance of respecting specific rules governing such things as visits, messages and delivery of special food as well as the general need for strict security in prisons. The implication was that Visiting Ministers were aware of the regulations but chose to ignore them. Chaplains also suggested that some Visiting Ministers had to overcome their naïveté about prisoners ('not being prison-aware') and their reluctance to ask for guidance. The theological challenge was summed up by one chaplain as the need for Visiting Ministers 'to relate their faith and theology to the issue of crime, punishment, concepts of justice, rehabilitation, guilt and forgiveness' (D031). Another formulated the challenge as the need 'to show how their faith and practice could be a positive influence in the reform and rehabilitation of offenders' (D100).

In addition to all these suggestions that Visiting Ministers showed insufficient respect for authority, small numbers of chaplains pointed out that some challenges were beyond Visiting Ministers' direct control. For example, racist and insensitive attitudes among some Prison Officers and the failure of staff to make Visiting Ministers feel accepted in their establishments were said to be challenges to which it was not easy to see how the other faith communities could make a constructive response on their own.

Even more chaplains considered that the major challenge facing other faith groups was simply to make suitable Visiting Ministers available. The obstacles in their path were said to be the lack of potential appointees in the vicinity of the establishment, the long distances that some Visiting Ministers had to travel to meet prisoners, the lack of time available for making pastoral visits and, in some cases, the shortage of adequate funds to pay for Visiting Ministers' services.

Despite the misgivings expressed by many chaplains about the unwillingness of Visiting Ministers to conform with the PSC's standards and to respect chaplains' authority, their general opinion about the future of other faiths' involvement in prison chaplaincy was positive. Of course, there was caution about the dangers of speculative thinking and about the need to bear in mind the diversity and complexity of all the relevant factors. Overall, however, chaplains were constructive and cautiously optimistic – with a few exceptions. In particular, there were two rather tetchy, dismissive statements. One simply noted that the way ahead for the involvement of other faiths in prison chaplaincy was 'to be avoided' (D081). The other warned that

We are in danger of over-reacting. For example, in order that 3% of this prison's population may have halal meat, all the other 97% have to have it. I foresee difficulties for the majority if non-Christian faiths are granted facilities over and above the numbers they represent. I believe the Prison Service Chaplaincy should remain a Christian provision with facilities for those who are of other faiths. (D096)

This view was also stated to us in uncompromising terms by a Roman Catholic nun working in a Young Offenders Institution. Several aspects of Visiting Ministers' work 'bugged' her. She was annoyed by what she considered to be the high fees paid to Visiting Ministers for relatively little responsibility. She claimed that Visiting Ministers 'swanned about' on high fees but actually needed 'nursemaiding'. She also complained about Visiting Ministers' lack of commitment to the prison and the prisoners; and she was critical of one particular Visiting Minister for bypassing chaplaincy channels and bringing external pressure to bear on the Governor in order to obtain preferential treatment. Significantly, however, she insisted that Christian chaplains should retain responsibility for facilitating the work of Visiting Ministers so that chaplains could keep proselytism in check. In her opinion, Visiting Ministers were not under the same pressure as Christian chaplains to work in a multi-faith way.

A few chaplains also hinted that if the numbers of other faiths prisoners continued to grow as a proportion of the inmate population it might be preferable to establish separate chaplaincy organisations for each major faith group. The majority did not, however, believe that such radical changes would be necessary. They expected that the current system would simply be adapted to accommodate increasing numbers of prisoners and Visiting Ministers from other faith communities. The expectation was that this could be achieved by making the following adjustments, beginning with the most frequently listed:

greater co-operation, sharing and inter-faith dialogue between faith groups

a stronger concern among Visiting Ministers with pastoral care for individual inmates

the possibility of appointing full-time 'chaplains' from other faiths and adding other faith representatives to the PSC headquarters staff

the need to redefine chaplaincy and prepare for a new Prison Act

more training for Visiting Ministers

> closer negotiation with national-level bodies representing other faiths
>
> more involvement of Visiting Ministers in day-to-day chaplaincy business.

In short, the majority of Church of England chaplains in our sample, as well as most of those whom we met in their chaplaincies, are open to the possibility that the provision of religious and pastoral care to members of other faiths in prison will be different in the future. But none of the chaplains' ideas about the forms which the re-organised provision may take would involve a radical re-structuring of the PSC or of its place in the Prison Service. The limits to which Church of England chaplains are prepared to go in re-organising chaplaincy will become fully apparent only in chapter 6.

Visiting Ministers' responses to Church of England chaplains

Relations between chaplains and Visiting Ministers tend to be weak but courteous in most chaplaincies. They centre on matters of routine and practice rather than on theology or principle; and they give rise to the authority relations discussed in the previous section. We now need to examine more closely the structures of chaplaincy from the point of view of Visiting Ministers, with special emphasis on their perceptions of the role of Church of England chaplains as 'facilitators'. In particular, we shall consider the Visiting Ministers' assessments of the way in which chaplains carry out their duties and organise things for members of other faith communities.

In the eyes of about one fifth of our Visiting Ministers the Anglican chaplains' role in relation to prisoners of other faiths was either unclear or badly performed. At worst, the role was described as 'unhelpful' (B029) or 'potentially hostile' (B027). By contrast, a much larger proportion of Visiting Ministers described the role of chaplains in neutral or positive terms, often making a connection between the fact that chaplains were the only full-time salaried religious professionals in the Prison Service and their special responsibilities towards all faiths. As many as one third of Visiting Ministers described Church of England chaplains' role performances as 'good', 'very good', 'supportive' or 'helpful'. Typical claims included: 'The chaplains at [a S. Midlands establishment] are very good and helpful. The [chaplain] is always helpful in every matter regarding helping the young prisoners' (B195) and 'generally sympathetic and supportive' (B021).

It was also common for Visiting Ministers to describe the role of Anglican chaplains in a variety of terms pointing to the idea of brokerage on behalf of other faiths. Some of the terms they used, such as 'broker', 'go between' and 'intermediary' speak for themselves, but it is a little more difficult to know whether 'link', 'mediator', 'messenger', 'post box' or 'contact' express the same positive image of brokerage. There can be no doubting, however, that the Visiting Ministers tended to perceive chaplains as channels of communication. None of them explicitly criticised the notion or the reality of 'facilitation' or 'brokerage', with the possible exception of a Muslim who alleged that 'Anglican chaplains monopolise prison activities' (B190).

In fact, chaplains played no part in organising activities for other faith groups as far as 57 per cent of Visiting Ministers were concerned, and the remainder reported either that the chaplains had been 'helpful', 'co-operative', 'supportive', etc. or that they had helped to facilitate things for other faiths. Examples included notifying Hindu inmates about the dates of festivals, arranging for Buddhist retreats and ensuring that Muslims could celebrate Eid and Ramadan. A Sikh Visiting Minister commented that 'the chaplain has given all possible facility and help, e.g. premises, service, use of kitchen/cutlery and crockery etc., and above all his company' (B127), while another commended the chaplain for 'arranging rooms, making arrangements at gates for extra persons coming in or extra items/food for the ceremonies' (B055). There were no complaints about anything that Anglican chaplains had done for other faith inmates. And, as we stated earlier, 79 per cent of Visiting Ministers denied that they felt under any pressure to model their own pastoral care on the Anglican pattern in ways that were not traditional to their own faith community. The exceptions included a Buddhist who described the pressure as 'a tendency to look for organised group worship rather than one to one meetings' (B012) and a Muslim who was less specific but more self-assertive in claiming that, 'There may be some pressure to conform. But I do pastoral care in the Islamic way' (B083).

Moreover, while Visiting Ministers acknowledged that the experience of chaplaincy had broadened their view of life, deepened their religious faith, clarified spiritual challenges, obliged them to make adjustments or made them more aware of other religions they did not feel that these changes were attributable to the influence of Anglican chaplains. There were also a few references to the frustrations of working in prisons, including:

> made me more tolerant of the petty bureaucratic nature of prisons and officers (B145);

the experience has made me more aware of how Muslims have been deprived of space and provision which, as a Muslim and Imam, I had taken for granted (B083);

I'm tired of fighting political battles and fed up with bureaucracy' (B013);

and 'I now feel that there is a stronger need and case for Government to support and finance a similar working structure of pastoral care for all faith communities (B185).

Yet, the Church of England did not figure even in these critical comments about the experience of chaplaincy work. In these circumstances, we feel confident that Visiting Ministers do not regard the ways in which Anglican chaplains mediate or facilitate things on behalf of other faiths as problematic in many cases.

Nevertheless, it was clear that relations between Visiting Ministers and chaplains were difficult in some cases. The underlying issues were diverse and, in some cases, interconnected in complex ways.[3] But, as we suggested in chapter 4 in the discussion of the conditions in which Visiting Ministers do their work in prison, questions of equality of treatment and resources could be particularly troublesome. Thus, complaints about meeting rooms, finances and the number of hours permitted for visits amounted to half of all the problems between Visiting Ministers and chaplains. They ranged from the straightforward claim from a Muslim that 'we do not have access to money and facilities' (B049) to the more elaborate identification of sources of tension with the Anglican chaplain as in the following list: 'My very existence. His budget. His desire to restrict the amount of time I can spend with very needy and often disturbed prisoners. Refusal to pay me for the necessary time this requires' (B029). Although some Visiting Ministers accused chaplains personally of treating them unfairly, the problematic issues were usually rooted in the organisational structure and resourcing levels of prisons. Chaplains were sometimes the targets of criticism which should have been directed at Prison Service policies or local management, but since Visiting Ministers were accustomed to dealing directly with chaplains there was a tendency to regard chaplains as the culprits. It is significant for our purposes, for example, that Visiting Ministers were resentful if they tried to raise problematic issues with governors but were simply referred back to chaplains. In fact, a number of Visiting Ministers complained about the inaccessibility of governors.

However, direct criticism of Anglican chaplains for causing tension with Visiting Ministers tended to centre more often on personal attitudes, concerns about communication, proselytism and arrangements for festivals and diets. Some issues were distinctly *ad hominem*, for example: 'interference; passing judgement without consultation with the Visiting Minister; bossy approach' (B162) or the problem of 'gaining access or to communicate with him' (B083).

By contrast, relations among Visiting Ministers, or between them and Christian clergy other than the Anglican chaplains, appeared to be unproblematic in virtually all cases. The reason for this tranquillity probably had a lot to do with the fact that non-Anglican chaplains were not perceived as having influence over chaplaincy policies and budgets. The only minor irritations which were reported concerned rumours of prejudice against certain faith groups or competition for favoured meeting rooms.

In short, it seems that the framework of chaplaincy regulations and the distribution of resources and authority between Anglicans and others combine to increase the likelihood that certain issues are going at best to require discussion and at worst to generate friction between chaplains and Visiting Ministers of other faiths. No doubt, changes in prison regimes, differences between establishments in terms of security status, and fluctuations in funding also help to determine the importance that Visiting Ministers attach to these issues. What is more, the degree of sensitivity and responsiveness that chaplains display to the issues, or are perceived to display, must not be discounted; but the evidence that we collected from Visiting Ministers suggested that these personal factors contributed towards tension with Visiting Ministers in only a small minority of cases. By comparison, the underlying structural factors associated with authority and resources were much more significant.

Practical and structural dimensions of chaplaincy

Very few Visiting Ministers were entirely dismissive of the current arrangements for chaplaincy. Most of them considered that there were definite advantages for them in these arrangements. About one third of Visiting Ministers considered that practical or material advantages were most important. They referred to such things as access to inmates, the availability of keys, the suitability of meeting rooms and the timing of visits. Slightly fewer than one third of Visiting Ministers identified the efficiency of current structures as the main advantage. They took into consideration such things as: the fact that Visiting Ministers had a single point of contact with the prison via the chaplaincy, the availability of back-up support if necessary, the fact that Church of England chaplains 'have "systems" worked out for their own ministry which I can appropriate and modify' (B181), 'less admin for me!' (B006), the fact that the chaplain 'is a link between me and my prisoners. He is full-time and helps when things are required of me' (B153), 'although problems can arise, it is generally helpful to negotiate access with one relatively sympathetic chaplain than with several (possibly less sympathetic) officers' (B021), and the 'possibility of delegating follow-up work to the chaplaincy as an organisation' (B218). The implication is that relationships between chaplains and Visiting Ministers tend to be satisfactory if the routine procedures and facilities work properly. Visiting Ministers appear to expect Anglican chaplains to ensure that day-to-day arrangements for chaplaincy should run smoothly. This facet of 'facilitation' presents problems to relatively few Visiting Ministers.

Only 16 per cent of Visiting Ministers saw religious or spiritual advantages in current arrangements for prison chaplaincy, and most of these claims were relatively modest. They included, for example, 'it is a chance to meet the inmates and help to aid their development and rehabilitation' (B087), 'contact and instilling of religious awareness' (B184), 'the prisoners feel more at home when I visit them' (B068) or to 'keep the faith alive in prison' (B082). None of these advantages makes any reference to Anglican brokerage. In fact, few Visiting Ministers saw the personal qualities or know-how of Church of England chaplains as current advantages from their point of view. Their perceptions included: 'at the moment it works but that is because of the nature of the individuals who are the Anglican chaplains' (B169), 'the main advantage is my access to the chaplain's knowledge and status whenever I need advice and help' (B127), and 'friendliness of chaplaincy staff' (B178).

Finally, three Visiting Ministers considered that the advantages of current arrangements lay in the independence which they enjoyed from the prisons where they worked. Thus, 'I'm not perceived as being part of, nor close to, the prison establishment' (B146), 'I am seen by the prisoners as entirely separate from the prison regime. Hence, confidentiality is viable' (B029), and 'I don't have to get too involved with prison bureaucracy and admin' (B013). These three responses raise the intriguing possibility that one of the unintended consequences of the Anglican 'brokerage' is that it deflects potential criticism away from the Visiting Ministers of other faiths. Chaplains sometimes talked to us about 'covering up for Visiting Ministers' or 'taking the rap for other faiths'. We shall show later that some Anglican chaplains are well aware of the luxury enjoyed by Visiting Ministers who can make use of all the practical advantages of chaplaincy without having to defend it or be associated with its problems and shortcomings. This is an aspect of the wider issue of accountability which looms large in the thinking of many chaplains, and it implies that Visiting Ministers should accept more responsibility for chaplaincy if they are to enjoy equal opportunities to participate in it.

Close to 40 per cent of Visiting Ministers were satisfied with current arrangements for chaplaincy, although some also voiced a few notes of resigned acceptance of the inevitable.[4] Seven out of the twelve Jewish Visiting Ministers were among those who seemed content with things as they were. But one third of Visiting Ministers believed that the practical arrangements or settings for Visiting Ministers' work could be improved in relation to such things as having longer and/or more frequent visits, better meeting rooms, improved distribution of keys to Visiting Ministers and more efficient ways of notifying Visiting Ministers about the number of prisoners of their faith group in each establishment. Only one proposed better rates of remuneration, but the reason for this was interesting because it touched on other aspects of the conditions in which some Visiting Ministers have to work in prison: 'We should be paid at a professional level since I have to take time off work. Twice I have been kept in [a central London prison] during a lock up, which means I cannot phone out, and was prevented from leaving for my next appointment; and not told what was going on' (B029). Suggestions that chaplains should consult Visiting Ministers more frequently and seriously came from two Muslims and three Sikhs. One of them added that it would also be helpful to have regular meetings with the Board of Visitors and governors as well as with chaplains.

Suggestions for changes to the organisational structure of chaplaincy were much less common and came exclusively from Buddhist Visiting Ministers. One proposal was to place all arrangements in the hands of a more even-handed chaplaincy team so that 'any faith could have a chaplain. The prison-appointed full-time chaplain could be from any faith and would represent the views of the chaplaincy team in terms of chaplaincy arrangements and administration. The chaplaincy would be more of a general religious centre than the sole domain of one particular faith' (B040). More radical proposals were to appoint a religiously neutral person to run chaplaincies or to give the administrative responsibility to prison Education Departments. Finally, there were three arguments for placing the administration of chaplaincy in the hands of secular agencies, possibly giving *all* participants the status of Visiting Ministers. The theme which ran through all these proposals for structural change was the imperative to remove overall control from the Church of England and to treat all faith groups equally. This theme was repeated in suggestions that the Prison Act 1952 should be replaced with more appropriate legislation.

In fact, one third of the proposals for legislative change involved removal of the Church of England's overall responsibility for running prison chaplaincy. They included the arguments that:

> 'the system by which the Anglican religion is the 'official' religion needs to be changed. The primary chaplaincy post should be open to all religions (or none?)' (B169);
>
> 'most essentially the abolition of [the law's] very strong bias in favour of the Church of England – all chaplains/minister/whatever and all faiths should be on the same footing within the prisons – an end to the chaplain as a figure in charge and an end to the distinction between the privileged chaplain and the visiting ministers' (B146);
>
> 'in an ideal world there would be no reference to Church of England, Roman Catholic, Methodist chaplains. Visiting Ministers, of any faith, would be appointed by the governor. Christian faiths would not be singled out for appointment to all prisons and would not have power over ministers of other faiths' (B166).

Other proposals in this vein stressed the need for transparency in chaplaincy budgets and for a neutral or secular person to run chaplaincies, but only one Visiting Minister explicitly criticised the assumptions underlying the 1952 Act:

the Act is based on the assumption that religion equals Christianity. Chaplains represent the major Christian denominations and Visiting Ministers the others. Other faiths have been tacked on to this set of assumptions. The religion part of the act needs to be re-written in more general terms to reflect the present multifaith community. It should also make better provision for prisoners to find out about other religions. (B040)

All of these proposals for radically re-distributing authority, responsibility and resources came from Buddhist respondents. Buddhists also proposed that inmates should be allowed to attend meetings of faith groups other than the one to which they officially belonged and that 'shopping around should be allowed/encouraged' (B027). In comparison, Visiting Ministers from communities other than the Buddhist tended to suggest legislative changes affecting specific features and practical modalities of chaplaincy rather than underlying assumptions or general principles.

Overall then, Visiting Ministers' suggestions for ways of improving chaplaincy arrangements corresponded generally with the pattern of their criticism of existing arrangements. They confirmed our view that levels of satisfaction with the current situation were quite high and that many Visiting Ministers emphasised the advantages which could be gained from making the practical arrangements work better. It is also clear that dissatisfaction with current arrangements for chaplaincy was unevenly distributed across faith groups and that pressure for wholesale reconstruction of the organisation of chaplaincy was expressed most strongly and consistently by the Buddhist Visiting Ministers. Other Visiting Ministers were certainly critical of the current arrangements, but their concern tended to centre on matters of practical detail rather than basic principle. The level of satisfaction with both structural and practical aspects of chaplaincy in its current forms was highest among Jewish Visiting Ministers.

However, we need to consider carefully three aspects of our findings at this point. Firstly we recognise the possibility that levels of dissatisfaction and demoralisation might be so high among the population of Visiting Ministers that the most serious critics of the current arrangements were too demoralised to communicate with us. There is always the risk in social scientific research that the samples of respondents and informants who volunteer information to researchers are not fully representative of any particular group. This is especially problematic when the response-rate in questionnaire surveys is low for some, but not all, categories of respondent. So, it is possible that the Visiting Ministers with whom we were able to make contact did not hold the kind of extremely critical opinions which might exist among the entire population of Visiting Ministers. However, we believe that our attempts to achieve higher response-rates and to contact as many Visiting Ministers as possible during our visits to prisons and in follow-up telephone conversations went a long way towards reducing the possibility that we had somehow failed to detect the true rate of dissatisfaction with chaplaincy arrangements for prisoners of other faiths. In any case, it seems equally plausible to us that Visiting Ministers who were thoroughly *satisfied* with current arrangements might be complacent and therefore also unlikely to complete questionnaires or to talk to us in person. If this were so, the absence of both extremes would not be such a problem. But, instead of second guessing the reasons for non-responses, we preferred to search for all available evidence that our data might not be representative of the full spectrum of opinion. We found no such evidence.

The second consideration is more subtle. Some of the comments which Visiting Ministers made to us in person suggested that wholesale reorganisation of the current arrangements for chaplaincy was not near the top of their list of priorities because they were preoccupied with the more immediate problems of, for example, trying to understand prison rules and procedures, finding time to visit their prisoners regularly or obtaining adequate facilities and support for their own work in their faith communities. In these circumstances, it would be unlikely that Visiting Ministers would press for proposals to restructure chaplaincy. Nevertheless, some of our informants accepted that *in an ideal world* they would be allowed to operate independently from the Church of England chaplains in prisons. In other words, the *long-term* aim of some Visiting Ministers was to be in a position where they did not need to use Anglican chaplains as intermediaries with prison authorities and where they could enjoy greater freedom in deciding how to provide religious care for prisoners of their faiths. The *short-term* aim of these Visiting Ministers was, however, more practical: they wanted better facilities for religious practice and better recognition of the religious requirements which their prisoners had to meet. The distinction between short-term and long-term aims is important because it shows that their opinions about the acceptability of current chaplaincy arrangements were not necessarily fixed for all time; their opinions need to be interpreted as an expression of priorities which reflected immediate pressures *and* longer-term aspirations. The discussion of Visiting Ministers' opinions was clearer in our interviews and conversations with them than in their questionnaire responses.

The third consideration relates to differences which we perceived between the opinions of individual Visiting Ministers and those of the co-ordinators of prison chaplaincy services in some other faith communities. In particular, the co-ordinators of Buddhist, Muslim and Sikh Visiting Ministers tended to be more critical of the current arrangements and more outspoken about the need for major structural changes than 'rank-and-file' Visiting Ministers. The main reason for the difference is quite straightforward: even the Visiting Ministers who visit prisoners in more than one establishment have few opportunities to know whether conditions for their fellow-Ministers in other places are better or worse. They have no way of knowing whether their experiences are typical and may therefore be reluctant to criticise the entire system. By contrast, the co-ordinators deal constantly with the difficulties encountered by many Visiting Ministers in a large number of prisons. Moreover, the co-ordinators have much more experience than Visiting Ministers of dealing with the Prison Service, the PSC, prison governors and the Home Office. As a result, their interest is in making the *structure* of chaplaincy more responsive to their complaints and proposals. They also make use of their twice-yearly consultations with the Chaplain General and his headquarters staff to voice the accumulated complaints of Visiting Ministers and to press for structural changes in chaplaincy provision. These meetings are often heated and confrontational.

This helps to explain why the thrust of the paper on 'Religion in the prisons of England and Wales'[5] which the co-ordinators of Buddhist,

Muslim and Sikh Visiting Ministers presented to the Home Secretary on 27 March 1996 was towards a radical re-structuring of prison chaplaincy services. As we reported in chapter 2, they seek to remove the Church of England's 'special privileges' in prison chaplaincy and to establish an Advisory Council on Religion in Prisons. These changes would require a new Prison Act to ensure that all religions were treated equally. Their objections to the current arrangements are based on the principle that 'a society which is proud of its diversity, equality and tolerance' should not 'confer special privileges on one denomination of one religion'. But our interviews with these co-ordinators revealed that their 'in principle' objection is actually based on years of daily frustrations with what they consider to be the inefficiency and insensitivity of a system which cannot, as it is presently constituted, deal fairly with non-Christian prisoners. So, the irritations experienced by individual Visiting Ministers are multiplied many times over in the co-ordinators' experience.

Rehabilitation and empowerment

This is the point at which we wish to return to the issue of how the Church of England affects the extent to which members of other faiths are able to make their voice heard in mainstream society. Visiting Ministers had a variety of reasons for believing that, if the conditions of their work in prisons were suitably improved, the effects of their religious and pastoral care would be beneficial. In particular, all the Visiting Ministers who commented on this matter argued that inmates of their faith group would be helped to feel more at home in the activities and institutions of the majority population outside prison.

The Visiting Ministers' main reasons for making this claim about the likelihood that prisoners' chances of being re-integrated into mainstream society after their release would be enhanced if their pastoral care was appropriate was the belief that religious activities fostered useful skills. They included the basic capacity for mixing with other people and thereby learning elementary social skills as well as 'the skills, knowledge and confidence through educational support to have a network of relationships and to build the motivation necessary for re-settlement' (B083). A Sikh Visiting Minister added that 'as well as teaching them their own religion I also preach tolerance of all people and practices, which will help them operate in society' (B096). Another aspect of religion's capacity to foster basic skills and personal strengths was the idea that religious activities would help to crystallise and develop the prisoners' self-understanding, identity and self-confidence. All of these suggestions fed into the general idea that religious and pastoral care helped to rehabilitate prisoners by virtue of the values and skills that it inculcated in them intentionally or otherwise.

Another reason that Visiting Ministers had for arguing that religious and pastoral care encouraged better participation in mainstream society and culture was that it helped to correct unfortunate attitudes or habits. As a Sikh Visiting Minister put it, 'At least [prisoners] will not develop an inferiority complex and feel ignored' (B077) if chaplaincy worked well, and 'they should become better behaved persons' (B108). A Muslim was more explicit about the correctional benefits of effective chaplaincy: 'Practising Muslims' behaviour is different from others' – decreased greed, trust in God and a caring, sharing attitude will help the mainstream society' (B036).

A third type of claim which some Visiting Ministers made for the benefits of improved chaplaincy concerned the effects of socialising inmates into religious ideas and practices which they had either abandoned or never known. In the words of a Buddhist, prisoners who developed 'more awareness of belonging to a religion rather than being a minor interest group' (B012) would be more likely to modify their conduct. A Sikh saw the benefits in terms of persuading prisoners to 'come back' to their religion and their community. The same theme was taken up by a Muslim who could see that the longer-term benefit of a return to religion in prison would be that new converts and 'returnees' 'would be able to attend the local mosque without any fear that they do not know anything about Islam or the Islamic tradition and how Muslims should participate in prayers' (B199).

Finally, a few Visiting Ministers developed the argument that it was good for members of faith groups outside prison to become involved in visiting prisoners and thereby creating the basis for stronger communities. In other words, prison chaplaincy ideally formed an integral part of any responsible faith community. This was an unusual argument but it had echoes in other Visiting Ministers' views about the benefits that could flow from enhancing the religious and pastoral services provided for other faiths in prison. For example, several Buddhists reasoned that a more visible appreciation of Buddhism in chaplaincies would help to strengthen the feeling of Buddhists inside and outside prison that 'Buddhism was openly accepted, rather than tolerated as a threat to Christianity' (B166). In other words, 'It does help to have one's religious faith practically recognised by Government bodies. It is also through participating in society that this recognition is given. The two things go together' (B040).

Questions about the contribution made by the religious and pastoral care of Buddhist, Hindu, Jewish, Muslim and Sikh prisoners in English gaols to their integration into mainstream society go to the heart of the issue of the Anglican Church's opportunity, capacity and readiness to enable other faiths to participate as fully as they wish in the national society. In practice, participation (in this sense) means being taken seriously, consulted, listened to, understood and having access to positions of influence, respect, authority and power. It is the opposite of being dismissed out-of-hand, excluded, ignored or discriminated against for being different from the nominally Christian majority of the country.

Visiting Ministers were clear on this point: they considered it very important to preserve and, in some cases, enhance the opportunities for the religious and pastoral care of prisoners from their faith communities. They supported this view with highly diverse, if not always consistent, arguments. But underlying this diversity was the widely shared view that it was essential to establish their chaplaincy work on the best possible footing if full participation in the life of the national society was going to be possible for their faith communities. Many Visiting Ministers took the view that this required the maintenance of the Church of England's statutory responsibility for chaplaincy, whereas others argued that the removal of Anglican privileges and responsibilities was a prerequisite for improving chaplaincy.

Conclusion

The picture which emerges of relations between Church of England chaplains and Visiting Ministers is mixed. The majority of chaplains and Visiting Ministers are reasonably content with the current provision of religious and pastoral care to prisoners belonging to other faiths. On the other hand, there are misgivings about the attitudes of some individuals or the unequal distribution of authority between Christians and non-Christians. And the co-ordinators of Visiting Ministers in three faith communities believe that the current structure of chaplaincy is not only ineffective but also unjust and unacceptable in a society as religiously diverse as England.

The next chapter will consider how far the Church of England's role of 'broker' for other faiths helps them to participate fully in prison chaplaincy and thereby to feel empowered to take their place in the life of the nation. This is, after all, one of the main justifications for the Church's ascendancy over the PSC. Special attention will be given to the degree of Visiting Ministers' inclusion in, and exclusion from, chaplaincy life as well as to their views on chaplains' receptiveness to cultural sensitivities. There will finally be a discussion of the limits to which chaplains are prepared to take the process of facilitating the involvement of other faiths in prison chaplaincy.

6   Inclusion and exclusion

Writings on ecumenical co-operation and inter-religious tolerance are extensive. It is not difficult to expound ideas about the common sympathies and affinities which, on a theoretical level, unite the practitioners of all religions in solidarity against the forces of secularism and indifference. It is widely believed that intolerance is the result of ignorance and misunderstanding on all sides. The solution is to make people knowledgeable about their own and others' religious traditions. The theory is that knowledge and understanding will cancel out ignorance and fear. This is a simple, liberal theory about the connection between knowledge, understanding and tolerance; and there is nothing wrong with it *as a theory*. But this way of thinking about the relations between religious and faith traditions fails to pay sufficient attention to the *practice* of social relations. We mean that the theory is silent about the fact that members of different religions do not interact in a vacuum (Séguy 1973). Rather, they meet as rivals for jobs, as competitors for resources and public esteem, as superiors and subordinates in organisations, as neighbours in residential areas, and so on. It is in these everyday social settings that religious faiths encounter one another. This is when the theory of religious tolerance is tested.

Prisons are 'extreme' social settings (Goffman 1968; Cohen & Taylor 1972). They amplify the 'noise' of ordinary social life by intensifying competition, rivalry, hostility, manipulativeness and vindictiveness – as well as friendship, altruism, solidarity and generosity. This is partly why religion becomes unusually important for some prisoners. Religion casts a new clarity on life for some; and for others prison life creates a new need for clarity about religion. So, although the proportion of prisoners who register as adherents of no religion continues to increase steadily and rapidly, demand for religious and pastoral care remains strong among others. In fact, some Anglican chaplains insist that even those prisoners who deliberately refuse to register as members of a religious faith community nevertheless look to the chaplains for help and comfort at times of difficulty such as bereavement or serious ill health.

The main question at issue in this chapter is how far Church of England chaplains can facilitate the religious observances of members of other faiths in the extreme conditions of prisons which are a stern test of the theory of religious tolerance. We shall draw together the threads from earlier chapters by considering, firstly, the extent to which the social life of chaplaincies includes or excludes Visiting Ministers. We shall then ask how well the cultural sensitivities of prisoners belonging to other faiths are respected in prison. And the third section will analyse chaplains' views about the limits of their facilitation and brokerage for other faiths as well as the implications for their own religious convictions.

Integration or omission?

According to some versions of multiculturalism, minorities have to as-similate to majority ways of thinking and acting in the public sphere but may preserve their different ways of life in the private sphere of home, friendship networks and sub-communities (Rex 1996; Modood 1994a. But see Ålund & Schierup 1992 for criticisms of multiculturalism). It usually follows from this way of thinking that minority religions are expected to be virtually invisible in public settings but to be active in private settings. The provision of religious and pastoral care in prisons seems to be based on this kind of multiculturalism in so far as the public and official side of chaplaincy remains firmly dominated by Christianity, the religion of the majority, while the other faiths, the minorities, are confined to private activities. What evidence is there to support our claim that other faiths are excluded from the public side of chaplaincy?

Formally and informally, 'chaplaincy teams' consisting of full-time and part-time chaplains as well as volunteers are known and expected to plan and deliver religious and pastoral care to prisoners and staff. This is the public face of chaplaincy, but fewer than ten per cent of the Visiting Ministers in our sample even knew of the teams' existence. They wrote,

> I think there is a Christian team (B010);
> I suppose there is one at [a London prison], but all I have noticed is that it is referred to by the chaplain on his answering ma-chine . . . Seems that it's only Church of England (B029);
> the Christians have a 'team' which they refer to all the time. It does not include me (B164);
> there was one at [a South Midlands prison] but I fell out with the chaplain and haven't heard a word from [there] for two years (B013).

In fact, only four Visiting Ministers declared unambiguously and without qualification that chaplaincy teams were in operation in their establishments.

Significantly for our purposes, many Church of England chaplains referred to their 'ecumenical teams', but none of these teams appeared to include any Visiting Ministers. Catholics and Methodists were included, of course, but ecumenism in prison did not extend to other faiths. Not surprisingly, only seven out of eighty-two chaplains reported that a multi-faith celebration or worship had taken place in their prison chapels.

Another possibility for Visiting Ministers to be included in the public side of chaplaincy activities is for them to engage regularly with prison staff and to offer training courses in the establishments that they visit. However, very few Visiting Ministers regularly participated in either of these activities. Apart from a few reports of, for example, trying 'my best to be co-operative with the prison staff' (B074) or being 'kind to everyone' (B051) and 'talking to them individually' (B012), only 19 per cent of our ninety-one Visiting Ministers listed activities specifically for staff. Even these activities were confined entirely to informal activities such as 'occasional intellectual discussion' (B181), answering 'requests for Buddhist teaching' (178) 'answering questions on Jewish faith' (B155), giving information about Muslim festivals, and translating documents to and from English. Four fifths of Visiting Ministers reported that they did nothing for prison staff. This is hardly evidence of the involvement of Visiting Ministers' in the aspects of chaplaincy which transcended their particular faith group.

The situation with regard to Visiting Ministers' involvement in helping to run training courses for prison staff was even clearer. Only six of our ninety-one Visiting Ministers had helped in such activities. They involved an exhibition on Buddhism at an open prison, training courses for new prison officers, a seminar for general prison staff, talks about particular faith groups and an 'inter-faith day'. All but one of these activities appeared to be one-off events. These findings therefore provided further support for the view that most Visiting Ministers are not firmly integrated into chaplaincies beyond the point of their routine visits to prisoners of their own faith groups – whether by choice or necessity.

No doubt some Visiting Ministers would prefer to describe themselves as 'independent' rather than 'isolated', for it would be a mistake to assume that they all wished to be integrated into chaplaincy teams – especially if this entailed further dependence on Anglican chaplains. Yet, the case for isolation cannot be easily dismissed, especially when further evidence is taken into account concerning invitations to events organised by chaplaincies. Of Visiting Ministers, 60 per cent reported that they had never been invited to any chaplaincy events. The next largest category (22 per cent) had been invited to Christmas Carol services and, in one case, to a Diwali celebration. Invitations to a variety of dinners, discussions, licensing of new chaplains, and conferences had been received by a further 14 per cent. Only three of the seventy-seven respondents mentioned invitations to multi-faith or interfaith gatherings. In short, a clear majority of Visiting Ministers were effectively excluded or omitted, intentionally or accidentally, from the kind of social gatherings that take place in and around prison chaplaincies.

Part of the explanation for Visiting Ministers' omission or exclusion from social events lies in the fear which some chaplains have of offending non-Christians by inviting them to, for example, Christmas celebrations. One chaplain was genuinely horrified when we asked her whether she had ever considered inviting Visiting Ministers to such occasions. She thought it would have been not only insensitive but also insulting to invite them into a room containing Christian symbols. Interestingly, the Imam had invited her to attend an Eid festival and had been disappointed that she had not been able to attend. Other chaplains were concerned about the risk of giving offence to Visiting Ministers by inviting them to Christian celebrations but chose to take the risk. Many of them believed that, although Visiting Ministers usually declined such invitations, it was still desirable to invite them on an equal footing with Christian ministers. It has to be added that very few Visiting Ministers expressed any doubts about the wisdom of inviting chaplains to their festive celebrations.

Perhaps, it might be argued, social events for the sake of being sociable are not a good indicator of the extent to which Visiting Ministers are included in the life of chaplaincies – however strong the evidence of their exclusion or omission. A better indicator might therefore be their participation in multi-faith initiatives in which representatives of more than one faith group could participate. At least multi-faith gatherings or programmes would have to count as evidence of a desire for inclusiveness in chaplaincy. Yet, our findings do not suggest that many Visiting Ministers had this opportunity to overcome their isolation.

Since prisons are among the few sites in English society where all the major religious groupings are represented on a daily basis, it would be reasonable to expect relatively high levels of communication and interaction among the groupings in multi-faith activities. By 'multi-faith' we mean the willing participation of the members of two or more faith groups in joint activities which draw on their different faith traditions. In fact, only seven chaplains were able to report any worship activities with even a vaguely multi-faith character in the prison chapel. They included a women's prayer group of Christians and Sikhs; a 'multi-faith day'; a 'sharing faith encounter'; visits to multi-faith meetings outside the establishment; 'an "Asian" celebration of "Christian" worship involving Sikhs, Hindus, Muslims in Urdu followed by traditional Asian food and liquid refreshment' (D085); and prayer groups for peace meeting alongside each other. The paucity of multi-faith activities was confirmed by Visiting Ministers, only 12 per cent of whom could identify multi-faith initiatives in any of the prisons they visited; and three of these initiatives were actually one-off events which had occurred only once in several years.

There was even less evidence of 'inter-faith' activity in which relations between faiths were explored. A Visiting Minister made the telling point that prison chaplaincy presented a 'lot of opportunity for inter-faith discussions' but that they never took place because 'each and every faith minister has different dates and days to visit' (B065). Those who had to travel long distances in their spare time to visit prisoners would probably have concurred with this statement. Time for visits is usually brief, so multi-faith or inter-faith initiatives might seem like a luxury or a diversion. Even so, the rarity of such initiatives supports the view that Visiting Ministers are relatively isolated from the rest of chaplaincy life. This interpretation was supported by the claim of a Buddhist Visiting Minister that 'the Christian chaplains have made it clear to me that they are not interested in inter-faith dialogue' (B182).

We did, of course, encounter situations where at least some Visiting Ministers were strongly integrated into chaplaincy life – formally or informally, but they were a very small minority of cases. It was much more often the case that chaplains facilitated Visiting Ministers' appointments and access to prisoners as a matter of routine but without considering it necessary to try to draw them further into the life of the prison or of the chaplaincy. This is one of the implicit boundaries of facilitation. The situation of most Visiting Ministers is that they are heavily dependent on Church of England chaplains for negotiating their access to prisoners and for many other services, but they remain isolated and marginal – perhaps even excluded – from chaplaincies as social entities. In some cases this is by choice and in others against their will. The PSC has no procedure for integrating Visiting Ministers into the public side of chaplaincy. On the contrary, its version of multiculturalism helps to keep them at a distance: dependent but distant.

Cultural sensitivities

If relations between Visiting Ministers and chaplains tend to be somewhat distant, do the Ministers none the less feel that the current arrangements for their visits are respectful of their particular religious and cultural values? Do Visiting Ministers believe, for example, that due recognition is given to their personal and religious qualifications for the work they do in prisons? Do Visiting Ministers consider that prison staff show appropriate sensitivity to the religious, spiritual and cultural requirements of prisoners in their faith groups? These questions all touch on the cultural aspects of inclusion and exclusion.

For example, the question of the titles by which Visiting Ministers are recognised presents problems to about one third of the Buddhists and to two Muslims in our sample who objected to their designation as 'Visiting Ministers'. One of the Muslim Visiting Ministers captured the sensitivity on this point very clearly: 'I am content with "Muslim Minister", but the term "Visiting" makes me feel like an outsider and not a fully contributing part of the Prison Service' (B199). He, in common with the Buddhists, preferred the title of 'chaplain' on the grounds that this was a better description of the work that he did and that it implied a stronger degree of inclusion in chaplaincy affairs. On the other hand, 90 per cent of Visiting Ministers appeared to be content with their title. In any case, some already enjoyed being called 'chaplain' or 'Buddhist chaplain'.

The Prison Act 1952 accords the title of 'chaplain' exclusively to clergy of the Church of England, referring to all other religious visitors as 'Visiting Ministers'. Over time, the title 'chaplain' has been extended to clergy of the Roman Catholic and the Methodist Church,[1] thereby aggravating the resentment expressed by some Buddhists at what they see as the symbolic exclusion of other faiths from full and equal participation in prison chaplaincy. The report for 1992–93 of Her Majesty's Chief Inspector of Prisons took a more robust approach to this problem: 'we have used the word "chaplains" to cover ministers of all religious faiths, although we appreciate that the Prison Act still restricts the word to the Church of England' (p.27).

Sensitivity to the designation of 'Visiting Minister' was only part of the story, however. There was greater concern about identity badges. Firstly, the distribution of badges is very uneven. Roughly half of our sample of ninety-one Visiting Ministers had identity badges, but the other half did not. Secondly, 78 per cent of those who did not have a badge declared that they would have liked one. Thirdly, the range of words to describe Visiting Ministers on their badge was wide: 'chaplain', 'visiting chaplain', 'minister', 'visiting minister', 'priest', 'visiting priest', 'Imam', 'chaplaincy visitor' and 'HMP Rabbi'.

Further issues of religious and cultural sensitivity arose in connection with, for example, the Sikh Visiting Ministers' requests for permission to carry the *kirpan* or ceremonial dagger on their visits to prisons. There have also been problems in some establishments when the food that

Visiting Ministers wanted to bring into prison on festival occasions was either rejected at the gate or subjected to security checks which were experienced as defiling. Strip searches of Muslim prisoners and lack of privacy in the area of showers have occasionally caused offence despite the official policy of allowing prisoners to keep the upper or lower part of their body covered while the other is being searched.

The high number of Hindu, Muslim and Sikh Visiting Ministers' complaints about the diet of their prisoners underlines the importance of cultural sensitivities about food. Some suggested that inmates of each faith group should be housed together in order to make it easier to meet their specific requirements for diet and food preparation. Others were more concerned to ensure that the appropriate food should be properly prepared and served on festivals and holy days. One, admittedly untypical, Muslim Visiting Minister went to the length of monitoring the quality of Halal meat by regularly checking orders and delivery invoices as well as the state of the kitchen. A Sikh also reported, 'I have discussions on diet problems, visit kitchen establishment, talk to Governors, look at the food and the labels on it' (B151). The co-ordinator of Visiting Ministers at the Islamic Cultural Centre is also preoccupied with questions about the authenticity of the food which prisons present as Halal. It is not just a question of honesty at local level but is also a matter concerning the *bona fides* of wholesalers and suppliers accredited to the Prison Service.

But the number of Visiting Ministers who explicitly claimed that their prisoners were deprived of the diet that they required was relatively small. Only 15 per cent declared themselves unable to ensure that there was satisfactory provision for the religious or cultural requirements of their prisoners' diets. There were no Jewish ministers in this category, but the other faith groups were proportionately represented. Some statements were straightforwardly critical of official responses to requests for dietary change, as in the case of a Sikh minister who wrote that '[I am] not satisfied with provision provided to my Sikh prisoners. I am trying my best to provide better facilities for the Sikh prisoners. Prison Governors not very co-operative about diets. Main comment I get is lack of funds for Sikh diets (why?)' (B074). Other difficulties centred on food preparation. For example, a Muslim stated that 'We are not satisfied with the provisions which are made for halal meat; and storage is not as it should be; halal meat should not be kept in a place with non-halal meat. We do not get the opportunity to cook it in the right manner' (B049).

Another issue concerns the quality of the special diet provided for vegetarian and vegan prisoners. According to a Buddhist minister, 'Many Buddhists are vegetarians and find it difficult to stay healthy on the vegetarian diet in prison. Some show signs of the effect of following this

diet' (B010). Again, complaints about insensitivity to dietary requirements based on religious or cultural considerations should be kept in
perspective. More than three quarters of Visiting Ministers appeared to
be satisfied with the current situation. Nevertheless, the accusations of
insensitivity were undoubtedly serious and heartfelt among the minority.

The serious accusations about insensitivity to religious or cultural
requirements ranged over various problems but fell into two main categories. Firstly, there was a cluster of concerns about the attitudes and
conduct of uniformed Prison Officers. Allegations included the non-
specific claim that 'I often receive complaints from [inmates] about the
unpleasant behaviour of the officers' (B034) and the more specific complaints that officers 'do not have background knowledge of Islamic rites
and rituals. It creates tension and problems' (B036) and that 'prison staff
do not respect the prisoners of my faith especially in food matters' (B043).

Secondly, some Visiting Ministers asserted that there was discrimination against prisoners of their faith as a category, as in the claim that
'Hindus find that they are not equally and well informed about their
rights. Thus, due to lack of knowledge their wishes are not respected'
(B092). This sentiment finds an echo in the views that prison authorities
'do not respect the religious aspects of Islam' (B049) and that 'Sikh
religious days and events are not all celebrated and they are neglected to
some extent. Inmates are not given the same opportunities as the main
religious and cultural events' (B151). In addition, an Imam with many
years of experience of visiting prisons in London resented the fact that
Methodists had better resources than Muslims. He felt that this was
discrimination against the Muslims who strongly outnumbered registered
Methodists in prison as well as in English society.

Cultural sensitivities were not the exclusive preserve of other faiths,
however. For example, the Senior Chaplain in a London prison pointed
out that some non-Muslim prisoners resented the fact that Muslim
prisoners did not have their pay reduced for the time they spent at daily
prayers. Another cause of resentment was the practice of allowing non-
Christian prisoners to receive the festive food served at Christmas time.

Visiting Ministers' thoughts about how the Prison Service could *ideally*
meet prisoners' religious and pastoral needs reveal each faith community's priorities and distinctive features.

Buddhists

First priority among the Buddhists was clearly for clean, quiet rooms in
which meditation could be taught and practised without interruption,
although the presence of shrines and Buddha rupas was closely connected

to this first requirement by only a few respondents. An equally frequent demand was for improved access to prisoners (in terms mainly of more frequent or longer visits) and for greater ease of prisoners' access to a shrine room. Other ideal requirements included, in declining order of popularity, a better supply of Buddhist reading material and ritual arte-facts, festivals and retreats as well as a regime of 'meaningful' work on the grounds that 'Religion does not exist in a vacuum, and some kind of activity that helps others and breaks down the kind of isolation or limited view of life that prison can engender would help' (B040). By contrast, other Buddhist ministers were opposed to trying to achieve ideal condi-tions in any prison for the reason that prisoners should 'recognise the way things are and make the best of adapting under the circumstances' (B001) and that 'anyone working in a prison would go crazy if they were con-cerned with obtaining ideal conditions. It's all about making do with the nth best. Good Buddhist practice too!' (B006).

Hindus

Hindu Visiting Ministers offered a number of concrete suggestions for ways of meeting religious or cultural needs in an ideal fashion, giving roughly equal weight to matters of diet and to the provision of religious texts or spiritual material on audio- and video-tapes. But the most distinc-tive feature of the conditions for meeting the religious or cultural needs of Hindu prisoners was the importance attached to ways of preserving or strengthening their relationships with fellow-Hindus outside prison. One Visiting Minister suggested, for example, that prisoners should be put in touch with community and religious leaders and that they should be encouraged to correspond with friends and relatives. Another view was that religion was 'essential to decrease the crime rate in society' and that prison should therefore be a place where prisoners' ignorance about religion should be remedied. 'Prisoners should be encouraged to attend regularly' (B215).

Jews

The Jewish Visiting Ministers' thoughts about ideal conditions for their prisoners were the most homogeneous. There was strong agreement on the importance of the conditions specified as follows:

meeting/prayer room dedicated for their use together with secure kosher kit-chen/storage of food facilities. Separate library for prayer and religious articles and books. Also video and tape library and facilities/opportunity (not always

available) for them to meet Friday night and Saturday morning and on festivals. (B095)

Suitable accommodation, kosher diet, religious literature and access to
prisoners recurred in about half of the responses from Jewish Visiting
Ministers. Additional suggestions included the appointment of a Jewish
chaplain and permission for prisoners to visit synagogues outside the
prison.

Muslims

One of the distinctive aspects of the Muslim Visiting Ministers' ways of
specifying the ideal conditions for meeting the religious or cultural needs
of their prisoners is that they supplied more detail about more conditions
than did the other ministers. Some of the answers were therefore lengthy
and closely reasoned. Four particular conditions seemed to be virtual
(and equally important) prerequisites in the opinion of most Muslim
Visiting Ministers. Suitable meeting rooms, diet, religious literature and
access to prisoners formed a bloc of allegedly ideal conditions. In some
cases, comparison with the provision of religious services and goods to
Christian prisoners loomed large. One respondent (B073) even composed a two-column table to underline how the Christians' resources
should be paralleled for Muslims.

Closely related to the Muslim Visiting Ministers' arguments about the
need for a better understanding of the requirements of Islam was the
proposal that Imams should be appointed as full-time chaplains and
should operate more independently from the Anglican chaplains. According to one respondent, these arguments are valid without regard to
the number of Muslim inmates:

I can see the great need of a full-time Imam in every prison. The number of
inmates makes no difference in having the need for someone to be there and see to
the needs of inmates, as it is the case for Christians in the prisons. Muslims are the
second largest faith in this country so we are not asking too much. If an inmate
comes into prison the first time, he or she has a lot of problems, inside and
outside. Moral help is essential especially for the minorities and people of different cultures and backgrounds, to fit themselves into this new place and people. It
needs a lot of adjustment. In some cases it takes anything between a week to
months before I get a chance to see the Muslims who have been inside for a long
time. Whether the delay is by prison officers or chaplaincy who do not pass the
message of the new arrivals, I do not know. But this is a very serious matter that
has to be looked into. (B110)

Echoing the theme of equality of treatment, another Visiting Minister
argued that vacancies for Imams should be publicly advertised and that

their terms and conditions of service should be equal to those of Christian chaplains.

In the absence of full-time Muslim chaplains, several Visiting Ministers argued for the necessity to have better training for themselves and for prison staff. This was unique to the Muslim respondents. Moreover, the two groups could be mutually beneficial, it was suggested, in the following way:

> Prison officers should receive training about other faiths. Visiting Ministers should be included in the training programmes and given a chance to speak to their new prison officers, and question/answer session be arranged between ministers and officers. Home Office guidelines are available, but none seems to have even read it.
>
> Visiting Ministers must be given instruction on all aspects of running the prisons. They are mostly kept in the dark about a lot of things, and as soon as they make a mistake the Governors come down very hard on them, and usually the Visiting Ministers are sacked. Ministers seem to be kept in the dark deliberately. (B002)

Sikhs

Many Sikh Visiting Ministers shared the same concern as their Hindu and Muslim counterparts with ensuring a proper diet for their prisoners and an adequate supply of books, tapes, etc. But the distinctive priority of the Sikhs was for ways of reproducing in prison as much as possible of the cultural, social and religious environment of the Sikh world on the 'outside'. The emphasis was on two particular aspects of this environment. On the one hand, there were suggestions that prison welfare officers who had relevant linguistic skills and knowledge of Sikh ways of life should be appointed and that members of the 'outside' Sikh community should be allowed to visit prisoners on festival occasions and to perform the full range of religious rituals inside the prison. On the other hand, Sikh Visiting Ministers drew attention to the need for programmes of cultural, and especially linguistic, instruction which would contribute towards strengthening the identity and cultural rootedness of Sikh inmates. The underlying belief was that,

> in this way a prisoner feels the environment from which he has come or is likely to go after release. If he is changed according to religious teachings, we can expect he can lead a normal happy life and by-pass all those bad acts, for which he is in prison. In these terms, through religious and cultural activities an environment is made where he can rehabilitate himself in a life to come. (B055)

In short, there are patterned, recognisable and understandable differences between the Visiting Ministers who tried to specify how the religious or cultural needs of their prisoners could ideally be met in prison. Only two out of the ninety-one thought that it was impossible to meet these needs. And only six of them described the current arrangements as ideal or as good as they could be. One of the reasons for devoting so much space to Visiting Ministers' depictions of their ideal ways of meeting prisoners' religious and cultural needs was to establish that none of the proposed arrangements would involve Church of England chaplains – except to negotiate or facilitate them in the first place, if necessary. The representatives of each faith community seemed to have no difficulty envisaging resources, facilities and activities which would be consistent with their traditions but which would also be quite independent of Anglican influence. We also found on our visits to chaplaincy sites and in our conversations with Visiting Ministers that many of them were grateful to the Church of England for facilitating their access to prisoners but that they would also prefer to operate independently from Anglican or Christian tutelage. It was more important for other faiths to preserve their religious and cultural traditions than to perpetuate Christian control of the PSC, according to Visiting Ministers.

Anglican facilitation and brokerage – and their limits

The notion that Anglican chaplains act as facilitators and 'brokers' for other faiths in prison chaplaincy has already occurred at several points. It is an idea which can help to explain many of the opportunities and costs for everybody involved in chaplaincy. As such, it requires more careful specification than it has so far received. We therefore intend to examine the multi-faceted character of facilitation or brokerage at this point and to draw together the numerous allusions to them which have already appeared above. This is also a good moment briefly to clarify the two terms and to distinguish between them.

'Facilitation' is the simpler of the two terms. It refers to the work done by Church of England and other Christian chaplains, firstly, to make facilities and resources available to Visiting Ministers and the prisoners in their care and, secondly, to enable other faith activities to take place. We use this term when referring to the actions which chaplains take without requiring the authorisation of prison managers. In other words, it is routine for chaplains to facilitate things for other faith communities by, for example, forwarding information or instructions to kitchen staff and security officers, ordering religious materials, booking rooms for Visiting Ministers, and so on.

In our usage of the term, 'facilitation' shades off into 'brokerage' at the point where chaplains negotiate with a third party on behalf of other faiths. In practice, the third party is usually local prison management but it could also be members of the Chaplain General's staff or a potential benefactor outside the Prison Service. Popular terms such as 'middle-man' and 'go-between' convey the non-technical sense of 'broker' quite faithfully. A broker occupies an intermediary position and has to deal with two parties more or less at the same time. As we stressed in chapter 1, there is sometimes the further implication that the two parties who are 'bridged' by the broker would find it difficult or impossible to reach agreement without the broker's 'good offices'. In these circumstances, brokerage is a difficult undertaking which sometimes borders on advo-cacy and which calls for goodwill on all sides if it is to be successful.

Facilitation and brokerage are different activities, then, but the overlap between them is also considerable, and their range is wide. They include:

> seeking new or replacement Visiting Ministers
> overseeing the appointment and induction of Visiting Ministers
> offering guidance to Visiting Ministers
> monitoring Visiting Ministers' pastoral work
> supporting respect for other faiths in prison
> supplying Visiting Ministers with information about inmates of their faith
> being available for consultation by other faith inmates, staff or Visiting Ministers
> conducting joint ventures with Visiting Ministers
> processing requests for resources and facilities for use by other faith groups
> offering models of good pastoral practice.

Most chaplains considered that it was their professional duty to carry out these tasks on behalf of other faith groups, although many of them also admitted that they encountered difficulties and challenges in doing so.

Relatively few chaplains reported relishing the role of broker; and only one seemed to regard it as an opportunity to talk about religious faith to a diverse audience. It was the dilemmas which loomed large in the minds of many of our sample of chaplains as well as those whom we met in their chaplaincies. For example, some chaplains resented the demands which brokerage for other faiths made on their time; and others were anxious about the possibility that Christian prisoners might come to resent the disproportionate amounts of time spent on catering for a small minority of inmates. Others found it painful and exhausting: 'it's like being called upon to go the extra mile, when I feel completely exhausted. And I know that Visiting Ministers of any tradition or faith need support and facili-tation' (076). There was a different consideration in the mind of the respondent who wrote that the challenge was 'to accept/facilitate/promote, when I am aware that this would be unlikely to be reciprocated in other countries, i.e. Muslim countries not facilitating Christian observance' (D126). This request for reciprocity between faiths was echoed in many of our conversations with chaplains. Yet, the vast majority of chaplains acted as brokers without complaint and, as we shall show in a later section, thought that they actually benefited from the experience.

We have no way of knowing for sure how effective their brokerage was, but chaplains' own assessments of the extent to which prisons met the needs of other faith inmates provide some clues. Table 6.1 summarises the data.

It would be unwise to place too much reliance on these data in isolation but, as a complement to our other findings, they do have some value. The view that the need for worship was one of the least adequately met among inmates' needs corresponds, for example, with the reservations expressed by many chaplains about the quality of accommodation provided for other faith Visiting Ministers and about the quality of the latter's own religious care.

The claim that prisoners' religious dietary needs were met very well was made by more chaplains than for any other religious need. This may also be connected with the fact that questions about diet figured prominently on the agenda of meetings between chaplains and Visiting Ministers. Similarly, the religious need that was the second most frequently classified as 'very well' met was the need for religious festivals. This item was top of the list of issues for discussion between chaplains and governors. In other words, the two religious needs which chaplains considered to be met more successfully than any others were the two over which they also probably had the greatest control. Moreover, these two areas of religious concern lend themselves to the exercise of the Anglican brokerage since they allow or require chaplains to act as the intermediary between other faith groups and several different prison departments.

Another aspect of the Anglican brokerage for other faiths concerns the supply of information to inmates about religious facilities and services. All but nine chaplains confirmed that the information about chaplaincy that prisoners received on arrival contained details of the provision for other faith groups. On the other hand, one third of chaplains reported that Visiting Ministers were not named in this information and that only the availability of religious care for other faith inmates was mentioned in information about chaplaincy. It was common for this information to specify that inmates should ask the Church of England chaplains for more details about religious provision. For example, one chaplaincy leaflet explained 'For those who belong to a faith other than Christian, if you

Table 6.1. *Chaplains' assessments of the extent to which their prisons met the needs of other faith inmates*

	Very well		Adequately		Inadequately		Not at all		Total[a]
	N	%	N	%	N	%	N	%	
Worship	23	(29)	31	(38)	20	(26)	4	(5)	78
Diet	30	(38)	44	(55)	6	(8)	0	(0)	80
Leaflets	15	(19)	53	(66)	10	(13)	2	(3)	80
Festivals	35	(45)	34	(44)	8	(10)	0	(0)	77
Registration	31	(39)	41	(52)	7	(9)	0	(0)	79
Re-registration	28	(36)	45	(58)	4	(5)	1	(1)	78
Access to VMs	31	(38)	48	(59)	2	(2)	0	(0)	81
Preservation of modesty	18	(25)	47	(66)	6	(8)	0	(0)	71

Note: [a] Variations in the totals for each row of the table are due to the fact that some chaplains did not answer all questions. One respondent failed to answer any questions on the grounds that it would have been impossibly complicated to take account of the differences between the training prison, the women's prison and the allocation centre for which he was responsible.

would like a visit from a minister of your religion, please ask the chaplain who will arrange it' (D039) or more abruptly 'apply to chaplain' (D032).

These examples represent a form of 'double brokerage' in the sense that chaplains acted as brokers in two linked phases. The first phase involved informing inmates that they had to contact a chaplain to receive more information. In other words, the only access to the services of a Visiting Minister was via the Anglican chaplain. The second phase of brokerage occurred when a chaplain either provided an inmate with information about religious care or put the inmate in contact with a Visiting Minister. This two-stage process seems to allow the chaplain a greater measure of control over other faith inmates and Visiting Ministers than would be possible if inmates had direct access to information and/or Visiting Ministers. Perhaps this is why it is the most frequently reported method of conveying information about the religious care provided to members of other faiths in prison.

The scope of Anglican brokerage was not unlimited, however. For example, chaplains have no responsibility for deciding whether Visiting Ministers should have keys during their prison visits, although a few mentioned that they had been consulted in this matter. In almost all cases, however, this responsibility falls to Governors, or Heads of Custody, HIAs or Security Officers. More importantly for our purposes, we discovered that chaplains imposed their own limits on how far to take their brokerage for other faiths.

'Tyranny of the majority'?

One of the clearest indicators of these self-imposed limits was that few chaplains were willing to share responsibility for chaplaincy with a committee representing the main faiths in each prison. In fact, only 7 per cent of the seventy-three chaplains who commented on the value of such a committee supported this idea without reservation. A further 12 per cent stated reservations about their conditional support, such as 'In theory it might be good. I wonder about the practicality of it being worked out' (D111) or 'depends on the composition of the committee' (D006). There was also a recurrent concern about achieving a properly proportional representation for other faith groups on any such committee. So, at most, roughly one fifth of our sample of chaplains did not reject the idea out of hand.

By contrast, the remaining 81 per cent of respondents dismissed the idea of sharing responsibility for chaplaincy with a representative committee. The range of reasons given was wide, but three main positions were evident. Firstly, a small group considered such a committee unnecessary because other faith groups already had representation in chaplaincy teams or were adequately represented by Anglican chaplains. Thus, 'while the large majority of prisoners are Christian, the present system is the right one. As a former Assistant Chaplain General I know of no chaplain who is not willing to act as an "enabler" for the minority faiths and groups' (D014). This amounts to an argument that no change is necessary because the current arrangement is appropriate.

Secondly, nearly one third of chaplains cited the inefficiency or counter-productivity of committees as their reason for a principled objection to any notion that chaplaincy would benefit from a representative committee structure. An indirect measure of the strength of their feelings is the fact that their answers to this question were adorned with more underlining, asterisks and exclamation marks than any other set of responses. The tone ranged from the priestly 'From committees Good Lord deliver us!' (D008), through the hackneyed 'The definition of a camel is a horse designed by a committee' (D012) to the insistent 'please no! We need responsible chaplains *not* committee managements' (D048). The substance of most reasoned responses in this category emphasised the inefficiency and ineffectiveness of committees, but one argument raised a different, more 'political' objection which is worth quoting in full: 'Unworkable. Senior management groups, of which chaplains used to be a part but now seldom are, need to have somewhere that the "buck" stops. It is impossible for the present chaotic situation within the Prison Service for people to deal with yet another committee' (D108). Incidentally, chaplains frequently expressed their dissatisfaction with committees. There seemed to be an affinity between their objections to committees on principle and their defence of a 'liberal' mode of chaplaincy in which Church of England chaplains supposedly played a pivotal, even-handed role on behalf of all faith groups. Again, we see the chaplains' self-image as honest brokers, motivated by ideals of fairness and altruism with a dash of 'noblesse oblige' and a pinch of paternalism in a few cases.

Nearly half of the reasons given by chaplains for rejecting a committee structure contained unconditional assertions such as 'unhelpful' or just 'not at all' as well as more carefully articulated arguments such as 'It would not be lawful under the Prison Act. It would undermine the line of authority from Prison Chaplaincy headquarters. It would muddy the waters unhelpfully' (D042). Another kind of argument was about the danger of excessive accountability: 'Totally unhelpful. The task of both chaplains and visiting ministers is clearly defined, and to be answerable to a committee as well as the Bishop, the Chaplain General, the Governor would be absolutely intolerable' (D062). This particular quotation is a useful reminder that Anglican chaplains enjoy extensive, but far from total, autonomy.

Finally, it is important to add that, scattered through all three categories of rejection, were a few suggestions that it might nevertheless be
helpful for chaplaincies to have consultative or advisory groups on which
the main faith groups could be represented. The implication was that
such groups could supply appropriate guidance and support for chaplains
but that the groups would not have managerial responsibility and that
chaplains would not be accountable to them. These suggestions could be
interpreted as ways of bolstering the Church of England's brokerage
function in a situation of increasing religious diversity.[2] Again, this
amounts to a recognition that there are limits to brokerage and that it
would be better to negotiate these limits than to have brokerage undermined or swept away.

The reasons that Anglican chaplains had for staking out the limits of
brokerage became clearer when we considered their views on the fact that
it is normal practice in many establishments for them to represent the
chaplaincy on internal prison committees. We quickly realised that this
practice was not normal in all establishments. In fact, close to one third
of our sample replied that their establishments did not insist on having
the Anglican chaplain as the representative of chaplaincy. Nevertheless,
although committee membership was undoubtedly shared among the
other Christian members of chaplaincy teams in some places, in practice
the Anglicans tended to represent chaplaincies much more frequently
than other ministers. It is also significant that only two chaplains mentioned that a Visiting Minister had been appointed to a prison committee, and both cases concerned membership of the Race Relations Management Committee. Thus, although the number of non-Anglican
ministers who have become representatives of chaplaincy has increased
in recent years, very few Visiting Ministers of other faiths have had this
opportunity.

In this respect, the Anglican chaplains were no longer necessarily alone
in the position of brokers for other faiths. Roman Catholic and Methodist
chaplains frequently shared this function. The boundary has undoubtedly shifted, but Visiting Ministers were rarely able to represent their own
faith groups (or, indeed, groups other than their own) on prison committees. In fact, we met only two Visiting Ministers who served on prison
committees. One was the Imam in a maximum security establishment
where disputes between Muslim prisoners siding with different 'schools'
of Islam had previously amounted to a serious problem. He was not only
skilled and experienced in 'race relations' good practice but was also
highly educated and knowledgeable about a variety of world religions. As
we moved around the prison in his company, it was evident that he
commanded the respect of prison officers and the inmates whom we met.

He seemed to be remarkably at ease in this high-tech and highly pressured environment; and his personal warmth contrasted sharply with the clinical coldness of the architecture and fittings. No doubt, his personal qualities and his command of the English language made him particularly suitable for service on the 'race relations committee', but he was far from unique among Visiting Ministers in these respects. The other Visiting Minister whom we met, who also served on a prison committee, could hardly have been a sharper contrast. He was the Imam of a local mosque and a retired factory worker who had come to the United Kingdom from Pakistan in the mid-1960s with few educational qualifications or skills. His command of English was very good and heavily overlain with a Yorkshire accent, but his interactions with prison staff were perfunctory and polite rather than friendly or relaxed. His weekly two-hour visit to the prison was purely for the purpose of leading prayers, so he spent no time with prisoners in their cells or anywhere outside the chaplaincy centre. He was escorted from the main gate to the room for other faiths and back again two hours later. He said that his relations with Christian chaplains were good but formal and distant. He had never been invited to social gatherings or seasonal celebrations in the chaplaincy but he was grateful for what he described as the Church of England's 'helping hand' whilst nevertheless expressing a strong preference for taking independent control over his prison visiting. Membership of the prison's Community Relations Management Group involved merely attending occasional meetings. He gave no indication that he wanted greater involvement in the life of the chaplaincy but he clearly wanted to have more freedom from the Christian chaplains because he thought that he would then be able to negotiate an increase in the number of hours that he could spend with the Muslim prisoners.

Some chaplains were quite sanguine, arguing for example that prison staff *expected* Anglicans to represent the whole chaplaincy especially in meetings with the Governor even in establishments where other Christian ministers occasionally represented the chaplaincy on committees. This is an important reminder that the brokerage performed by Church of England chaplains is not only an activity which they freely choose to conduct but is also a function which other people in the Prison Service expect them to fulfil. There may be little statutory authority for this function but it is nonetheless an integral part of the organisational structure and process of prisons.

Almost two thirds of our sample of Anglican chaplains argued that it was normal for them to represent chaplaincy on prison committees in their establishments, and they supported this state of affairs with four types of arguments.

1. Just over one quarter of chaplains argued that Anglicans should represent chaplaincy because they were usually the only full-time chaplains in most establishments and/or that the prisoners registered as belonging to the Church of England usually formed the largest proportion of inmates. For example, 'Where there is a full-time chaplain there is a general expectation that he will represent the chaplaincy on internal committees because of his "all hours worked" commitment' (D107). An interesting variant of this first type of justification for the current arrangements emphasised that the chaplains' long hours of work were also an institutional investment which deserved recognition: 'The Anglican Church is the only one to give the services of their priests and ministers to a great extent. Anglican commitment to the prisons is high and should not be ignored or put down. There is considerable expertise amongst the Anglican chaplains' (D027). All the arguments in the first category of justifications for retaining the practice of having Church of England chaplains as the sole representatives of chaplaincy on prison committees revolved around the force of Anglican numbers.

2. The second category of arguments has much more to do with the *quality* of the contributions that Anglican chaplains were believed to make to prison life. One of the most succinct statements of this position was 'There is an Anglican tradition of care for all within a geographical area. It still is alive and often works' (D022). Other respondents elaborated on the distinctiveness of the care offered by Anglicans by making comparisons with other faith groups as follows:

I feel that the Anglican chaplain is used to the Church of England ethos that 'everyone is in their care' – this is not patronising nor is it insulting if there is sufficient mutual respect. I find that most of my other colleagues are 'denominationally driven', i.e. the Rabbi will only see Jews – (his choice) the Roman Catholic will direct the majority of his attention towards the Roman Catholics (his choice) whilst the Church of England is used to caring for all. (D036)

Only the Anglican clergy allegedly 'have responsibility in conscience and in fact for people of other beliefs or none' (D048).

A closely related idea was that Anglicanism *eschewed extremism*. According to one chaplain, 'Traditional Anglicanism is probably more laid-back and the least aggressive of faiths to preserve the integrity between respect for the religious quest and the danger of proselytising' (D033). The positive implications for brokerage were also tied to the avoidance of extreme views:

In theory a full time presence should make for greater opportunity to fight the corner for all religious observance. This presupposes a theological position which can support a broker. Extreme views do not encompass this task. I believe prospective chaplains should be questioned on this matter and appointed with this aspect of their role in mind. (D111)

3. A third set of justifications for the status quo was based on claims about the legal or *constitutional responsibilities* of Anglican chaplains. The starting point was often along the lines of: 'While the Church of England is the established church it would appear appropriate. I regard myself as a civil servant as well as a priest. I have certain duties to perform as a civil servant. This includes facilitating ministry to minority faiths in the prison' (D008). This was closely related to the Church of England's responsibility to the entire prison staff as well as to the inmates of all faith groups: 'The Anglican chaplain remains the principal chaplain charged with chaplaincy to the *entire function of the prison*. This is in my view what he/she is trained and paid for' (D031). The legal primacy of Anglican chaplains allegedly helped to enhance their effectiveness. They were 'central' to the establishment and therefore capable of acting as 'enablers' and as 'links' between all parts of their prisons. They also had the 'overall understanding' of prison life as well as skills and expertise not available to other ministers. Consequently, 'It remains a good and workable system, however much spokespersons for some small minority groups would wish otherwise' (D057).

4. Finally, a small but distinctive category of reasons for supporting the Anglican chaplains' practice of representing chaplaincy on prison committees drew upon the idea that the Church of England was itself representative of the *nation's culture*. One view was that 'It is appropriate that the roots of British society in the Judaeo-Christian tradition lead to the retention of the established church as the key representative focus' (D124). There was also evidence that if the Church of England were relegated to the position of one 'permitted religious observance' among others it would fail to 'reflect the fuller critical and creative involvement throughout the life of a prison community and of the Judaeo-Christian moral/ethical inheritance' (D031). A Deputy Chaplain in one of London's busiest prisons with a large number of prisoners from other faith traditions expanded on this point at some length in an interview. She described herself as being 'comfortable' helping prisoners from non-Christian backgrounds; and she was happy with the idea that some day there might be Imams working full-time in chaplaincy work. But she 'drew the line' at having a Muslim in the position of Senior Chaplain because she was worried about what such an appointment would signify about the meaning of being British. She said she felt the need to preserve 'our culture' in an 'increasingly pluralistic society', and this was why she objected to the idea of entrusting overall responsibility for a chaplaincy to a Muslim. In fact, she thought that she would be happier if chaplaincy

were in the hands of a religiously neutral administrator than if it were under Muslim influence. This was not a flippant remark or even an answer to one of our direct questions: she had clearly given the matter prior consideration and she offered us her thoughts freely but carefully.

The strength of chaplains' feelings about the desirability of defending the Anglicans' claims to be representative of chaplaincy was clearly apparent. We also detected some notes of defensiveness and sensitivity in connection with the Church of England's legal rights and responsibilities. One chaplain went to the length of crossing out the word 'Anglican' in the questionnaire and of referring us to the Prison Act, 1952, possibly to accentuate the link between the law and the established church in England. Representation of chaplaincy was an aspect of brokerage which was not yet negotiable in the eyes of the majority of our Anglican chaplains. It seemed to be firmly rooted in complex assumptions about what was 'natural' or 'commonsensical' in regard to religion in general and chaplaincy in particular. The corollary was that, since most Visiting Ministers were only occasional visitors to prison, they were thought to have relatively little time for other responsibilities and could not become more involved in prison affairs. Yet, there was also a strong undercurrent of intimations in chaplains' comments that Visiting Ministers tended to lack the ideological commitment to toleration and even-handedness that would be required of any would-be representatives of chaplaincy.

The senior Anglican chaplain in an Allocations Prison provided a good example of this concern about Visiting Ministers' alleged lack of commitment to the interests of all people in the prison system in contrast to the Anglicans' 'impartiality'. He was unhappy about the attempts of a Buddhist Visiting Minister to obtain permission to erect a small statue (a 'rupa') of the Buddha in the prison – not because he was opposed to Buddhism but because such a statue would have given undue prominence to one religion only. Since there were no visible symbols of Christianity outside the chapel, he thought it was inappropriate to show favour to one religion over others. Another member of the chaplaincy staff supported this position on the grounds that it would 'open the floodgates', although no requests had actually been received for similar recognition of other religions. To make matters worse, from the chaplain's point of view, the Visiting Minister had tried to argue his case for the Buddha rupa directly with the Governor. Again, this seemed to convince the chaplain that the Visiting Minister was 'too pushy' and exclusively concerned for his own religious group – as reportedly was the Orthodox Rabbi who refused to visit Jewish prisoners belonging to the Reform tradition. We encountered similar concerns in other chaplaincies where it was largely taken for granted that the Church of England had an important role to play in preventing any single religious group from gaining advantages over others. However, this outlook did not amount to religious neutrality, for Anglican chaplains invariably preferred their own religion to any others; but, like liberal theories of the state, this outlook signified that Anglicans regarded themselves as somehow 'above the fray'.

How do Visiting Ministers respond to Anglican facilitation and brokerage? Nearly two thirds of them expressed positive opinions about the Anglicans' responsibility for overseeing chaplaincy. Their opinions ranged from the laconic 'seems OK' (B011) and 'satisfied' (B184), through the practical 'I have no objection because he is the person who is there most of the time to look after chaplaincy arrangements' (B179) to the more enthusiastic 'it is a very good idea for all to "relate" to the chaplain' (B127) and 'all the chaplains I deal with seem happy and able to appreciate other faiths' requirements and act as excellent conduits for information to myself when necessary' (B095). A few legitimated the Anglican ascendancy on the grounds that 'this is how it should be. It is a Christian country' (B005), but it was more common for Visiting Ministers to offer legitimation in terms of efficiency.

We quote in full the opinion of a Buddhist Visiting Minister who captured very well the dilemma facing those who could see advantages *and* disadvantages in the current situation:

How other faiths are treated is entirely dependent on the character and views of the chaplain. This can be a problem or it can work well. It is necessary to have someone who can relate to staff and know how the prison operates so that religious activities can practically take place. If this was in the hands of the prison administration I wonder if there wouldn't be a new set of problems. Religion is a minority activity, and I could imagine pressure being brought to bear on the chapel space used for other more popular inmate activities. Someone needs to be there to do the job of overseeing. If they have a narrow view of other religions, then there is a problem. (B040)

This nuanced position was not shared by many other Visiting Ministers. They tended to be more categorical in their opinions, as we shall now show.

Eighteen Buddhists, two Hindus, one Jew, six Muslims and four Sikhs, or 38 per cent of the sample, judged that it was inappropriate, unfair or just plain unacceptable for Anglican chaplains to have overall responsibility for chaplaincy. Although they were all agreed on the need to abolish the structural ascendancy of Anglican chaplains, their reasons for doing so varied widely.

1. At one extreme were those who believed that their particular faith group was actually or potentially disadvantaged by the current arrange-

ments. For example, 'This is wrong and should be changed. If the chaplain does not tolerate Muslims or Islam, then he can make things very difficult for us' (B087) or 'This is unfair as the other faiths are suppressed by the views of the Anglican chaplain, and as he does not have knowledge of the Islamic needs of the Muslim inmates, therefore he is unqualified to oversee any Islamic needs' (B189).

2. At the other extreme was the argument that the existing system of brokerage was unfair to the Anglicans (alone or with others). For example, 'I do not really blame the Anglicans for the short-comings. Maybe they are very busy with their own problems. This is why I think there is a great need for a full-time Imam in our area at least to see about our problems rather than complaining' (B110) or 'not always good for the Anglican chaplain or prisoners registered as belonging to other faiths, as there can be conflict of interest' (B168).

3. The middle ground was occupied by arguments about the desirability of a system which was fair to all faith groups. One suggestion was that 'it would be best if this were a secular post with no bias to a particular religion. *All* chaplains should be visiting chaplains' (B169, emphasis original). It was also recognised that 'it puts [the chaplain] in an impossible position. How can I expect him to provide facilities equal to those he enjoys? The sooner the Church is disestablished, the better for everyone concerned' (B166), and 'someone needs to do this time-consuming work, and at present there seem to be plenty of Anglican chaplains willing to do it – but I see no reason why it should not be done by someone of another religion; in fact, I think it would be an advantage for everyone if this happened' (B025).

The range of Visiting Ministers' opinions about Anglican facilitation and brokerage is not in itself surprising. After all, Church of England chaplains are far from unanimously enthusiastic about this aspect of their work. But our findings show that Anglican brokerage for other faiths is complex, subtle and variable and that it elicits equally varied responses. It has the support of the majority of chaplains with whom we discussed it; and it seems to be compatible with some degree of shared responsibility with other Christian chaplains for administering chaplaincies. But it probably accentuates the dependency of Visiting Ministers of other faiths on Church of England chaplains; and chaplains draw the line at brokering the entry of Visiting Ministers into chaplaincy committees or representative positions in prisons.

The Methodist and Roman Catholic chaplains with whom we discussed these issues tended to agree that it was not appropriate for Visiting Ministers to act as representatives of chaplaincy on prison committees. In a few cases this was because, in the words of a Methodist chaplain,

'Visiting Ministers are responsible only for their prisoners; we're for the whole prison', but the majority of non-Anglican chaplains among our informants argued that it was only because Visiting Ministers had relatively little time to visit prisons that they were unable or unwilling to join prison committees. It was a female Methodist chaplain who added that 'Prison Officers would be very suspicious of an Imam' if he participated in a committee at her prison.

Implications of religious diversity for Anglican Chaplains

Our analysis of the relations between the Church of England and other faiths in prison chaplaincies may have given the impression that the Anglican chaplains retained a great deal of autonomy and power by virtue of their legal mandate, the weight of custom and practice, and the brokerage that they exercised on behalf of other faith groups. Such an impression would be an exaggeration and a simplification of complex social relationships. In practice, Church of England chaplains have been subjected to many external influences and have had to adapt to circumstances not necessarily of their choosing. The extent of their autonomy and power is limited – increasingly so, if one believes the numerous expressions of frustration which spiced their questionnaire responses and their conversations with us.[3] Some chaplains were also concerned that they might become redundant in establishments where counsellors and therapists were being employed to undertake essentially pastoral duties. Indeed, the Acting Governor of an open prison in the Midlands speculated that chaplaincy would eventually cease to be necessary. We were having lunch in the panelled dining room of a converted private house at the time. The governor made no secret of his lack of faith in the current chaplaincy system, even joking about the 'Catholic mafia' at Prison Service headquarters, thus adding to the chaplains' fears for the future of the Prison Service Chaplaincy. The governor seemed to have lost patience with what he saw as the chaplains' attempts to reconcile their own position of privilege with the requirement to facilitate religious and pastoral care for members of other faiths. We sensed that his preference was to sweep the whole structure of chaplaincy away and to appoint more therapists in its place.

We were particularly interested in their own perceptions of how the growing religious diversity of inmates had affected their view of prison chaplaincy and of how their own religious faith had adapted to any changes. The opportunity to 'learn from differences' seemed to be the main benefit that chaplains perceived in the increase of religious diversity among prisoners. It was closely associated with the belief that mutual respect would flourish between people who came to understand each other's cultural and religious differences. One respondent extended this line of reasoning to the religious 'nones' as well: 'Increased awareness of religious diversity heightens awareness of cultural differences which, in turn, should increase sensitivity to the needs of non-religious but ethnically, culturally diverse prisoners. The Church of England chaplain is chaplain to the "nil" religion inmates too!' (D057).

Another frequently perceived implication of religious diversity for pastoral care was that it enriched the religious or spiritual experience of believers. 'I think it encourages broad sympathies and is a salutary reminder of the mystery of faiths and a need to be tentative and reticent in our dealing with it' (D111) was the view of one respondent. Probably more representative of the 35 per cent of chaplains whose views fell into this category were claims that religious diversity created opportunities for inter-faith dialogue and a recognition of 'that of God in all others' (D076). Others stressed the benefits that they had personally derived from having their Christian faith challenged by members of other faith groups. Self-questioning was considered almost inevitable in religious mixed settings. But a relatively small proportion of our sample went further than the others in arguing that religious diversity in prisons provided opportunities to expose the problems of discrimination and intolerance and to affirm the prisoners' rights to practise their religion even if they were tiny minorities. There was also a claim that the campaigns waged by some other faith groups for equality of rights and treatment could be beneficial for the whole establishment if they succeeded in revealing unexamined prejudices. In short, the equal opportunities aspects of the pursuit of religious freedom were seen as a potential boon not just for chaplaincies but for the ethos of entire prisons.

Nearly one third of chaplains reported that religious diversity among inmates had made little or no difference to the way they performed their own role. In some cases this was because the number of other faith inmates in their establishments was too low to be significant. But in other cases respondents took the view that their role had always been defined as a ministry to all people in prisons and that the growth of diversity had not caused them to act any differently.

Roughly one quarter of respondents argued that practical aspects of their role had changed in response to religious diversity, while another quarter of respondents claimed that their work had become more demanding and/or interesting. The first group contained a number of chaplains who complained openly about the additional work that prisoners and Visiting Ministers of other faiths had generated for them. For example:

A disproportionate amount of my time is taken up in dealing with 'other faiths'. The total time spent in organising such things as festivals far exceeds the time I spend, e.g., with C of E inmates who form the largest group. (D017)

Gives me less time to fulfil my responsibility to members of the Anglican faith. (D018)

Another variant on this theme was that increasing religious diversity had given rise to jealousy and resentment over the distribution of facilities and that chaplains had to spend more time trying to resolve disputes. By contrast, one chaplain wrote that religious diversity 'increases my workload! But it is gladly accepted' (D057).

The second group of chaplains emphasised the capacity of other faiths to enrich the chaplains' role by, for example, permitting inter-faith dialogue, creating fresh challenges which would be unlikely to arise in other circumstances and providing insight into otherwise inaccessible worldviews. There was also the less predictable realisation that chaplains who successfully dealt with members of other faiths had had to achieve their status instead of relying on ascribed privilege. This was said to be inherently satisfying and 'more interesting than living in a religious vacuum' (D098). Moreover, 'it adds an enormous dimension (beyond numbers) to how the chaplain's role is perceived in the prison' (D076). Another benefit to be derived from working in a religiously diverse situation was the perception that 'often the devotion of those of other faiths is an example to Christians' (D111). Some chaplains believed that these experiences had made them more sensitive about religious or cultural differences and therefore better fitted for the chaplain's role.

Not all responses to religious diversity were positive, however. A few chaplains implied that the PSC had lost its direction or that the mission of Christian chaplains had become ambiguous. There was even a note of resignation in the claim that the old certainties had been undermined and that radical change was therefore inevitable in the near future. But only one chaplain argued that the growth of religious diversity might be exploited by prison management 'in order to diminish the authority and valuation of the chaplain. This applies to other denomination chaplains too' (D031). Most chaplains saw no reason to adjust their approach to pastoral care in the face of religious diversity, but a quarter of them said that they had become more sensitive to cultural and religious differences and had acquired more sympathy for demands from other faiths for distinctive diets, clothing and festivals in the context of trying to support inmates pastorally.

Yet, not a single chaplain attributed changes in pastoral care to the influence of theological, philosophical or spiritual currents emanating from other faith groups or individuals. Such influence may have taken place, of course, but it was certainly not recorded. On the contrary, chaplains gave the clear impression that any changes which had occurred in their approach to pastoral care had originated in their Anglican traditions and were extrapolations from, or adaptations of, Christian spiritual resources. For example, growing familiarity with other faiths 'has broadened my knowledge, enhanced my ability to relate better on a variety of levels with people not of my own culture, background or faith, but not to the extent that I am now a syncretist! I have also had to develop concise arguments to support e.g. doctrines that most Christians take for granted' (D057, emphasis original). Indeed, many Anglican chaplains were insistent that the broadening of their outlook had at the same time confirmed and deepened their Christian faith. One case was particularly clear: 'I remain a Church of England priest of the traditional school who nonetheless accepts the right of others to share their faith within their own culture. This acceptance does little to my understanding of Christian ministry or of theology' (D094).

In sum, most Anglican chaplains reported that contact with other faiths had broadened and/or confirmed their own understanding of ministry and theology but that, as in the case of pastoral care, the effects tended to take the form of extrapolations from, or adaptations of, Anglican traditions of thought. The clearest example of this was the recurrent accent on liberal notions of understanding, mutual respect and toleration. We found no evidence that chaplains had adopted any new ideas about ministry or theology from other faith traditions. Even the relatively few insights into 'common ground' between faith traditions were modest and guarded.

Conclusion

Although Visiting Ministers are heavily dependent on Church of England chaplains for overseeing their appointment, induction and access to prisoners, we found little evidence that they were integrated into the social life of chaplaincies. This is no doubt partly because Visiting Ministers choose to remain independent as far as possible, but there was very little evidence of attempts to invite them to play a more central role. It is not surprising, therefore, that Visiting Ministers felt that more could be done to improve sensitivity among prison staff to the cultural requirements associated with their faith traditions and that their visions of the ideal way of meeting these requirements in prisons made no reference to the role of Anglican chaplains. This is not to claim that Visiting Ministers were ungrateful for the assistance which they received from chaplains but it is to stress that their preference was to enjoy greater independence. Few Church of England chaplains were prepared to concede greater independence for Visiting Ministers in their ways of administering chaplaincies.

We have shown that our Church of England chaplains, for all their differences of training and experience, tended to agree that serving the religious needs of all prisoners or staff in their establishments and, in particular, enabling prisoners from other faith communities to meet the requirements of their faith were essential and central to their work. It is also clear that this facilitation or 'brokerage' gave rise to various challenges and difficulties, some of which were attributed to the fact that Visiting Ministers did not always share Christian notions and styles of pastoral care. Chaplains attributed other problems to the constraints imposed by prison security, the lack of suitable accommodation and the shortage of resources.

The spectrum of Anglican chaplains' opinions was broad, but very few of them seemed to think that the provision of religious and pastoral care for prisoners of other faiths was in general inadequate or that the main difficulties facing other faith communities in relation to providing care for prisoners were attributable to prisons or chaplains. The majority view was that modest adjustments to the present arrangements would enable better provision to be made in the future. But there was very little support for the idea that chaplaincy should be placed in the hands of committees representing all the main faiths in each establishment or that non-Christian ministers should represent chaplaincies on prison committees. Nor did chaplains believe that the growing numbers of prisoners from other faith communities had modified their approach to pastoral care. They seemed to believe that their mission to the entire prison community was strong enough to enable them to cope with the growth of religious diversity among prisoners. Very few of them thought that the interests of other faith prisoners would be well served by replacing the PSC's oversight of chaplaincy with a religiously neutral administration in the hands of purely secular staff. The next chapter will compare these opinions with those of chaplains working within the very different frameworks for prison chaplaincy in the United States.

7   Prison chaplaincy in the United States

The speed with which the prison population expanded and became religiously diverse after 1960 created many challenges for the Prison Service of England and Wales. One of the most intriguing but least publicised of these challenges concerns the provision of religious and spiritual care for inmates from all religious, ethnic and cultural backgrounds. Any chaplaincy system would probably have found it difficult to adjust to such rapid and radical changes. The fact that the Prison Service Chaplaincy (PSC) remained a predominantly Christian and Anglican organisation produced both positive and negative consequences. The positive benefits included continuity of ethos, privileged access to leading officials in government and state, the maintenance of a relatively sound reputation for chaplains in the Prison Service, and an affinity with the country's most representative religious organisation. On the negative side, the Church of England's ascendancy over prison chaplaincy made non-Christian faith communities appear marginal to the PSC, perpetuated the dependence of other faiths on Anglican patronage and brokerage, kept Visiting Ministers of other faiths in a subservient position and gave rise to a fear that chaplains were being expected to devote a disproportionately large amount of their time to facilitating the religious observances of prisoners belonging to other faiths.

The close relationship between the established Church of England and the PSC is therefore at the centre of our interest in the capacity of chaplaincy to cope with the increase of religious diversity among staff and prisoners. The main purpose of this chapter is to examine prison chaplaincy in the USA in order to throw into sharper relief the implications for prison chaplaincy of the Church of England's established status in the United Kingdom and, by contrast, the constitutional obstacles against the 'entanglement' of religion and the state in the United States. Our aim will be to show that, on the one hand, federal and state prison systems have responded to religious diversity in the United States in ways which tend to promote 'equal respect' between faith communities more transparently and convincingly than has been achieved in England and Wales

172 Religion in prison

but that, on the other, the cost of the American achievement has been a relative lack of flexibility and generosity of provision in comparison with the situation in England and Wales.

We need to establish what we mean by 'religious diversity' in the United States. It is popularly assumed that, as a country populated mainly by immigrants from all parts of the world, the United States must have a much more diverse religious composition than an Old World country like the United Kingdom. This is indeed true if diversity is measured by the number of different religious groupings represented in the United States. But this simple measure of diversity neglects the fact that the thousands of small religious groups outside the mainstream of Protestant and Roman Catholic churches amount to no more than a tiny proportion of the total American population. Thus, a Bureau of the Census survey of religious affiliations in 1957 showed that 66.2 per cent were Protestants, 25.7 per cent were Roman Catholics, 3.2 per cent were Jews, 2.7 per cent reported no religion and only 1.3 per cent were classified as 'Other Religion' (Kosmin & Lachman 1993). The National Survey of Religious Identification, conducted in 1990, showed that the situation had not changed significantly in the interim as far as the small, minority groups were concerned. Buddhists, Hindus, Jews, Muslims and Sikhs together accounted for fewer than 3 per cent of the 113,723 people surveyed (Kosmin & Lachman 1993). One of the reasons for this surprisingly low figure is that about one half of all migrants from Asia to the United States since about 1960 have been Christians. Another relevant factor is that 'Eastern religions face a very arduous task simply maintaining the loyalty of their traditional Asian adherents in America' (Kosmin & Lachman 1993). In short, the religious diversity of the United States is unquestionable but different from that of England and Wales where 'other faith' communities constitute a larger proportion of the population. It is therefore ironic that prison chaplaincy in the United States appears to be far more even-handed than its counterpart in England and Wales in its treatment of 'other faiths'.

We can establish only the outlines of our argument in the compass of a single chapter. Our evidence is based on visits to a small number of federal prisons and one state prison in a North Central state as well as on our interviews with several leading chaplaincy administrators at the federal and state level. This is an admittedly limited body of evidence but it is supported by our reading of relevant literature on United States prisons and on the place of religion in American public life. There is clearly a need for much more comparative research on prison chaplaincies (Shaw 1995), but for present purposes we are content to offer our insights as hypotheses for other scholars to test.

The US frameworks

The Mission of the Bureau of Prisons is to protect society by confining offenders in the controlled environments of prison and community-based facilities that are safe, humane, appropriately secure, and provide work and other self-improvement opportunities to assist offenders in becoming law-abiding citizens. (US Department of Justice 1993: 2)

One of the ways in which this Federal Bureau of Prisons mission statement is fulfilled is through the activities of various 'departments' in each Federal penal institution. These include 'psychology services', 'food service operations', and 'religious programs' – also known as chaplaincy. To this end, the 'Bureau of Prisons provides inmates of all faith groups with reasonable and equitable opportunities to pursue religious beliefs and practices, within the constraints of budgetary limitations and consistent with the security and orderly running of the institution' (US Department of Justice 1995b: 1). Before looking at the work of United States prison chaplains in more detail to see how their role compares with that of their English counterparts and to see how they meet the Bureau's aims, some consideration needs to be given to the different structural arrangements for prisons in general in America. According to whether an institution is under Federal, State, County or City control, different regulations govern its management and operation, and thus also its chaplaincy arrangements. This chapter will pay special attention to the relevant differences between Federal and State systems, beginning with a description of their differing perspectives and policies on the appointment of chaplains.

The Federal system

The Federal Bureau of Prisons acts as an agency within the United States Department of Justice. Though Federal prisons were already in existence by the turn of the century, the Bureau itself did not become a separate agency until 1930. It provides a wide range of institutions and programmes, reflecting the diversity of sentences meted out to offenders sentenced or held on remand under Federal law. Currently there are some eighty-five Federal prisons across the States, with others under construction. The Bureau divides these institutions into six different regional systems, each with a regional director of chaplaincy. There are special prisons for women, and until recently there were separate programmes for young offenders.

All Federal prisons have at least one chaplain. Some of the larger institutions have up to five. The general ratio of chaplains to prisoners is one per five hundred inmates. However, it is the prerogative of the Warden (Governor) to decide how to allocate positions in the institution, and how many chaplains to appoint. The Bureau has interpreted the constitutional principle of the 'non-establishment of religion' and the 'non-interference with religious practice' by *favouring* the appointment of chaplains to ensure that the second clause in the First Amendment to the United States Federal Constitution is protected. The First Amendment holds that 'Congress shall make no law respecting an establishment of religion, or prohibiting the free exercise thereof' (Tribe 1982: 31).

The State system

Each of the fifty States in the United States also has its own prison system. Convicted offenders against State laws will be incarcerated under State jurisdiction in institutions managed separately from the Federal system. Some States interpret the First Amendment by not funding chaplains out of taxpayers' money. The State of Virginia, for example, operates this policy, and there are no chaplains on the payroll. However, some prisons in Virginia have arranged for chaplains to be available in their institutions, with funding from church sources.

The State of Michigan takes a different approach, however. Weighing up the separation of church and state with the constitutional right of prisoners to practise their religion, it has decided to use state funds in order to ensure that the spiritual needs of inmates are met whilst they are incarcerated. Under this arrangement, institutional chaplains are hired as civil service employees, by each individual prison, in accordance with Michigan's interpretation of the First Amendment of the US federal constitution.

The Religious Freedom Restoration Act (RFRA)

States that formerly did not employ chaplains have in some instances reviewed their policy in the wake of the Religious Freedom Restoration Act, passed by the United States Congress in November 1993. More chaplains have subsequently been employed in State institutions since, particularly in prisons that did not formerly have a chaplaincy department. The new law has made an impact on many areas of social life and particularly on the whole question of religion in correctional institutions. But it remains to be seen whether this impact will remain effective in the longer term, since the United States Supreme Court ruled in June 1997 that the Religious Freedom Restoration Act was unconstitutional.

What is the background to the Act, and how has it changed prison chaplaincy? RFRA partly came about as a result of action taken by two Native American prison employees. They were fired for smoking a hallucinatory drug as part of their religious devotions. They filed a case against the Bureau of Prisons, claiming that it was their religious right to smoke. Other cases also gave rise to judicial review. For example, in 1972, a Buddhist prisoner in Texas challenged restrictions imposed upon him (a) denying him use of the prison chapel, (b) forbidding correspondence with spiritual advisors, and (c) preventing him sharing his religious material with other inmates. The case resulted in a legal opinion suggesting that there was a valid claim for judicial review. The Court found that if the prisoner's allegations were true, the State had clearly discriminated against the Buddhist religion because the First Amendment prevents government from making a law prohibiting the free exercise of religion. This case, and others like it, paved the way for RFRA (see Moore 1995).

The Religious Freedom Restoration Act prevents the state from taking action that substantially burdens religious exercise, unless its action furthers a compelling state interest and is the least restrictive means of addressing that interest. The act overturned the theory that an inmate's right to observe his or her faith could be refused if penological interests were considered to be at stake. Now the state/institution has to *prove* any suspected security risk, and the least restrictive alternative has to be put forward, since

> virtually every judicially approved restriction on inmate religious practice . . . is now open to a new legal challenge. It is a brand new ball game for institution-imposed restrictions on inmate religious practices and this new ball game will be played under new rules which put a much greater burden on corrections to justify restrictions on inmate religious practices. (Anon. 1994: 65)

Long before the RFRA had been enacted, prisoners in the United States had begun to make effective use of courts of law as a means of challenging prison regimes. According to Feeley and Hanson (1990: 12, cited in Moore 1995), 'the federal courts have become one of the "principal agents of change in the nation's jails and prisons"'. But the 1993 legislation nevertheless led to a sharp increase in the number of test cases in American courts. Fear of litigation under RFRA has meant that it is often in the best interests of prisons to employ a chaplain to ensure that religious services are conducted equitably, and that any restrictions on religious practice are identified and alternatives sought. The State of Michigan, for example, now employs more chaplains than ever before, largely as a result of RFRA. Soon it will have chaplains at all its institutions. The new Act seemed likely to bring a fresh examination of such things as religious diets, 'hair and beard lengths, cross-gender pat searches of inmates who object on religious grounds, restrictions on religious clothing, hats and medallions, limitations on religious services inmates may attend, access to religious leaders, and religious paraphernalia' (Anon. 1994: 66). A later section of this chapter will examine current policies relating to these various aspects of religious practice, but it is too early to know whether or how RFRA's impact will be weakened by the United States Supreme Court's ruling in June 1997 that the Act was unconstitutional.

Having sketched the broad framework of policies and structures that govern the hiring of chaplains in prisons – something that has been taken for granted for decades in the English prison system – we need to consider the kind of role that United States prison chaplains fulfil, and in particular, the responsibility that they have for ensuring that the needs of all faith groups are met in jail.

The role of chaplains

The Federal Bureau of Prisons considers the three primary roles of chaplains to be:

> Pastor-as-prophet
> Pastor-as-community liaison
> Pastor-as-manager of cultural diversity

It is the last of these functions that is the most revealing about the assumptions that the Bureau makes about the nature of prison communities and the role of chaplains. It is described as a 'critical role' in view of the multicultural workforce and inmate population. Meeting the demands posed by diversity is an 'integral component' of correctional management, and the chaplain stands at the forefront of leading institutions in 'a system-wide focus on the enhancement of cultural, ethical and religious diversity issues' (US Department of Justice 1995a: 3). It is taken for granted that Federal prisons reflect the vast array of different traditions in America, and that chaplaincy stands at the cutting edge in highlighting awareness. The theory is that chaplains,

as they identify and affirm cultural differences, they foster the recognition that diversity, far from being detrimental, is acceptable, even preferable. Through their sensitivity to the special needs of minority staff and inmates, chaplains confront attitudes felt to be demeaning and they highlight the vitality which diversity brings to the correctional environment. (US Department of Justice 1995a: 3)

This does not necessarily entail facilitating 'equal' treatment, but it does involve 'equity'. 'Differences do exist; they demand attention' (US Department of Justice: 1995a: 3). This attention to faith differences and needs does not extend to chaplains themselves, however. In order to ensure 'impartial religious leadership to meet the diversity of faith groups', involving supervising programmes, managing resources and collaborative teamwork, 'chaplains, regardless of their own faith backgrounds, are expected to be pastors to all who live and work in the institution' (US Department of Justice 1995a: B-1). This involves surrendering some aspects of their own religious identity. Impartiality, taken to its logical conclusion, means that 'there are no "Protestant, Muslim, Jewish, Catholic etc." chaplains in the Bureau – only *staff* chaplains who happen to be Protestant, Muslim, Jewish (or) Catholic' (US Department of Justice 1995a: B-1). Avoiding the use of denominational titles such as 'Imam' or 'Reverend' in favour of the more general and generic word 'chaplain' helps to convey the message of impartiality to the wider prison community and to portray the ethos of chaplaincy as being based upon 'a team of professionals'(US Department of Justice 1995a: B-1). None of this implies that chaplains are expected to compromise their own ministerial integrity, however, since leading services for inmates of their *own* tradition remains one of their roles. But their denominational identity cannot be allowed to stand in the way of 'a healthy interfaith approach to correctional ministry' (US Department of Justice 1995a: B-1).

Vignettes of two chaplains: a Muslim and a Lutheran

How does all this work out in practice? Descriptions of two Federal prison chaplains, one a Lutheran Christian, the other a Sunni Muslim, will help to illustrate how the theory of impartial ministry towards a religiously diverse prison population works in practice. Their experiences highlight the fact that to some extent meeting the needs of all faith groups in prison is more about 'facilitation' (if this is understood as making available and/or managing a service) than 'brokerage' – where one faith group (in the United Kingdom the Church of England) acts on behalf of, or as an intermediary for, others. Chaplains of one faith group or another do not stand over or above any other in terms of priority; likewise inmates. There is no assumption that one faith group or a chaplain of a particular denomination or tradition is the 'default value'. Where an English prison inmate who seems uncertain of his or her religious identity during reception may be automatically registered as 'C of E', there is no such possibility in America.

Muhammad Salim, the fictional name we have given to an African-American Muslim in his late thirties, is a full-time chaplain at a maximum security US Penitentiary (USP) in a Southern state. It holds some 3,000 inmates in the three facilities in the complex, of whom about 6 per cent are Muslim. In terms of qualifications, length of service, and general experience, he qualifies for the title 'senior' chaplain, although he is not department-head. However, when the department-head is absent from the institution, he becomes the 'acting head of department'.

Having converted to Islam, he decided to learn more about his new faith by living and studying for six years in Saudi Arabia. Although he did not intend to work in the Bureau of Prisons on his return to America, his eventual involvement with several mosques in the South led to him being encouraged by colleagues to consider prison work. He worked in three other prisons before being hired by the USP in a Southern state in 1992. His Islamic education was certified by an organisation called ISNA – the Islamic Society of North America.

Chaplain Salim accepts the title 'chaplain', and he regards himself as a pastoral carer for all the prison inmates, regardless of their faith. This self-identity enables him to support and care for all staff and inmates, though he is clearly unable to lead worship for people other than Muslims. For administrative purposes, different groups of inmates are allocated to different members of the full-time chaplaincy staff, of whom there are five. Chaplain Salim has responsibility for Muslims, Rastafarians, The Nation of Islam, and the Moorish Science Temple of America (a forerunner of the Nation of Islam). His daily work involves meeting the administrative needs of these groups, such as arranging for them to be allocated the 'Common Fare Diet' (see below) or facilitating their weekly programme of worship and classes. Like chaplains in England and Wales, he also has to ensure that inmates on the segregation unit are visited regularly. The majority of such prisoners will not be members of the faith groups for which he has administrative responsibility, let alone from his own school of thought within Islam. He therefore takes a selection of different faith texts and other literature in a variety of languages when visiting the segregation unit in order to be prepared for all kinds of religious requests for reading matter.

During his daily work in the prison, many African-American inmates (of all faith backgrounds) approach Chaplain Salim for help. Common ethnic and cultural factors mean that some inmates see him as the natural source of assistance and advocacy. Not so the smaller Muslim groups, however. Intra-faith tensions lead some Muslim groups in the prison to prefer to approach non-Muslim members of the chaplaincy with their requests. Although Chaplain Salim noted that he could not afford to 'see denominations or colours' during his 'ministry', inmates nevertheless do.

Chaplain Salim feels that the Bureau of Prisons has realised the advantage of having a member of the chaplaincy staff who represents Islam. Prior to his appointment, there were clashes and misunderstandings between Muslim inmates and prison staff. The manipulative streak in some inmates led them to make illegitimate religious claims, as Chaplain Salim illustrated with the following example:

the guy will say 'well, it is Ramadan. I cannot be around food, I cannot see food, and if someone is eating I will have to go back to my cell'. That way he gets to lie around all day doing nothing. So when you have a ready reference – the imam – they just call me if something seems too way out of line, and the inmate will have to deal with me!

In another Federal prison in New York City, a young Lutheran Christian chaplain is responsible for the religious needs of another diverse and equally demanding inmate population. He sees his responsibility as largely 'administrative' in the sense of co-ordinating religious services, the 'contractors' and 'volunteers' (see below), and facilitating the same sort of needs as his Muslim colleague in the South, such as the 'Common Fare Diet'. However, he adds that ensuring equity for inmates who have committed especially violent crimes is also part of his role:

now we have maximum security world terrorists in this facility and they happen to affiliate themselves with the religion of Islam. It has been easy for some staff members to forget objectivity . . . So I need the advocacy of my superiors to help me at certain points to ensure that these men are treated fairly and equally even though their crimes are abhorrent.

But in what other ways does Chaplain Hill exercise his Bureau-defined role as a 'manager of cultural diversity'? To some extent it has involved immersing himself in the particular needs and traditions of the different faith groups that practise in the institution. Though this has largely involved gathering information about such needs and administering services – for which it is not necessary to be a clergyman, he says – nevertheless, he has a role over and above this practical facilitation. His position enables him 'to be understanding and compassionate and to have a feel for advocating for the rights and rites of individuals'. For him, one of the essential tasks of a correctional chaplain in the 1990s is to 'somehow extend yourself to another person of another faith group in such a way that they feel supported and cared for and empowered'. But how does this manifest itself on a practical level?

A good example concerns those ultimate symbols of power and authority in prison – keys. Federal regulations dictate that only full-time staff who have undergone three weeks of Bureau training at a Federal Law Enforcement Training Center can draw keys. None of the religious volunteers or contractors will be entitled to carry keys, no matter how long they have served in an institution, and regardless of the respect with which they may be held by the chaplain(s) and/or Warden. But when circumstances dictate, Chaplain Hill likes to share the authority to which key-holding entitles him with the contract Rabbi or Imam. If, for example, they need access to his office in order to make a telephone call whilst he is in the chaplaincy area, he will temporarily lend them his keys so that they can unlock the door. He affirms that, 'I have the authority to open any office in here. So while those guys are with me, I'll share that authority with them . . .'.

Another example of equitable facilitation, this time for inmates, is found in the allocation of time for different religious programmes. Chaplain Hill likes to ensure that access to religious activities is the same for all the faith groups: 'what I do for one group . . . I like to do for the other group. If I am going to let the Muslims come down for an additional service, a second service in the week, then I want to let the Buddhists have the same thing'. This strict attention to parity between faith groups ensures that 'religious programs' are seen to be acting equitably. Chaplains, chaplaincy administrators at headquarters and Bureau literature all emphasise that the attitude of 'neutrality' towards diversity that permeates all chaplaincy discourse is intended to safeguard chaplaincy against threats of favouritism, and possible litigation on these grounds. Such an attitude leaves little space for active faith groups with a particular interest in prison issues to further the interests or opportunities of their co-religionists in prison. For example, the recent inauguration of 'Buddha Groves' in some English prisons, donated by the Buddhist Prison Chaplaincy Organisation, would be out of the question in a US Federal jail.

Flexibility in the face of particular circumstances or inmate representation may take second place behind 'neutrality' and even-handedness, as is evident in the refusal to cater for the fine distinctions within all the faith groups. This was especially clear in a North Central state prison where inmates belonging to a major faith group attend only one weekly worship service together. Particular denominational interests are catered for through religious literature, not congregational gatherings. According to the Special Activities Director for the Department of Corrections in this particular state,

It does not matter whether you see yourself as part of the Sunni tradition or the Shi'ite tradition, if you want to participate in Jummah prayers, then there's only going to be one Jummah prayer session. Now, we do that for the Protestants. This country has a multitude of denominations within that larger designation, and we will say 'There is a Protestant service'; we will not say 'We're going to have a Methodist service or we're going to have a Presbyterian service, or a Baptist service'. We say 'We're going to have a Protestant service'.

This clearly sets some limits upon the number of religious meetings facilitated by chaplaincies each week. However, in many prisons, whether under Federal or State jurisdiction, it is necessary to bring outsiders into the chaplaincy in order to lead weekly worship and/or religious classes, especially in smaller institutions where there may only be one full-time chaplain.

Contractors and volunteers

As we showed in chapter 3, Visiting Ministers play an important role in the prisons of England and Wales in providing religious and spiritual care to inmates of their faith or denomination for which there is no full-time member of chaplaincy staff. Likewise, American prisons have a similar system of bringing volunteers and contract imams, rabbis, priests and others into institutions to assist with the chaplaincy programme. But the US systems operate on very different bases as far as the selection and appointment of contractors and/or volunteers are concerned. Their conditions of service are also significantly different from those of their counterparts in England and Wales. These differences derive from the distinctive frameworks of law and custom which have shaped prison chaplaincy on each side of the Atlantic.

Contractors. A substantial percentage of most chaplaincy budgets in the United States is devoted to the payment of contract priests, rabbis, imams, and so on. Chaplain Hill estimates that up to 50 per cent of his budget will be allocated to the services of contractors. Contractors are appointed to perform any services or ministry that cannot be undertaken by staff chaplains such as leading worship or taking classes. There are two particular circumstances when contractors are recruited. In the first case, although there may be a full-time Catholic staff chaplain, a contract priest may act as a regular part-time assistant if there is an especially large number of Catholic inmates or if the layout of the institution warrants a number of separate Catholic services (such as a high-rise prison building). In the second case, a contract imam will be appointed to meet the worship needs of Islamic inmates if there is no full-time staff chaplain to lead worship for Muslims. Currently most Federal prisons without an imam on the full-time staff will have a contract imam instead. This exemplifies the general principle that most major faith groups with a significant number of inmates in the institution will be represented by a contractor as distinct from a volunteer. However, contractors may enlist the help of volunteers to support them in their ministry, in conjunction with the chaplain.

The appointment of contractors has a formal character. Posts are advertised in the local press, and a selection and interview process takes place. Candidates are expected to be qualified religious professionals, teachers or leaders within their own tradition, and they will receive remuneration for their services, based upon three to four hourly 'sessions'. Contractors and volunteers are carefully screened in terms of their motives for wishing to work in prison. Proselytism is against the Bureau's policy, and it is the chaplain's duty to monitor this, particularly among staff members. (Proselytism among inmates happens all the time, but chaplains feel less empowered to prevent this.) However, Chaplain Hill keeps a close eye upon any violations or misguided intentions among contractors or volunteers: 'if they are coming in to proselytise, then they need to go do that some place else'.

Fortunately for Chaplain Hill, there was no shortage of qualified Muslims who could act as the contract imam in the New York prison where he works when he needed to find a replacement for the previous Muslim contractor. Furthermore, some of his Muslim colleagues in the Bureau of Prisons were able to direct him towards mosques and Islamic centres that might have been able to supply a suitably qualified contract imam. The precise nature of qualification will vary between faith groups, but in this case, Chaplain Hill was only interested in individuals with formal and certifiable training in mainstream Islamic theology, a reasonable level of general education, and an ability to understand the diversity within Islam.

Volunteers. In accordance with the Bureau of Prisons' recognition that 'the involvement of community volunteers in various correctional programs is vital to both staff and inmates' (US Department of Justice 1993) volunteers are recruited to assist with a wide variety of activities in prisons. State prisons operate similar systems, although the detailed arrangements vary from state to state. Substance abuse counselling, literacy programmes, as well as chaplaincy fall within the remit of volunteer activities. The Bureau defines a volunteer as any adult (over the age of 18) who performs a 'non-compensated service in a Bureau facility' (US Department of Justice 1993). In other words, in most circumstances they are not paid any fees and they cannot expect any compensation in terms of their time or expenses. Each Federal prison usually has a Volunteer Co-ordinator to monitor the appointment of volunteers and the implementation of volunteer programmes. However, actual recruitment is likely to be carried out by a department-head seeking assistance. The most senior chaplain in an institution, as the head of 'religious programs', thus undertakes the recruitment of volunteers whom he or she requires for the chaplaincy, in conjunction with the Volunteer Co-ordinator.

Volunteers are carefully screened prior to admittance to a prison and, once accepted, they then undergo at least four hours of institutional safety and security training covering topics such as emergency procedures, discipline, contraband, entrance/exit procedures, confidentiality, and so on. Each year this training is supplemented by a refresher course which, for the sake of convenience, is usually held during the week of 'recognition'. Their contribution to the institution is recognised during National Volunteer Recognition Week held annually in April. This may take the form of a dinner held for their benefit, or a material gift which serves as a token of appreciation.

Volunteers are recruited by chaplains to add variety to the chaplaincy programme and to offer inmates a 'presence that will complement, rather than duplicate, the ministry of Staff Chaplains' (Department of Justice 1995a: B-8). To fulfil this goal, chaplains are encouraged to recruit volunteers on an on-going basis, paying attention to their qualifications and to the ethnic and religious mix of the prison. Chaplain Hill has about forty-five volunteers serving in his chaplaincy, representing a variety of Christian denominations, Buddhism, Islam and Judaism.

Despite the rapid growth in the number of registered Buddhists in his institution (about fifty, mostly Chinese) Chaplain Hill still has only voluntary support to meet their spiritual needs. This takes the form of a weekly 'service' during which they meditate and recite mantras. About sixteen Buddhist inmates attend. Since the prison is located in a part of New York City where there are many Chinese residents, it was not difficult for Chaplain Hill to find temples and monasteries that might have been able to supply volunteers. However, he encountered difficulties in finding voluntary support from individuals with suitable qualifications and the ability to communicate fluently in English. Rather than act too hastily, running the risk of recruiting unsuitable volunteers, Chaplain Hill allowed the process of finding support for Buddhist inmates to take several years. His visits to local Buddhist temples and the slow introduction of Buddhist volunteers into the prison was a way for him to ensure that he recruited only those individuals who were committed to the service of the inmates and adequately qualified to lead their meetings. The process of making them feel confident and comfortable in the prison environment required 'a lot of encouragement' from him.

The decision to recruit a contractor rather than a volunteer appears to depend on the judgement of the chaplain, the demands of the inmates, and an assessment as to whether a faith group is significantly 'major' or not. However, finances are also a factor in the decision-making process.

Chaplain Salim admitted that 'if we can get a volunteer, then we can use the money for something else . . . materials, because that is one of our most expensive expenditures – the contract people'.

Facilities and resources

Neutral 'sacred' spaces

In English and Welsh prisons there are a variety of different arrangements for accommodating weekly meetings for religious groups. For example, some of the large Victorian jails have synagogues. Over the last decade the increase in the number of Muslim inmates has led some establishments to allocate permanent worship space for Muslims that is referred to, and serves as, a mosque; 'Buddha Groves' have been inaugurated in various prisons over the past five years; other jails have developed 'multi-faith rooms'. Regardless of these changes in provision as a response to increasing diversity, it is rare for prisons in the United Kingdom to be without a Christian chapel. Indeed, some have two or even three – one for Anglicans, one for Catholics and one for Free Church members.

In the United States, the principle of the non-establishment of religion means that the tax dollars of American citizens are not used to build separate facilities for different religious groups, whether in Federal or State prisons. The only exception is the American Indian 'sweat lodge' which Federal rules specify is to be 'maintained in a suitable secure and private location for the spiritual needs of American Indian inmates, except in institutions where building design would prohibit the construction of a sweat lodge' (US Department of Justice, Federal Bureau of Prisons 1995b: 4).

Federal prison policy dictates that in worship areas:

the space assigned for group prayer and worship should be large enough for the congregation, functional and neutral in design. This neutrality presumes that any religious group would feel comfortable and not be affronted by symbols of other faiths groups; it does not imply a space that is cold, bare, or unattractive. (US Department of Justice 1995a: B-6)

Religious spaces therefore have to be shared between all faith groups. The space may be called a 'chapel' but it will be a multi-purpose room and there will be no permanent religious fixtures or furniture. Federal prison 'Program Review Guidelines' and audit documents specify that everything used by inmates has to be neutral. A senior administrator of Religious Services for the Bureau of Prisons, reflecting on his earlier experience of using such neutralised space, recalled that in a prison where he had previously served, we did Mass [and] then we did a Protestant service, and then we'd remove all the chairs . . . and all the Islamics [sic] would come in and have their prayers. We can't get into a position where we say 'This is a Jewish room' or 'This is a Christian room'. You know, we have thirty five to forty different groups meeting, and we just don't have that kind of facility . . .

By contrast, the provision of worship space at a large complex of prisons in a North Central state and at some of the older prisons in this state is different. For historical reasons, the chaplaincy centre, which is housed in a cluster of buildings at the centre of the compound, includes separate provision for three faith groupings. It comprises a large 'all faiths' chapel of a conventional Protestant type; a Catholic chapel with an attached room for storing artefacts and books; and a Jewish worship room with an attached office for the Rabbi. A screen is used to cover the permanently fixed Cross in the 'all faiths' chapel, but all other decorations that may be offensive to other traditions have been removed. However, all new State prisons in this particular state now have to ensure that all religious symbols are removable. Newly constructed facilities may also drop the word 'chapel' in favour of the more neutral word 'auditorium', especially if the general layout of the room bears little resemblance to a 'chapel'. The semantics are less critical than the physical structure to which they refer.

Chaplains have to compete with other departments for use of religious spaces and for adequate facilities to store artefacts. In fact, there is strict separation between the different faith groups when it comes to the storage of artefacts. There might be a locker for the Christians containing altar ware, a cupboard for Muslims with prayer rugs and prayer caps, and separate storage space for Catholic icons, and so on. The only principle governing the allocation of space is that it must be 'sufficient to secure the religious accoutrements of the various religious inmates groups reverently and equitably' (US Department of Justice 1995a: B-6).

Religious artefacts and holy books

Federal policy dictates that chaplaincy funds cannot be used to purchase religious items that will become the personal property of inmates. '*Unless they are returned to the chaplains after inmate use*, (when the inmate leaves the institution) items such as kufis, yarmulkes, rosaries, prayer rugs, shawls, statues, religious books, icons, etc., will be purchased by the inmates out of their own funds' (US Department of Justice 1995a: B-5). Chaplains may facilitate such purchases by supplying inmates with catalogues and providing 'special purchase orders'. Some State prisons may only purchase artefacts or books for inmates from approved suppliers.

For corporate worship the chaplaincy is expected to provide all the necessary items, provided that they are not considered as contraband (with the exception of sacramental wine for Christian services). Inmates can request the purchase of books or tapes for the library through the chaplain(s), but personal copies of holy books have to be purchased by inmates, though there are often donated copies of, for example, the Qur'an or the Bible for free distribution. Chaplaincies cannot solicit donations of holy books or other materials, but they can make donating agencies aware of the kinds of texts or materials that can be accepted by the chaplaincy. Furthermore, 'a reasonable portion of the Chaplaincy Department's budget should be used to equitably make available to all inmates a variety of religious periodicals and magazines' (US Department of Justice 1995b: 6).

Chaplains are permitted to buy food items for liturgical use from their budgets, such as wafers or sacramental wine. However, Chaplain Salim noted that not every prison will take the view that dates for breaking the daily Ramadan fast are 'liturgical', although in each facility in which he has served, dates have been purchased from the chaplaincy budget. Where the prison will not supply dates through the chaplaincy, viewing them as a food item rather than a liturgical item, arrangements are made for inmates to purchase their own from the commissary (similar to the English prison 'canteen'). Not surprisingly, Chaplain Salim was critical of the policy in such institutions: 'I do not think that it is fair or equitable because you don't make the Jews or Christians buy their sacraments . . . With the dates for Ramadan, for us it is no less than the blood and the body – the wafers and the wine, because this is a sacrament when we break our fast.'

Chaplain Salim takes the principle of even-handedness and strict application of the rules on religious purchases seriously. On the one hand 'if you don't make Christians buy chairs for the chapel, [then] you can buy rugs' for Muslim worship. But he added:

I don't buy those small rugs because you invite the guy to take it. I buy the big rugs at least four feet by six feet and get several of those for the services. If a guy does not want to buy a ten dollar prayer rug for himself, how religious does he want to be? That is not equitable either. If he wants one he can buy it. If he can't buy it then I can find him one that has been donated or his family can send him a towel. If he wants to pray, he doesn't need decoration.

The issue of religious property was more complex for Chaplain Hill in New York. The limitations of space were such that there is 'barely enough room to store the soups [and] the tuna fish, let alone the religious materials'. This constraint meant that personal religious items were obtained by inmates on a 'property authorisation form'. Inmates could write to their family or to a religious vendor in order for items to be sent into the prison. However, this system was beginning to break down. Too many contraband items were getting into the jail, and the administration of the paperwork was a time-consuming and lengthy process. The system was especially unsatisfactory in view of the fact that most inmates were only being held for three to nine months. Many would have been transferred to another facility by the time the item they had ordered arrived. At the time of our visit, plans were in hand for the development of a small inmate commissary that would supply general personal religious items, such as prayer rugs. In the meantime, Chaplain Hill was in a difficult position as to the basis on which to supply smaller religious items:

The United States taxpayer on average does not want to have their taxpaying dollars go to provide or pay for religious items such as headwear for inmates. They say, "Why should I pay for that stuff?". So the Bureau says to me as a Department head, "We do not want you to spend any more of your money on things like that. You need to spend it on books, VCR's . . . things to edify your inmates' faith, but not something that is personal property".

But in the interim period, until the commissary is established, Chaplain Hill is keen to meet the personal needs of inmates, such as supplying kufis for Muslims. He has therefore purchased small bulk orders of such items in order to give them to inmates, unofficially. He was aware that some would steal religious items such as these unless a prison stamp was placed on them . . . but this was something he was hesitant to do. He viewed religious items for personal use in a different way from things like tables and chairs used in worship.

Regardless of the means by which inmates obtain religious items, strict rules govern what can or cannot be given to inmates. Another role of the chaplaincy is the inspection and distribution of any religious items/litera-ture donated to the prison to ensure that it does not violate prison policies. Books or other materials that might be considered as racist or prejudicial towards another faith are strictly forbidden. Many chaplains in England and Wales are also involved in monitoring, as well as facilitat-ing, the circulation of religious artefacts and literature, but they seem to be constrained or guided by fewer rules and regulations in this respect than are their American counterparts.

The Common Fare diet and festival foods

Each prison in England and Wales seems to have its own approach to the question of religious diets; and, generally, separate faith groups have their own specific arrangements. These become more complicated at times of religious festivals when special ceremonial meals or foods may be appropriate, sometimes supplied by local faith communities, at others by the prison itself. Although most British prison kitchens will take responsibility for the day-to-day provision of different religious diets, following guidelines in the *Directory and Guide to Religious Practices in HM Prisons*, chaplains nevertheless have some interest in the religious dietary arrangements. This is particularly the case if there are complaints from inmates or their Visiting Minister about the authenticity of a religious diet, since these will generally be referred to the chaplain. There is little disputing the fact that provision of a 'halal' diet for Muslims remains a sensitive and politicised issue at both local and national level.

In the United States a very different approach is taken to religious diets. Each Federal prison offers the 'Common Fare' diet to any inmate who wishes to have a different menu on religious grounds. It is not necessary to change religious registration in order to be allocated the diet. According to a senior Administrator for Religious Services, 'as a Christian, if I say, "I don't eat meat, or I don't eat chicken because the Bible says I have to honour my body and this is the best way for me to do that", then I can go on the diet'. The diet is nutritionally sound, if somewhat simple. The diet is considered more or less suitable for all religious groups. So how have the complexities of different religious requirements been simplified so that they satisfactorily accommodate most faith groups in one diet?

The Common Fare diet was designed to be equitable for all religious groups. Before its inception, prisons provided food for all inmates from the main line, although there was a separate kosher diet for Jews. But an increasing number of requests were received from Muslims, Seventh Day Adventists, Rastafarians, and so on, for their own special diets as well. The Kosher diet was relatively acceptable for most of them, but not for Muslims who could not have kosher wine, nor for Hindus who did not wish to eat meat. Since it was considered unfeasible for each faith group to have its own kitchen, the Common Fare diet was introduced as the best way of meeting all needs. Problems remain for those who wish to have a vegetarian diet, however, since the Common Fare includes three meat entrées per week, but for all others it is considered acceptable. The meat has been approved as kosher by Jewish authorities, and Islamic consultants have confirmed that Muslims can eat meat slaughtered by 'the people of the Book' – Jews or Christians. This does not mean that it is strictly 'halal', but it is acceptable to most Muslims where there is no alternative. Common Fare foods are usually served with re-usable plates and cutlery, but they are designated for Common Fare use only. Disposable utensils are provided when necessary. Personally, Chaplain Salim chooses not to eat the meat offered on the Common Fare at his penitentiary, but he accepts that for inmates who do not have the luxury of choice in buying their own groceries, the meat provided can be considered as legal, if not halal. Those who do not wish to eat the three meat entrées each week can chose food from the salad bar instead.

According to a senior Administrator for Religious Services at the Bureau headquarters in Washington DC, there have been few complaints about the Common Fare diet on religious grounds. 'In fact', he added,

we have many States calling us about our diet. We have few complaints on religious grounds. We have problems about quantity and quality. And we have problems about who should and shouldn't go on it, [and] if, when, and how they should be removed. Except for this vegetarian issue [and] we are looking at some other kind of alternatives, there is very little question any more about the meat . . .

Inmates have to apply to the chaplaincy in order to be placed on the Common Fare diet, and chaplains act as the 'approving officials'. They then inform the Food Service Administrator about the number and identity of inmates on the diet. Inmates who have chosen Common Fare must choose food from that menu, and not from the main food lines. Inmates who violate the integrity of the Common Fare programme in any way are put on probation, and if they miss six consecutive Common Fare meals, the Food Service Administrator will recommend their removal from the diet to the chaplain. There is a sliding scale of punishments for violation of the religious diet programme. After the first offence, the inmate is removed from the Common Fare for sixty days. Following a second offence, they will be removed for ninety days. After a third violation, removal is permanent. The final decision rests ultimately with the Chaplain.

Special celebratory meals or fasting are important aspects of many religious festivals. In order to make such occasions as straightforward as possible, the Bureau of Prisons has a clear set of general guidelines and policies, as well as provision for specific religious needs. As a general principle, no festival food can be donated to the institution from faith communities. It must all be obtained through the Food Services Administration in the prison and from the institution's master menu. Each autumn, chaplains provide kitchen staff with a list of the ceremonial meals that should be catered for over the following twelve month period. They must supply the date of the festival, the name of the religious group, an estimate of the number of participants, and instructions as to any special food orders that should be placed. Each faith group is permitted one ceremonial meal per year, and only those inmates registered with that group may attend the meal. Within this general framework, special arrangements are made for Muslim and Jews during Ramadan and Passover respectively.

Muslims who wish to participate in the Ramadan fast receive their Common Fare evening meal after sunset. In some places, Muslim inmates receive a bag breakfast containing non-perishable foods, but in others they are permitted to go to Food Services for a breakfast meal.

Any inmate, whether Muslim or not, who undertakes a fast, is required to sign a form relieving the Bureau of two main liabilities. An inmate on fast must declare that he or she is 'fully aware that during participation in the fast, he or she is exceeding the 14 hour limit between meal times ordinarily required by policy, [and] the inmate is aware that, since he or she is fasting, he or she will not necessarily be getting the number of calories the normal menus provide' (US Department of Justice 1995c: 5).

Jews who wish to observe Passover are required to submit an application to the chaplain three weeks in advance for food that meets the 'kosher-for-Passover' standard. It is supplied to all Jews who make a request, regardless of whether they normally take the Common Fare diet or not.

Festivals and holidays

During religious festivals arrangements have to be made not only for special dietary provision but also for adjustments to the prison regime. This might include exemption from work on holy days, or delaying the normal evening count, one of the five daily 'counts' during which each inmate must be in his or her cell, standing by the bed.

Chaplains play a key role in facilitating the necessary arrangements, including the processing of written requests from inmates to observe festivals, verifying with community representatives the significance of festivals, and ensuring that events take place in an appropriate manner. The Bureau's Central Office Chaplaincy Administrator maintains a list, which can be consulted by Wardens or chaplains, of recognised holy days for twelve faith groups (including Christianity).

To take just one example of how a faith group observes a fast and festival, Muslim inmates spend the month of Ramadan at a Federal Penitentiary in the South as follows: 'Everything changes during Ramadan. Instead of being locked down for the count at eight thirty, they stay up till ten o'clock with me. We do the special prayers and all of that.'

Furthermore, as the month draws to a close, Bureau rules accommodate the need to observe the last ten days in particular. Thus, 'the *Night of Power* during the last ten days of Ramadan is an important time for the chaplain to help inmates properly observe this holy month . . . Making the chapel available for evening prayer may entail altering normal work schedules . . . clear communication and co-ordination with correctional services is essential for this ritual' (US Department of Justice 1995a: A-6, emphasis original).

Converts and registrations

The attraction to Christian prisoners of sharing the Eid festival with Muslims is one of the reasons why some prison chaplains in England and Wales notice an increase in the number of inmates wishing to change their religious registration to 'Islam' just prior to the festival. Prison inmates appear to be similarly ingenious in the United States as well, as the number of requests to change inmate registrations increases prior to Eid. However, Chaplain Hill exercises caution before making any changes:

I can check against their religious preference how they identified themselves when they first came in. If they first came into the institution and are indeed Protestant, and then when Ramadan comes and they are suddenly Muslim and they write me a request coming in for Ramadan, I write them back and say "your religious preference is Protestant. If you have followed the teachings of Islam and you would like to change your religious preference, fill out an application to have that done with your counsellor". I kind of circuitously work it so that if they are really real they will take the steps, otherwise they will just blow it off.

Chaplains in the United States walk a tightrope when it comes to such matters. They cannot interfere with the right of inmates to practise a faith, and Bureau rules specify that all religious activities are open to all inmates regardless of their 'race', colour, nationality or creed. Yet on the other hand, there have to be some rules and regulations which limit or prevent the abuse of this right. What steps are taken to achieve this delicate balance?

When inmates enter a Federal prison, they receive information about the chaplaincy during the Admission and Orientation programme. The Bureau encourages the chaplaincy to present details of activities, inmates' religious rights (in the light of RFRA), and the availability of resources. Each inmate's religious preference (if any) will be recorded on the Bureau of Prisons computer system – SENTRY. He or she is free to change this designation at any time by writing to the chaplain. Once a chaplain has approved a request he or she will notify the inmate's case manager who will then alter the computer records. Chaplains therefore function as one way of preventing abuse of this freedom by monitoring patterns of changes in declarations of religious preference. Unusual patterns which may indicate abuse will be investigated. Another means of reducing abuse of religious rights amongst those inmates who choose not to indicate a religious preference during Admission and Orientation is to deny them the right to participate subsequently in those religious activities which are considered suitable for registered members only. Yet, none of these administrative measures can fully resolve what Shaw (1995: 150) regards as the 'dramatic story, yet to be told' of the competition between Christians and Muslims for the loyalty of African-American prisoners. Echoing an earlier claim that 'imprisoned Muslims remain "strange, strident and separatist"' (Butler 1978), Shaw describes religion in general as 'a battle-ground' in US prisons (Shaw 1995: 39).

Further conditions may be imposed on re-registration in state prisons. For example, a North Central state specifies that inmates are only free to change their religious preference twice in a three month period, and they are allowed to attend the activities of only one faith group at a time. If inmates fail to attend the religious activities relating to their faith more than twice in a six month period without a good reason (such as medical need), they are dropped from its activities. Should they then wish to resume attendance, an interval of three months must elapse before they can take up this right. These stringent rules go some way towards preventing the abuse of religious freedom, while at the same time allowing inmates who genuinely wish to follow a different religious path the opportunity to do so. These regulations also protect chaplains from any accusations of bias or prejudice towards particular inmates or faith groups, while limiting their capacity to influence inmates unduly towards their own religious tradition. This protection has been strengthened by recent changes in procedures for report-writing by chaplains.

Until recently, chaplains working in Federal prisons used to write parole reports, consisting of a paragraph of comment about each inmate. However, this practice was challenged by an inmate in court who asked, 'Why is the chaplain doing that for me? . . . I have no interest in religion'. The result of the case led to a change in practice, and eventually the parole system was abolished for other reasons. However, chaplains are still involved in writing reports, but the basis upon which this is done is regulated, again after weaknesses were found in the existing system. The following case paved the way for changes.

A judge was faced with a wholly favourable parole report written by a chaplain, at the request of an inmate with whom he had a good relationship. The inmate's case manager also had to write a report for the judge on behalf of the institution, but the comments about the inmate directly contradicted those of the chaplain. The judge then brought this to the attention of the Director of the Bureau of Prisons, and policy changes were implemented. Under present regulations, any report written by a chaplain (only at the request of an inmate) is now incorporated into the main institution report. The changes have meant that chaplains are now rarely involved in report-writing.

'Inmate religions'

The First Amendment to the United States federal constitution protects the right of American prison inmates to practise their religion, within certain constraints. However, unlike the Prison Service Chaplaincy in England and Wales which is in the privileged position of being able to define which faith groups it will 'recognise', and which faith groups are 'permitted' in prison, no such list exists in America. But with the advent of RFRA in 1993, it has become even more urgent to determine which religious faiths are worthy of constitutional protection – in order to establish whether an institution is burdening religious practice unnecessarily. Making such decisions has become especially complex when inmates have founded their own religions, sometimes out of genuine conviction, and at other times as a deceptive means of running gangs and/or exercising the right to hold inmate meetings on 'religious' grounds (Shaw 1995). 'Inmate religions' with names such as 'The Melanic Palace', the '5 Percenters' and 'MOVE' take chaplains into unfamiliar territory; certainly into realms that would be very unusual in English and Welsh gaols where Rastafarianism, Scientology and the Nation of Islam are still denied the status of 'permitted religions'.

Since Congress passed the RFRA, a number of cases have been brought to court by inmates who have founded their own religions and who have sought constitutional protection for their rights to practise their faith under the new Act. But in order for a case challenging a restriction on religious grounds to be brought before the court, it has to be established that a religion is at issue. Two cases particularly highlight whether 'inmate religions' can be considered as rightfully deserving of constitutional protection.

Faced with a legal challenge from an inmate who founded the religion MOVE, the court used a number of principles to judge whether MOVE was indeed a valid faith tradition. The court asked, 'Is it concerned with ultimate questions of life?', 'Does it have a comprehensive doctrine?', and 'What external factors indicate that it is a religion?'. Placing these questions alongside the tenets and practices of MOVE, the court ruled that it was not a religion. It had no official governing body, no worship practices, no scriptures, and no ceremonial or sacred festivals. They judged that it was better considered as a 'way of life', and thus exempt from the constitutional protection of religion.

However, in a later case involving another 'inmate religion' called the '5 Percenters', although there were – as in the MOVE case – similarly debatable grounds for ruling that the '5 Percenters' was a religious faith, the court rejected the three test questions used in the MOVE case and ruled that the '5 Percenters' was a religion by applying a more subjective test based upon the state of mind of the individual. If believers conceived of their beliefs as being religious in nature and similar to those held by individuals following major world faiths, then their beliefs, the court ruled, were worthy of constitutional protection.

Whereas prison chaplains in England and Wales are faced with clear, if restrictive, guidelines as to which faith groups are permitted to practise in gaol, American chaplains never know which new faith they might have to facilitate next. An increase in the number of American inmates practising Satanism has led to some prison chaplains leaving their prison ministry. They have felt compromised by their duty to facilitate Satanist worship. However, the decision about which traditions are permissible in the United States is at least decided in public courts of law rather than privately by the central chaplaincy administration. A comparable situation for making similar decisions in Britain is one that some minority faith groups would be likely to prefer compared to the present system whereby the Prison Service Chaplaincy determines which faith groups are permissible without visible or transparent consultation with interested parties.

Evaluating chaplaincy

One of the resources which guides chaplains through the minefield of religion in American prisons is a Bureau document known as the 'Program Review Guidelines – Chaplaincy Services'. It serves two main functions. It outlines how chaplaincy should be organised, but secondly and more importantly, it is a guide for Bureau reviewers when assessing the adequacy of religious services in each institution. Compared to the documents used for compiling the Annual Reports on each prison chaplaincy in England and Wales, the 'Program Review Guidelines' are presented and written as if for the world of business, and there is little disputing their comprehensiveness or concern with equity between faith groups. Perhaps more than any other Bureau document, the 'Program Review Guidelines' indicate some of the concrete ways in which 'impartial religious leadership . . . to meet the needs of diverse faith groups' is evaluated and assessed (US Department of Justice 1996: 2).

The inmate Admission and Orientation program is reviewed by careful examination of documents used by chaplains, and unit staff are interviewed to ensure that SENTRY records which indicate religious preferences are up-to-date and accurate. To ensure that chaplaincy activity schedules divide time between faith groups equitably, inmates from at least five major faith groups are interviewed and questioned about the adequacy of their meeting time. Chaplaincy reading matter is assessed when Bureau reviewers 'look at the bookshelves, racks and library to determine that the displayed literature is representative, and current of, the broad spectrum of religious groups and is not disrespectful to any' (US Department of Justice 1996: 11). The physical facilities in the chaplaincy have to conform to a range of requirements, but one of them is 'interfaith neutrality'. The suitability and adequacy of contributions to the chaplaincy by the contractors and volunteers are scrutinised by interviewing five inmates served by them – 'to determine their effectiveness in providing spiritual leadership' (US Department of Justice 1996: 16). At least three contractors and three volunteers are also interviewed, 'to determine that they receive direction and support for their activities . . . that they are invited to have input in religious programming . . . [and] feel as though their contributions are respected by institution staff' (US Department of Justice 1996: 16). Examination of documents and interviews provides a measure of the extent to which chaplains 'facilitate staff awareness of the diversity and complexity of inmate religious needs . . . avoid[ing] misunderstanding, conflict and potential litigation' (US Department of Justice 1996: 18). Chaplains are expected to use every opportunity to communicate with staff about the needs of a religiously diverse prison population, whether through annual training or institutional publications and memoranda. They are also expected to attend and participate in institutional 'Affirmative Action' meetings.

These rigorous standards reflect the high level of expectation placed upon chaplains by inmates, institution staff, and the Bureau of Prisons. But, as we shall see, chaplains have access to a variety of resources to guide and support their responses to these tough demands arising from their work among religiously diverse prisoners.

Chaplaincy organisations

One of the key resources for chaplains is the 'American Correctional Association' (ACA) – a large organisation with about fifty smaller affiliated bodies. One such body is the 'American Correctional Chaplains Association' (ACCA) which again has *ad hoc* groups of denominational and different faith chaplains within it. ACCA is one of the key Federal Bureau organisations for chaplains, but most States also have their own separate groups. The Correctional Chaplains sponsor workshops at the larger ACA conferences on themes such as RFRA, ageing, and so on.

The National Association of Muslim Chaplains, which has been in existence for ten to fifteen years, is most active in the northern States, and primarily represents correctional chaplains, though some Muslims active in health care and other chaplaincy work are also involved. Chaplain

Salim described it as a 'progressive' body. During ACCA conferences, the eleven imams currently employed by the Bureau of Prisons meet together to discuss matters of common concern, although Chaplain Salim feels that they are included in the total ACCA conference programme despite the fact that most of the delegates are Christian. Any conference organised by the Bureau will allegedly reflect its concern for equity among faith groups inside institutions as well as at its own professional meetings. But, he added, much depends upon the organiser of the conference as to how creatively this inclusion is communicated. A senior administrator for chaplaincy in the Bureau of Prisons noted that with the increasing input of Muslims into correctional chaplaincy he 'would not be surprised in a couple of years if we don't see an Islamic imam as one of our Executive Officers in the ACCA'.

Jews have had a long history of involvement with ACCA, and they also have their own small informal sub-group within it. But the large number and concentration of Rabbis in New York City has led to a strong regional network of Jewish correctional chaplains based there, and this body acts as the focus for national Jewish chaplaincy support.

Bureau chaplains are expected to keep themselves 'professionally current and personally renewed' (US Department of Justice 1995a: C-2) by attending conferences, whether of a denominational, professional, or spiritual nature, at least annually. Attendance at meetings of these kinds is not supported by Bureau funds, though chaplains are entitled to administrative leave in order to attend such programmes. For some chaplains, attendance at a conference is also necessary in order to renew their endorsement from their own denomination to work in prison.

Chaplaincy training

Strongly related to professional chaplaincy bodies is the training and certification of chaplains prior to full-time correctional ministry. For Federal prison chaplains, a certain level of general education is required (a Master's Degree) as well as some kind of formal ecclesiastical consecration/ordination, at least two years of autonomous pastoral experience, and some kind of current denominational endorsement. The Bureau also places an upper age limit upon Protestant applicants. Unless there are special circumstances, candidates over the age of thirty-seven will not be considered, although this age condition is waived more frequently for applicants from other Christian denominations and other world faiths. The Central Chaplaincy staff are critical of the stricter adherence to this upper limit for Protestants. They find that pastoral identity is not adequately formed in younger candidates, often not until their late thirties.

The age limit also prevents otherwise suitable applicants, who view prison work as a second vocation in their life, from joining the profession. It might be argued that the attitude of even-handedness that characterises the attitude towards religious beliefs and practices within prisons is thus not entirely reflected in the recruitment of chaplains.

Similarly, applicants from Jewish and Muslim traditions are faced with different entry standards from their Christian counterparts. An Assistant Chaplaincy Administrator for the Bureau of Prisons explained why, particularly in relation to Muslim applicants:

> Our requirement is that besides their formal training in the study of Islam they also have a Master's Degree and twelve courses in general Judeo-Christian theology outside of their study of Islam. The reason for that is that 90 per cent – more than 90 per cent – of our inmates who express a religious preference express a preference for Christian religions. You see, when an imam is hired, or a rabbi is hired, he is not hired to be an imam or rabbi. He is hired to be a chaplain for all faiths. And so we have to be sure that they have enough theological background to be able to provide ministry for that faith even though they wouldn't be doing sacramental ministry.

On the surface this concern appears well-founded. But beneath it there are some striking assumptions. Even though Judaism and Christianity are forerunners of Islam, it is assumed that Muslim applicants will not have enough knowledge, based upon their own experience of Islamic theology, to understand the Judeo-Christian tradition. In comparison, Christian applicants, for whom Clinical Pastoral Education (which places strong emphasis upon psychological-spiritual models of chaplaincy) is the most likely form of training for correctional ministry, are not required to study the particular needs or traditions of other faith groups. It is assumed that their training in clinical settings is adequate preparation for ministry in a multi-faith environment.

Despite claims that Clinical Pastoral Education is a suitable basis for chaplaincy training regardless of the faith of the student, Chaplain Salim is critical of the realities upon which it is based. He agrees that the CPE concept is ostensibly a good one, based as it is in the clinical environment in which pastoral care takes place. However, despite looking into the possibilities of doing CPE himself, Chaplain Salim concluded that 'it is not relevant to the Muslim experience right now. You see, when you have a Muslim in the class and you want to relate to him on the basis of the Trinity, or as Jesus as being the Son of God . . . we have Christ in a different role so we don't relate that way.' At least for the time being, chaplains of different faiths who embark upon correctional ministry are likely to have come from very different training backgrounds, certainly in Federal prisons.

However, this situation differs somewhat in State prisons. In a Northern state, for example, chaplains are hired as civil service employees at four different levels according to their standard of general education. The Special Activities Director for the Department of Corrections in this particular state explained how the graded scale of appointments operates:

> In Islam, most Imams are selected by the local group. Formal education may, or may not, be a part of that selection process. And so we don't say 'You have to have a divinity degree in order to be a chaplain'. We say, 'If you want to be a chaplain at level eleven or twelve you have to have that divinity degree' but there are other faith groups and other denominational groups that don't require that so we hire them at, say, the nine level. And, yes, there is some pay difference in those levels.

This rather more flexible system offers a most accessible pathway into chaplaincy for those with lower educational standards but with the endorsement from their religious community and the commitment to prison work.

Conclusion

In some respects the prison chaplaincy systems in the United States and in England and Wales are mirror opposites of each other. For example, equal respect and even-handedness are sought by strict neutrality between faiths in the United States but by close identification with Anglicanism, Methodism and Roman Catholicism in England and Wales. Similarly, chaplaincy is merely one part of various support services in American prisons but is a separate and distinctive part of the Prison Service in England and Wales. Finally, volunteers and contractors enjoy a formal and central status in American chaplaincies whereas the Visiting Ministers who are their closest counterparts in the PSC tend to lack formal recognition and to be marginal to the life of chaplaincies.

These fundamental polarities in the structure of chaplaincies in the United States and England and Wales have a direct bearing on the practical ways in which chaplains in the respective systems respond to religious diversity and an indirect bearing on issues of equal respect and multiculturalism. The established nature of the Church of England has clearly given the Anglican church a privileged position in prisons. It is the ultimate reference point for all matters concerning religion in gaols and the axis around which other faith groups have had to turn in order to meet the needs of their own faith groups. The basis upon which chaplains in England and Wales help to facilitate other faiths' observance of their religious practices is therefore very different from that in America. Anglican chaplains operate from a position of authority closely associated with their church's established status, so that the Anglican position might be considered as the 'norm' from which others depart. When Anglican chaplains act as 'brokers' for other traditions, it is partly as if they are 'doing a favour' for them, however well-intentioned they may be. They share their power as hosts might welcome guests; and the quality of the latter's reception depends a great deal upon the hospitality of their hosts.

The policy and regulation-driven climate of US prisons places chaplains in a very different position. The principles of the First Amendment, and fear of litigation associated with them, mean that correctional chaplains act less as 'landlords' and rather more as 'tenants'. Their authority and power are not based on the privileged position of one particular church or faith. When they facilitate allocation of the Common Fare diet or exemption from work on holy days they do so as a matter of institutional regulations and inmate rights rather than as a concession or as an extension of their own privileged position. So pervasive is the awareness of the need for equitable treatment of all religious groups in the context of religious diversity that few chaplains would be likely to enter correctional ministry unless they found such an approach acceptable. There is no sense in which one church is the norm (Shaw 1995); and it cannot be assumed that any particular faith or denomination is the 'default value'. This means that chaplains, whatever their faith, are less likely to see themselves as members of a majority or minority community in prison, regardless of the number of other chaplains from their background. They are there as staff chaplains, not as 'imams' or 'rabbis' or 'priests'.

No doubt there are extensive parallels between the kinds of pastoral, religious and spiritual care provided by prison chaplains in the United States and in England and Wales, but there are also sharp differences between the two systems in terms of the spirit in which this care is delivered and the organisational frameworks within which American and English chaplains work. These differences have a direct effect on the likelihood that equal respect is perceived to be shown to all faiths and that all prisoners have the same opportunities to practise their faiths.

Our evidence points to the conclusion that US Federal prisons and some State prisons operate more detailed, more standardised, more transparent and more accountable systems of chaplaincy than does the PSC of England and Wales. The involvement of volunteers and contractors in American prison chaplaincies also tends to be much more formal, public and routinised than are the arrangements for Visiting Ministers in the PSC. These features of American chaplaincies promote multicultural ideals and equality of respect for all faiths.

On the other hand, our evidence also suggests that a price is paid for the neutrality to which American chaplaincies seem to aspire. By comparison, chaplains in England and Wales enjoy greater freedom of manoeuvre within their own sphere of influence. They are less bound by system-wide regulations and by the pressure to observe standardised procedures. Within limits, they have the freedom to be creative about the arrangements made for other faiths; and they can take 'affirmative action' if they believe that extra support should be given to one or more faith communities. Most significantly, chaplains in England and Wales can facilitate as many religious activities as their budgets and their staff can sustain without feeling constrained to ensure that every faith community receives equal opportunity or equal benefit. As a result, the amount of chaplaincy-sponsored religious activity in prisons in England and Wales is proportionally greater than in American prisons. But the relative 'generosity' of the provision in England and Wales depends heavily on the personality and disposition of individual chaplains as well as on local resources. In this sense, the provision is vulnerable to arbitrariness, variability and unfairness. It is not easy for prisoners or religious groups to challenge or change existing arrangements.

The overall picture is therefore mixed. American prison chaplaincy is distinctive for being relatively standardised, predictable, equitable and accountable, but the level of provision for religious and pastoral care is also relatively low. It seems as if neutrality and equal respect between faiths are sought at the expense of flexibility and generosity of provision. Litigation, or at least its threat, is the means to shift this balance between neutrality and rigidity. The advent of the Religious Freedom Restoration Act in 1993 made it easier for prisoners and religious organisations to challenge the existing balance. The US Supreme Court's ruling in June 1997 that the Act was unconstitutional may make such challenges more difficult in future.

8   Conclusions: state, church and diversity

There are good reasons for trying to avoid the blunt category of 'other faiths' when we refer collectively to faith communities as different from each other as Buddhists, Hindus, Jews, Muslims and Sikhs. 'Other faiths' is a category which smacks of condescension and superiority on the part of Christianity. It also implies that other faiths are a departure from the Christian norm. On the other hand, our study of religion in prisons has shown that this questionable category is in daily use in the Prison Service of England and Wales and that it is not simply a matter of terminology. Many important, practical things follow from the categorisation of prisoners and Visiting Ministers as members of other faiths. A summary list of the main implications, all of which are findings from this study, includes:

> No member of an 'other faith' community has been appointed as a full-time or part-time prison chaplain;
>
> The appointment of Visiting Ministers of other faiths and their visits to prisoners are usually facilitated by Church of England chaplains, who also have heavy responsibilities for many other facets of chaplaincy work;
>
> The Prison Service Chaplaincy provided its first training course for Visiting Ministers in April 1997;
>
> Facilities for meetings between Visiting Ministers and prisoners belonging to their faith communities are highly variable and fully adequate in some prisons only;
>
> Relations between Visiting Ministers and prison authorities are usually mediated or brokered by Church of England chaplains;
>
> Opportunities for collective worship, prayer, study and fellowship are not the same for members of all faith groups;
>
> Visiting Ministers are marginal to most chaplaincy teams and are rarely appointed to prison committees;
>
> Opportunities for leading representatives of other faith communities to influence, or to be officially consulted about, the

> Prison Service Chaplaincy's policies and practices are virtually confined to meetings of twice-yearly consultations.

This list is eloquent proof of our argument that the category of 'other faiths' has an undeniable reality in the Prison Service and must therefore be taken seriously in any sociological study of religion in prisons. Indeed, the distinction between Christianity and other faiths is one of the structural principles of prison chaplaincy in all parts of the United Kingdom. As we showed in chapter 7, however, it is virtually unthinkable in US prisons.

The category of 'other faiths' has important implications not only for Visiting Ministers and their prisoners but also for Christian chaplains. The latter are under a variety of statutory, contractual, customary and moral obligations to compensate for the lack of full-time or part-time ministers from other faith communities. In a context of difficult working conditions, insufficient resources and inadequate staffing for their work with members of their own churches they find themselves under pressure in many establishments to undertake more and more tasks on behalf of other faiths.

Yet, the evident force of the category 'other faiths' in prison chaplaincy should not obscure the fact that Buddhists, Hindus, Jews, Muslims and Sikhs differ from each other in many aspects of religious and pastoral care. Their respective understandings of what it means to offer religious and pastoral care to prisoners are distinctive, and the importance that they attach to the role of Visiting Ministers also varies from community to community. Change has occurred over time in their perceptions of how they should be involved in chaplaincy work. And leading representatives of some, but not all, faiths have come to adopt a critical attitude towards what they consider to be unfair discrimination against prisoners belonging to their communities.

Our findings about the structural differences between Christianity and other faiths in prison chaplaincy bring us back to the questions about multiculturalism and equal opportunities in prisons that we raised in chapter 1. In particular, they draw attention to the way in which the Prison Service is implementing the Prison Act 1952 and its own policy on 'race' relations. The policy states that 'all prisoners should be treated impartially and without discrimination on grounds of colour, race or religion'. The two main issues are whether it is fair and reasonable to expect one religious organisation, the Church of England, to act impartially on behalf of others and whether 'other faith' communities should have more responsibility for the religious and pastoral care of their members in prison. The unique position of the Church of England is relevant to both issues and therefore requires close scrutiny at this point.

The Church of England

Three features of the religious landscape in England are particularly relevant to our study of religion in prisons. Of course, the sphere of religion is far more complicated than this, but for the sake of clarity we need only sketch the outlines rather than attempt to record its every detail. The three most salient features are:

(a) The establishment in law of the Church of England;[1]
(b) The long-running, slow decline in the number of people who identify themselves with, and/or participate regularly in the services of, the Church of England;
(c) The growth in the absolute and proportional numbers of people associated with some non-Christian faith communities, especially Hinduism, Islam and Sikhism.

This combination of features means that the Anglican Church retains much of its prestige, privilege and power, while its claim to be the most representative religious organisation in the nation becomes more and more questionable. There is a tension between the Church's universalist aspiration to be always and everywhere available to people who call for its help and two other forces at work in England and Wales. On the one hand, indifference to organised religion is increasing, and, on the other, identification with some non-Anglican Christian churches and other faith communities is also growing (Beckford 1994; Davie 1994). The result is that the religious landscape, which has displayed a rich variety of mainstream and marginal Christian churches for several centuries, is beginning to reveal extensive areas of indifference punctuated by small bursts of colourful enthusiasms. Large holes are appearing in the canopy provided by the Church of England. At least one Anglican observer accuses other Anglicans in the General Synod of making the holes bigger than necessary: 'the "privileged position" of the Church of England as a national church by law established is one which gives it the responsibility of ministering, if required, to every citizen, without qualification. The Church needs the residual involvement with the State in order to preserve that duty against the iconoclastic tendencies of the General Synod' (Austin 1995: 87–8).

    In the eyes of many observers of the religious scene, these changes are simply the product of choices exercised by millions of individuals. The changes are supposedly voluntary responses to processes such as rationalisation, disenchantment or individuation. This may be true but it is only one part of the truth. For the choices that individuals make about their religious beliefs, feelings and actions are also influenced by social and cultural factors. In other words, collective considerations and constraints help to shape the options that are available and the choices that individuals make. Sociological studies of religion should emphasise this aspect of religion (Wilson 1985; Bruce 1992).

Yet, many sociological studies of religion have a surprising tendency to focus entirely on the beliefs, values and attitudes of *individual* human beings. Measurements of the strength of religious belief and opinion often occupy pride of place, even when the aim is to demonstrate trends of disbelief or unbelief (Greeley 1972; Dobbelaere & Jagodzinski 1995). A fascination with indicators of individuals' attachment to, or identification with, churches, sects, 'cults' or movements is also common (Robbins 1988). This may be one reason why the relation between individual believing and individual belonging is a major preoccupation among sociologists of religion at present (see Davie 1990; Hastings 1991). This concern with individual beliefs and actions has produced some excellent results but it throws relatively little light on relations of power between religious collectives or on relations between them and other social forces. Our study of religion in prisons has tried to remedy this situation by examining the structure of relations between religious collectivities in milieux controlled by prison authorities.

The reason for highlighting the structural setting of religion in prison rather than the beliefs and actions of individuals was to expose the social, organisational and cultural factors which shape the opportunities for prisoners to receive religious and pastoral care. More precisely, our aim was to discover the extent to which the Church of England's commanding position in prison chaplaincies in England and Wales enables prisoners to cultivate and practise religions other than Christianity.

The wider importance of studying the structural setting of prison chaplaincy lies in what it reveals about multiculturalism and equal opportunities in a country where the diversity of faith communities has increased dramatically since the 1960s but where the Church of England, as the established church, remains in a relatively privileged and powerful position.

Establishment and secularisation

The legal basis for the Church of England's established status is complex if not arcane (Robilliard 1984; Hastings 1991; Archbishop's Commission 1985; Montefiore 1990). Fortunately, the constitutional niceties are not central to our argument, so they can be briefly summarised without seriously jeopardising or unduly biasing our analysis. The salient points of the framework within which establishment operates in England are as follows:

1. The monarch holds the title of 'Supreme Governor of the Church';
2. The Archbishop of Canterbury is the monarch's 'first subject', taking precedence over the Prime Minister and the Lord Chancellor'
3. The Archbishop of Canterbury crowns the monarch during the coronation ceremony;
4. The two archbishops and twenty-four senior bishops have the right to sit in the House of Lords;
5. A Crown Appointments Commission draws up a list of two nominees for vacant bishoprics. The Prime Minister makes the final choice of the name to be recommended to the monarch;
6. Parliament retains certain rights to determine aspects of the Church's doctrine, liturgy, financial management and ecclesiastical organisation;
7. Some judicial matters are delegated to ecclesiastical courts in the first instance.

It is undeniable that the established Church of England has enjoyed powers, privileges and advantages to which no other religious organisation has been granted access in the country's history since the late sixteenth century. The fact that establishment has also entailed numerous and, in some cases, onerous responsibilities and constraints on the Church's autonomy[2] does not alter the basic picture of Anglican privilege. There are also good grounds for extending this argument to the claim that other religious organisations have been disadvantaged in both general and particular respects by the Anglicans' relatively powerful position. All of these considerations have figured prominently in debates about the respective merits of establishment and disestablishment (see Cornwall 1983; Habgood 1983, 1988; Hastings 1986, 1991; Medhurst & Moyser 1988; Wolffe 1994).

In some respects, the power of Anglican personnel and organisations can be traced directly to constitutional arrangements which unambiguously exclude other churches, to say nothing of other faiths, from the very possibility of fulfilling the established Church's functions. This is most obviously the case as far as the prerogatives of the Church in Parliament and in state rituals are concerned. In other respects, however, the continuing power of Anglicanism is dependent less on constitutional law and more on historical precedent or accident. For example, the fact that the Church of England was sufficiently wealthy and geographically distributed across the entire country placed it in a strong position to preserve late medieval schools and to develop a network of schools in virtually every town and, eventually, in many villages as well. A similar pattern of development occurred in hospices and hospitals. Even when competitiors were no longer subject to legal restrictions, Anglican arrangements tended to dominate provision of schools and hospitals until a series of Acts of Parliament in the late nineteenth and early twentieth centuries standardised local government formations and required local authorities to provide educational, health and welfare services alongside or in place of the Church's framework.

Yet, in 1995, the Church of England was still responsible for 21.7 per cent of maintained schools in England and for 12.17 per cent of all the children educated in England.[3] By comparison, the Roman Catholic Church did not enter the modern era with a ready-made school system in the United Kingdom but invested heavily in the creation and expansion of parochial schools from the mid nineteenth century onwards. Maintained Catholic schools accounted for 9.65 per cent of all schools in England and for 9.71 per cent of pupils in English schools in 1995. Anglican and Catholic church schools together contained 21.88 per cent of all pupils in state schools in England. 31.35 per cent of state maintained schools in England belonged to these two main churches (see Davie 1994: 137; Hornsby-Smith 1987; McLaughlin *et al.* 1996). The extent of religious involvement in the state school system is easily underestimated, but the precise magnitude of religious interests in education can only be calculated by taking account of the fee paying schools and the teacher training establishments owned by all the major religious organisations as well.

Nevertheless, it is a central tenet of most accounts of secularisation that the power of the Church of England, like that of all state and national churches, was weakened by the growth of state agencies for delivering services which had previously been the Church's responsibility (Wilson 1966, 1985; Dobbelaere 1981). Indeed, this scenario has been identified as the ideal-typical process of secularisation in countries where Protestant churches were legally established (Baubérot 1994; Champion 1993). The process amounts to a progressive evacuation of some of the Church's functions, regardless of any changes in its members' beliefs and practices.

The claim that Protestant established churches have typically been subject to this aspect of secularisation (akin to 'laïcization' in Dobbelaere's [1981] analysis) has gone one stage further in Casanova's argument that Protestantism itself contains a secularising dynamic which is accelerated by constitutional establishment (Casanova 1994). The Reformation allegedly undermined church-type claims to universalism and opened the door to pluralism. When religious dissent became too difficult for the state to handle, Casanova argues, it was politically expedient to create even more distance between church and state. Although the establishment of some Protestant churches has survived the consolidation of fully modern nation states, according to Casanova, the price that has been paid includes internal weakness and an inability to 'emancipate them-selves from the state' because 'of all religions, the "established" churches of secular states, caught as they are between a secular state which no longer needs them and people who prefer to go elsewhere if and when they want to satisfy their individual religious needs, are the least able to weather the winds of secularization' (Casanova 1994: 22). Although Casanova does not explain why predominantly Catholic countries, lack-ing the same pressure towards pluralism, dissent and tolerance, also contributed towards the secularisation dynamic he does at least claim that

It was the caesaropapist embrace of throne and altar under absolutism that perhaps more than anything else determined the decline of church religion in Europe . . . One may say that it was the very attempt to preserve and prolong Christendom in every nation state and thus to resist modern functional differenti-ation that nearly destroyed the churches in Europe. (Casanova 1994: 29)

In other words, the claim is that establishment is bad for religion. Not surprisingly, Casanova's explanation of the new-found democratic effec-tiveness of national churches in Spain, Poland and Brazil turns on the argument that they have 'stopped viewing themselves as integrative com-munity cults of the national state and adopted a new transnational, global identity which permitted them to confront prophetically both the national state and the given social order' (Casanova 1994: 225–6).

Casanova's claim about the weakness of established churches accords with the currently fashionable thesis of Rational Choice Theory that religion flourishes in conditions of market-like competition but lan-guishes when the religious market is monopolised by a single church, especially if the state acts in support of this monopoly (see Finke & Starke 1992; Bruce 1993). The advocates of Rational Choice Theory place religion on the same footing as all other human action. That is, they assume that humans have good reasons for engaging in religion. The practice of religion is therefore defined as rational in so far as its practi-tioners believe that the associated benefits outweigh the associated costs and that the calculation of costs and benefits can take non-tangible or non-material things into account. Whereas many of the rewards that humans pursue in their everyday life are specific and practical benefits in the here-and-now, other are so general and intangible that they have to be postponed to the distant future. Thus, 'So long as humans intensely seek certain rewards of great magnitude that remain unavailable through direct actions, they will be able to obtain credible compensators only from sources predicated on the supernatural' (Stark & Bainbridge 1985: 7–8). Religions are therefore understood as human organisations for 'providing general compensators based on supernatural assumptions' (Stark & Bain-

bridge 1985: 8). The relationship between costs and benefits may therefore seem less direct in religion than in, for example, economic activity,
but from the point of view of Rational Choice theorists the optimising of
behaviour is common to both areas.

The next stage in thinking about religion from a Rational Choice
viewpoint starts from the premise that individual religious actors choose
their religious groups in roughly the same way as consumers in an economic market make decisions about goods and services. That is, they
optimise the balance between the costs and benefits associated with each
option. This means that the collective fortunes of religious organisations
competing with each other in the religious market depend largely on the
aggregate of choices made by individual, rational actors. This is a 'supply
side' way of explaining the changing fortunes of religious organisations as
collectives in rational choice terms.

The historical data assembled by Rational Choice theorists for the
United States show some surprising tendencies. They suggest, for
example, that the proportion of the US population that is affiliated to
Christian churches and denominations increased steadily from no more
than 30 per cent in the eighteenth century to about 60 per cent in the
1990s and that the rate of membership growth in American churches has
been higher in urban than in rural areas. But the most far-reaching claim
is that the strength of American churches and denominations derives
from the relative lack of governmental regulation of the religious market-
place. The lower levels of participation in religious organisations in
Western Europe, by contrast, can therefore be attributed to the historical
entanglement of states with religious organisations.

Against these theories, it is important to emphasise the distinctiveness
of the statutory and customary intertwining of the Church of England and
the Prison Service of England and Wales. The status of the Prison Service
Chaplaincy and the dominant role played in it by Anglican chaplains
confirm the point that the United Kingdom is anything but 'laïc' or 'lay'.
Not only is there no formal separation of church and state in the United
Kingdom, but the level of anticlerical sentiment is also low in comparison
with many other European countries. The United Kingdom is a clear
exception to Emile Poulat's (1990) claim that 'We are all laïc now' and a
refutation of Jean-Paul Willaime's belief that European countries are
characterised by a 'cultural laïcity' involving the religious neutrality of the
state and a formal recognition of religious freedom and the autonomy of
personal conscience (Willaime 1996: 158). The United Kingdom does
not display any of these characteristics unambiguously. The Prison Service Chaplaincy's manner of accommodating other faiths is a clear instance of the decidedly non-laïc framework within which it operates.

Other examples of the interpenetration of church and state in the United Kingdom include the employment of full-time chaplains in all branches of the armed forces, the virtually unquestioned use of Anglican personnel and buildings on the occasion of state rituals and the exclusive protection afforded by the law on blasphemy to the Church of England's doctrines. In short, the established status of the Church extends more broadly and more deeply into England's social fabric than is suggested by the list of features with which we began this chapter. The continuing decline in the number of people who attend Anglican services regularly and in various other indicators of the Church's activities cannot therefore be taken as unambiguous evidence of secularisation on their own. This undoubted decline must be interpreted in the context of the Church's persisting power and influence in England's public life. The ascendancy of the Church of England over prison chaplaincy in England and Wales is a clear illustration of the continuing intertwining of religion and the British state. The implications of this close relationship for the possibility that other faith communities might obtain access to public resources and recognition have a direct bearing on community relations in the United Kingdom.

Establishment and other faiths

Our study has indirectly tested some of these ideas about establishment by examining the implications of the Church of England's established status for the practice of other faiths in prisons. The findings clearly do not confirm the simplistic idea that the established Church of England uses its privileges merely to exclude minority faiths from prison chaplaincy. The Church's relations with other faith communities in the Prison Service Chaplaincy are actually complex, mixed and rather ambiguous.

In the first place, the personal endeavours and goodwill of numerous chaplains have contributed strongly towards the provision of religious and pastoral care for members of other faiths. Had it not been for these personal initiatives, it is conceivable that the Prison Service would have taken much longer to accept the need to place such provision on a regular basis. In addition, some Anglican chaplains go to considerable lengths to foster and protect opportunities for prisoners belonging to other faith groups to strengthen their religious interests. Numerous Visiting Ministers told us how much they appreciated the willingness of some Anglican and other Christian chaplains to 'go the extra mile' in order to facilitate the religious practice of prisoners coming from other faith traditions. These individual chaplains were known by name and often cited as models of how to conduct chaplaincy in a multi-faith society. Visiting

Ministers often attributed the success or failure of chaplaincy work in particular establishments to the influence, for good or bad, of named chaplains. 'Things changed overnight when x came' or 'when x left' was commonly offered to us as sufficient explanation of the changing circumstances in which Visiting Ministers carried out their prison work.

Chaplains who are known to promote the interests of other faith groups run the risk of meeting or provoking opposition from prison staff who are prejudiced against ethnic or religious minorities. But King and McDermott's survey findings indicated that Birmingham was the only prison among the five establishments in their sample where 'the chaplaincy seems to us to approach fulfilment of its ecumenical goals and demonstrate a genuinely tolerant attitude towards social and cultural as well as religious differences' (King & McDermott 1995: 178). And, although most of the 642 prisoners in their study generally held chaplaincies in quite high regard, there were clearly significant differences between the ratings accorded to them in different prisons. We also found that Visiting Ministers with direct or indirect knowledge of more than one prison found it relatively easy to distinguish between establishments in terms of the goodwill with which they perceived that chaplains facilitated their visits to prisoners belonging to other faiths.

Secondly, the majority of Church of England chaplains regard it as part of their professional obligations to facilitate the religious and pastoral care of prisoners belonging to other faiths. Often in conjunction with Methodist and Catholic chaplains, they do what is required to ensure that appropriate Visiting Ministers are appointed and that the latter's visits take place without problems. Misgivings about the quality of the care provided by Visiting Ministers or about the motivation of prisoners who switch their religious registration from Christianity to other faiths do not deter these chaplains from their role as facilitators for other faith communities. On the other hand, they tend to resist the ideas of augmenting the provision of religious care for members of other faiths and of including Visiting Ministers in the administration of chaplaincies. Their relations with Visiting Ministers are likely to be polite but distant.

Thirdly, the Chaplain General and his headquarters staff have recognised the importance of collecting and disseminating information about other faiths by means of the *Directory and Guide on Religious Practices in HM Prisons* and training courses for chaplains. Meetings of the Consultation on Religion in Prison, scheduled at six-monthly intervals, also give leading representatives of other faith communities the opportunity to be informed about developments in the PSC and to convey their opinions to its leadership. However, the level of satisfaction with this consultation seems to be low among our informants.

In short, there is a gradient in the Church of England's relations with other faiths in prison chaplaincy ranging from enthusiastic co-operation at one end to purely formal consultation at the other. Leaders of Jewish communities appear to find this situation acceptable, and the majority of chaplains and Visiting Ministers in our sample regard the current arrangements for facilitating the religious and pastoral care of prisoners who belong to other faiths as acceptable but not ideal. Improvements are sought most urgently in the supply of information about prisoners, in raising awareness of religious and cultural sensitivities, in the provision of suitable rooms and religious artefacts, in ways of celebrating religious festivals and in increasing the time that Visiting Ministers can spend with prisoners. But leaders of the Buddhist, Muslim and Sikh communities who are actively involved in prison chaplaincy are frustrated by what they regard as the unfairness of the present arrangements for prison chaplaincy and as the unwillingness of the PSC leaders to consider establishing a more equitable system. They have reached the point of believing that responsibility for prison chaplaincy should be removed from the PSC and transferred to a religiously neutral agency which should aim to ensure equality of opportunity for prisoners belonging to all faith groups to practise their faith in appropriate fashion. This argument is not unlike the claim that, since state funding for some Church of England, Roman Catholic, Methodist and Jewish schools is unfair to Muslims (Davie 1994: 131), it might be better either to abolish subsidies to *all* 'denominational' schools or to distribute subsidies to all faith communities wishing to run their own schools with the state's financial assistance.

Whilst these proposals for a radical re-organisation of prison chaplaincy are primarily concerned with the quality of religious care supplied separately to prisoners of all faith groups they do not fully address one of the major reasons advanced for the PSC's mission and for the Church of England's ascendancy over it. We are referring to the fact that Christian chaplains are supposed to serve the entire Prison Service as prophets, pastors and priests (Lynne 1975; Macquiban 1995) and that their presence acts as a form of legitimation for the Prison Service's work. Part of the chaplains' role involves counselling, consoling and encouraging prisoners and prison staff alike, but a less obvious aspect of chaplains' collective presence is to act as a check on potential abuses of power and as a symbol of institutional integrity. As the three most senior Anglican, Catholic and Free Church chaplains put it in 1989:

A thoroughgoing chaplaincy does not stop at a ministry to individuals. The chaplain is therefore concerned with the social values of justice and peace, fairness

and equitable dealing, growth and opportunity, the values of the Kingdom of God
... Chaplaincy includes a ministry to the structures. (Pound, Atherton & Davies
1989: 53)

In this respect prison chaplains function like military chaplains or chaplains to emergency services who can also perform the roles of 'whistle
blowers' and of relatively independent arbiters of complaints and pro-
tests. A 'lightning rod' is how one prison chaplain described his function.
According to Shaw (1995: 127), his fellow American chaplains are 'the
only honest "snitch" group in the organization' because they are the only
prison personnel who can speak freely to people outside prisons. The
question in some chaplains' minds is whether members of other faith
communities are able or willing to perform the same function.

This question about the capacity of non-Christians to function as
legitimators and watchdogs arises from the ideological assumption that
only clergy of the most representative church in England could be above
sectional interests and rivalries. It is assumed that only Anglicans can be
identified with England in its entirety and can therefore occupy the
position of symbolic representatives of the nation thereby warranting the
integrity of its major institutions such as prisons. The fact that about 10
per cent of prisoners who choose to register any form of religious affiliation are nowadays members of non-Christian faith communities casts
these assumptions in a new light. The growing proportion of prisoners
from other faiths does not, of course, invalidate claims about the Church
of England's representativeness but it raises questions about the manner
in which it fulfils its representative functions.

Until the mid-1990s, for example, the representatives of the 'national
church' did not assign high priority to the provision of training for Visiting
Ministers. Of course, there may have been some theological reasons for
their reluctance to become involved in preparing Visiting Ministers to
deliver spiritual and religious services in faith traditions different from
their own. Yet, there were generic chaplaincy issues for which at least
preliminary training could have been offered. For example, many of the
practicalities of gaining access to prisoners, preparing reports, seeking
permission for the celebration of festivals, and advising prisoners on
personal problems could have been the subject of initial training, to say
nothing of the possibilities for in-service conferences, development
courses and the involvement of Visiting Ministers in discussion of penological issues. At present, each chaplain decides how much assistance
and guidance to offer to the Visiting Ministers in his or her establishment.
We came across very little evidence that written guidelines were prepared
for Visiting Ministers, with the result that their induction tended to be *ad*

hoc and contingent on Anglican chaplains' willingness or ability to make themselves available. In the eyes of some Visiting Ministers, this helps to keep them dependent for information on each chaplain's goodwill but it does nothing to integrate them into chaplaincy teams.

Nevertheless, staff at PSC headquarters began planning to provide training for Visiting Ministers in the mid-1990s but were prevented by policy changes in the Training Services Division and by reductions in the budget from implementing a course initially designed for Imams. Despite the uncertainty about Prison Service policy, a one-day course at the Prison Service College was taken by forty-four Visiting Ministers in the Spring of 1997. There are plans to provide further courses designed by various faith groups in the future. Although leading representatives of two faith communities either did not encourage their Visiting Ministers to participate or were critical of the practical arrangements, it is clear that responsibility for the training of Visiting Ministers is now on the PSC's agenda.

The development of a programme for training Visiting Ministers ironically symbolises the strengths and weaknesses of the Church of England's facilitation of other faiths' religious practices in prisons. On the one hand, the Church is able to capitalise on its position of power and influence in the Prison Service to ensure that decisions are made, and the resources are deployed, to instigate the training of Visiting Ministers from various faith communities. This is a clear example of how the Established Church's brokerage function can work to the benefit of the Prison Service and of other faith communities. It is debatable whether such a result could have been achieved without the intervention of a third party acting as broker. In this respect it seems as if the Church's established status, contrary to Casanova's (1994) interpretation, can at least produce beneficial results for the place of religion in public life. On the other hand, of course, the PSC's involvement in running a training course for Visiting Ministers perpetuates a relationship of patronage and dependence between the Church of England and other faith communities. For, if Visiting Ministers wish to be informed about chaplaincy policies and procedures they have to accept that Anglican chaplains are likely to be their teachers, mentors and gatekeepers. So long as the Church continues to dominate the PSC, there is no alternative channel through which 'official' training for Visiting Ministers can be supplied. To use an economic image, the Church of England comes close to having a monopolistic position. In the eyes of Rational Choice Theorists it is difficult for monopolies, spiritual or material, to be efficient or fair in the long term.

An Anglican chaplain captured her Church's dilemma very well with the despairing adage that 'we're damned if we do; and we're damned if we don't'. If the Church of England arranges training for Visiting Ministers it exposes itself to the charge of being patronising. If it fails to arrange the training of Visiting Ministers it exposes itself to the charge of exclusivism. As we have repeatedly asserted in this book, the basic structure of prison chaplaincy is coming under increasing pressure from changes in the prison population and changes in the degree to which other faith communities are growing in size, self-confidence, resources and capacity for mobilisation (Rex 1994).

Public discussion of this dilemma is necessary and long overdue. In the absence of such discussion radical proposals for stripping the Church of England of its ascendancy over the PSC have come forward. Regardless of these proposals' merits, the case for a reconsideration of the scope, quality and purpose of the religious and pastoral care offered to prisoners in England and Wales is extremely strong in our opinion. At the very least, greater transparency of policies and practices is required. More extensive machinery for consulting other faith communities and for involving them in policy debates would also be necessary if the full benefits of the United Kingdom's religious diversity are to be realised rather than merely tolerated.

The State, the nation and religious diversity

The structure of the PSC means that only Christian chaplains are currently in a position to represent, legitimate or, from an insider's vantage point, criticise the Prison Service. Visiting Ministers are not in a position to fulfil the same functions. The main point at issue in the closing section of our book is what this situation signifies about the changing nature of British society.

'The fragile legitimacy of the prison system' (Sparks 1996: 88) is frequently under attack or in need of affirmation or defence. The presence of Church of England chaplains has long helped to legitimate the Prison Service (to itself and to others), but it is now time to consider the chaplains' capacity to continue to do so in view of the growing proportion of prisoners who come from other faith backgrounds. We sensed a strong feeling among Church of England chaplains, however, that their Church's historical links with the English nation, the British state and the majority of the population made them the only natural agents of legitimation. Some even suggested that the growth of religious diversity was a good reason for insisting that only the most representative religious organisation in England and Wales could perform the task of legitimating and criticising institutions of the state. The fact that British society was becoming more and more mixed only increased the need, they argued, for a single, fixed point of symbolic reference, i.e. the Church of England. Some chaplains added that, since they were already acting as 'brokers' for other faiths, they clearly could be of service to the entire Prison Service and therefore *should continue* in this role. Fact and value were conflated. Other chaplains were also sceptical about the loyalty of other faith communities towards the British state. Indeed, there were distinct echoes in these statements of Norman Tebbitt's infamous question about the loyalties of Britain's ethnic minorities when the English cricket team played teams from India, Pakistan, Sri Lanka or the West Indies.[4]

These issues of the symbolic integrity of the Prison Service are of only secondary concern to the other faith communities which are campaigning for the repeal of legislation giving the Church of England effective control over the PSC. Their priority is to obtain better resourcing for their work and freedom from the necessity to rely on the goodwill and brokerage of Anglican chaplains. But the defenders of the Church's position regard questions of national representativeness and of even-handed service to the entire prison system as crucial for its legitimacy and well-being. This is one of those points at which the nature of the Church's establishment and its roots in the history and identity of the nation come to the surface. It is also one of the points at which some Anglican and Catholic chaplains insist on the need for a full-time chaplaincy service to prisons as well as to prisoners. Whilst the usefulness of part-time chaplains is widely recognised, there is also resistance to the idea that all chaplains could be supplied by parish churches in the vicinity of prisons. Contrary to Vivien Stern's (1987: 248) proposal that 'If chaplaincy services were provided by the local churches then benefits could be great', we often heard the argument that prisons require chaplains who are not only professionally qualified for this specialist work but also free to devote their energies to their demanding tasks on a full-time basis. The same argument is deployed against suggestions that it would be fair to place all chaplains and Visiting Ministers on an equal footing as part-time volunteers.

Debates and disputes about the representativeness of the PSC are not simply about the distribution of resources or esteem between Christian churches and other faith communities. They also reflect deep-seated tensions and uncertainties arising from the British state's need to have legitimation for its Prison Service in universalist terms at a time when the Anglican Church is faced with the increasingly difficult task of speaking for a diverse and divided nation. The leaders of some other faith communities no longer find it acceptable to be represented by the Church of England in prison establishments run by the state. They expect to make their own contributions to the Prison Service and to public life by articulating their own views. For them, it is no longer acceptable to be merely tolerated or to be allowed to participate in public life by special concession.

The challenge to state and society alike is therefore to find ways of drawing on the contributions of faith communities outside the Christian sphere which are claiming equal opportunities to contribute directly to public life in their own terms rather than via the intermediary of agencies which claim to represent the whole nation. The question is whether greater contributions can be made by Visiting Ministers of other faiths whilst the exclusively Christian Prison Service Chaplaincy retains overall control and performs the role of legitimating the Prison Service. A case can be made for arguing that if other faith communities wish to take their place in public life they should also lend their symbolic support and their criticisms to public institutions. This is not an argument about assimilation or differential incorporation of minorities into British society: it is a question about how to equalise the opportunities for full engagement in public life and about how to ensure that the rich diversity of religious and cultural resources in multi-faith Britain can contribute towards the improvement of its prison system.

This is also a challenge for other faith communities, of course, for they are faced with the problem of deciding whether they wish to be represented in state-run establishments, who could represent them, how they could be consulted and to whom their representatives could be accountable. Moreover, they must consider the risk of co-optation, manipulation or exploitation by agents of the state. The Church of England has hundreds of years of experience of working with British state agencies and has encountered many difficulties in trying to achieve an appropriate balance between relative autonomy from, and relative subjection to, the state or governments. It is unlikely that other faith communities will find it any easier to achieve this balance.

The issues surrounding prison chaplaincy and other faiths are a microcosm of broader issues concerning much more than the inclusiveness of the Prison Service Chaplaincy. They reflect the deeper problem of societal cohesion in a society divided into numerous faith communities and pervaded by indifference to organised religion. The claim that Britain is still a Christian society is defensible but it misses the point that sizeable minorities of, for example, British Hindus, Muslims and Sikhs want respect for their religious values in public institutions such as prisons. They do not expect to have to put aside their religious and cultural identity in order to enjoy the full benefits and responsibilities of citizenship. Since the state sponsors religious and pastoral care in prisons, it might seem to follow that 'other faith' communities should have equal rights to receive and to deliver the kind of care appropriate to their communities. They also claim an equal right to participate in discussions about the resourcing and delivery of chaplaincy services. Grace Davie (1994: 136) was therefore correct to argue that the majority of British citizens should become more aware of the 'existence of important religious minorities, whether Christian or not' and that 'an acceptable framework in which those of diverse opinions . . . can cohabit with confidence' should be sought. We would agree that the relationship between Christian churches and the British state is an 'essential part of the framework', but the full involvement of other faith communities in designing and implementing such a framework is no less important in our opinion.

The corollary of these claims is the view that it is unfair to apportion a supposedly universal benefit such as the opportunity for religious care in accordance with each faith community's proportional size in the prison population. If the Prison Act 1952 allows 'a minister of any denomination other than the Church of England to visit prisoners of his denomination in a prison to which no minister of that denomination has been appointed',[5] it is inequitable, according to critics of the current system of chaplaincy, to tie the frequency of such visits to the proportion of prisoners belonging to that minister's faith community.

This disagreement reflects the difference between 'liberal' and 'radical' approaches to equal opportunities. The liberal approach involves an insistence on procedural proprieties in order to ensure strictly equal chances for all parties to apply for sought after goods regardless of the differences between the parties in terms of, for example, their 'cultural capital' (Bourdieu 1984) or their political power. Equality in this case means having objective and transparent rules and procedures for advertising opportunities and for processing applications. It is mainly a quality of in-put procedures and therefore 'ignores or has great difficulty in accommodating the structural sources of social capacities and skills – and, hence, the structural sources of social inequality' (Jewson & Mason 1992: 221). A variant of this liberal approach concerns out-put: it insists on the distribution of goods in strict proportion to the relative numerical strength of applicants in society.

By contrast, a radical approach to equal opportunities emphasises the need to ensure that goods are eventually distributed in such a way that injustices are cancelled out. This may involve political decisions and positive action in favour of applicants from disadvantaged backgrounds.

Defenders of the Church of England's current ascendancy over prison chaplaincy tend to adopt a liberal approach to questions about the distribution of resources and responsibilities between faith traditions. Critics of the current system favour a radical approach. Jewson and Mason have demonstrated that liberal approaches to equal opportunities cannot produce outcomes acceptable to proponents of radical doctrines.

All of these issues about equal opportunities and proportionality are complicated by the fact that it is the established Church which largely controls prison chaplaincy. Critics of the Prison Service Chaplaincy's treatment of other faiths are not therefore contending directly or solely with the British state but are also grappling with the Church of England's claim to transcend religious divisions in its even-handed service to the nation. The Home Office and the Prison Service can therefore count on the Church to handle questions about religion in prisons on their behalf and to keep religious critics of their policies somewhat at bay. It remains to be seen for how long the Church can credibly continue to fulfil this function on behalf of the state at a time when its claim to represent all the main religious interests in the country is increasingly called into question.

Those who believe that the establishment of the Church of England means very little to people except Anglican Bishops and Archbishops are probably unaware of its implications for prison chaplaincy, health care chaplaincy and civic religion (Beckford & Gilliat 1996). Similarly, the view that 'non-Christian religions . . . seem increasingly to regard the Church of England, and its spokesmen in the House of Lords, as convenient representatives of religion in general' (Hastings 1991: 71) takes no account of the tensions which arise from Anglican ascendancy over prison chaplaincy. There is a world of difference between representing religion in general and having ascendancy over a religious agency funded from the public purse. It may also be true that 'the Archbishop of Canterbury can increasingly be counted upon to speak up for the interests of Muslims and Jews when that is needed' (Hastings 1991: 71), but the evidence from our study shows that leading representatives of some faith traditions would like the opportunity to speak for themselves and to be heard in the corridors of power without wishing to appear ungrateful for all offers of Anglican support or mediation. For the same reason it may be true that members of other faith communities prefer to live in a country where at least one religious organisation is established in law, even if it does not represent their particular faith, rather than to be citizens of a secular state (Modood 1994a). But they are not necessarily content for the established Church to act on their behalf, especially if it marginalises them, in prison chaplaincies. An analogous situation exists in schools. Many Hindus, Muslims and Sikhs support the principle that the British state should fund schools run by the Church of England, the Roman Catholic Church and some Jewish organisations. But they cannot understand why the principle has never been extended to them (Duncan 1992).

We must not forget that a small minority of Church of England chaplains and of other Church members are also in favour of disestablishment if it were to mean that Anglican clergy would no longer be expected to act as facilitators and brokers for other faiths. In addition to arguing for the need to throw off Parliament's shackles on the Church's doctrine, liturgy and finances, some advocates of disestablishment claim that it is no longer healthy for one Church to be representative of such a religiously diverse society as the United Kingdom and that the Church's Christian mission in prison would be more successful if it did not have to spend so much time working on behalf of other faiths. It is unclear, however, whether these supporters of disestablishment would be content for prison chaplaincy to be organised by an entirely neutral agency and for the Church of England to lose its ascendancy. We suspect that they would continue to regard even a disestablished Church of England as somehow the 'natural' body for administering prison chaplaincy.

The majority of Anglican prison chaplains probably agree with Keith Ward's depiction of a 'Christian society' as

one which is concerned to provide spiritual resources for its people, especially at key moments in their lives, and which takes the Christian tradition in one of its forms as its main resource, without excluding others . . . [I]t seems right that Christianity, as the main historical resource in Britain, should have a major part to play. But other forms of faith may be brought in, wherever possible, to complement this tradition. (Ward 1992: 14, 15)

Ward is confident that the idea of a Christian society is not a contradiction but he is also unsure whether the Church of England is ready to encourage other denominations and other faiths to play a role in giving 'vision, insight and inspiration' to the nation. The results of our study of relations between the Church of England and other faiths in prison chaplaincies suggest that the issue of giving the members of other faith communities the same opportunities as Christians to participate fully in publicly-funded prison chaplaincy is becoming more pressing. Adapting Ward's phrase, we ask whether a multi-faith state is a contradiction or a realistic possibility.

Notes

1 EQUAL OPPORTUNITIES AND MULTICULTURALISM IN PRISONS

1 The term 'other faiths' is contentious but has been chosen as the least unacceptable way of designating religions and philosophies of life such as Buddhism, Hinduism, Judaism, Islam and Sikhism. There is no implication that Christianity is the norm from which these other faiths have departed; nor is it implied that other faiths are all alike.
2 'Saris, samosas and steel bands' in the late Barry Troyna's unforgettable words. Troyna (1987).
3 Prisons in England and Wales contain almost 90 per cent of all prisoners in the United Kingdom.

2 CHAPLAINCY, CHAPLAINS, CHAPELS AND OTHER FAITHS

1 New legislation for Scottish prisons was enacted in 1994.
2 It may seem strange to use the word 'remind' in this context, given that the 1952 Prison Act is still in force. But this is the construction employed by Lord Avebury in his written question to the Government about the procedures for prisoners to change their religion. He asked when the Government 'expect to issue the reminder to governors of prisons in England and Wales of the procedures that should be followed so that prisoners are not forced to register in a new religion before meeting a minister to discuss the change'. Earl Ferrers, replying for Government, wrote that 'The reminder to governors was issued on 20th January'. *Debates* (House of Lords), 27 January 1992, WA 39.
3 This issue was raised in Helsinki Watch (1982) p. 29.
4 See General Synod (1974).
5 Report of HM Chief Inspector of Prisons for England and Wales. *Annual Report*, April 1994 – March 1995, p. 17.
6 HM Chief Inspector of Prisons for Scotland. *Report for 1994–95*. Cm 2938, p. 22.
7 Prison Service Chaplaincy (1993).
8 'Religion in the prisons of England and Wales', discussion paper presented by Lord Avebury, the Venerable Khemadhammo Mahathera, Bashir Ebrahim-Khan and Indarjit Singh, House of Commons, 27 March 1996, text located at http://www.penlex.org.uk, p. 2.

Notes to pages 34-95

9 Prison Service Chaplaincy, 'Chaplain's Job Description', H1.B 132885, nd, emphasis added.
10 Prison Service Chaplaincy (1990), p. 9.
11 See T. MacQuiban, 1995 for insights into the challenges which face part-time prison chaplains, many of whom 'come to chaplaincy work not out of choice but accept it as a duty of the local circuit or church to find someone to fill this role' (p. 2).
12 Prison Service Chaplaincy, 'Prison Service Chaplaincy Concordat' (1983).
13 Co-ordination of Sikh Visiting Ministers in the Midlands region is now undertaken by Dr Kartar Surindar Singh in association with Mr Indarjit Singh.
14 Four of them were run by private companies.

3 CHURCH OF ENGLAND PRISON CHAPLAINS

1 Quotations are identified by an index number referring to respondents to the questionnaires completed anonymously by chaplains and Visiting Ministers.
2 The two prisoners concerned had given their permission for one of us to be present, but it would be unnecessary and unethical for us to reveal any details of their identity or circumstances.
3 Incidentally, chaplains gave a variety of different accounts of exactly what these formalities entailed.
4 See chapter 1 for a discussion of the terms 'brokerage' and 'facilitation'.
5 Interview at PSC headquarters, 22 April 1996.

4 VISITING MINISTERS OF OTHER FAITHS

1 *Prison Rules, Scotland*, 1994, Section 35 (1).
2 HM Prison Service, *Race Relations and Religion. A Pocket Book for Prison Staff.* London, nd, p. 7.
3 The low response rate among Hindus, Muslims and Sikhs is a warning to us to be cautious about assuming that our respondents are fully representative of all the Visiting Ministers from these faith communities. It is a reasonable expectation that religious professionals would be more likely than the lay members to complete a time-consuming and complicated questionnaire, although some religious professionals who came to this country as adults may have been reluctant to try to complete our questionnaire because their grasp of the English language was not good enough for this purpose. The responses of religious professionals and lay members should not be assumed to be necessarily similar.
4 Another Visiting Minister offered an interesting insight into the possible sources of any differences that might exist between Sikhs: 'I recognise no division within the Sikh tradition. Any such practices are due to Sikhs' ongoing suppression in India and the ignorance being boosted by the Government of India. They have "improved" on the British policy of "divide and rule" and now practice "divide and kill"' (B127). This particular Visiting Minister also wrote five paragraphs at the end of the questionnaire about the allegedly iniquitous conditions in which Sikhs had to live in India.

5 It remains for other researchers to try to discover whether ecumenically minded people are drawn to serve as Visiting Ministers or whether the experience of being a Visiting Minister induces them to become more tolerant of factional differences within their own tradition.

6 Incidentally, the Director of chaplaincies in a large American state correctional system informed us that it was not uncommon for prisoners to enter prison with very little interest in religious differences but to develop strong interests in them in the 'hothouse' atmosphere of a closed situation. Marginal differences between tiny sectarian groupings can assume huge proportions in the minds of prisoners who brood on very little else.

7 'Our sole interest', according to one of Angulimala's leaflets, 'has been to make Buddhism available in the prisons of the United Kingdom and we have tried to make this an offering and to go about it in the spirit of Dána or Giving . . . All we have ever asked for are reasonable facilities and the right to go about our business unhindered' (Forest Hermitage 1996).

8 The Chaplain General has issued guidance about reception procedures. It emphasises the need to register prisoners as far as possible in exactly the way requested by them. Members of small minority groups should not be included for reasons of convenience in larger groupings or under generic labels such as 'Pentecostal'.

9 For example, a Jewish Visiting Minister stated that, 'very often non-Jews ask to be registered as Jews – sometimes Jews do not register for fear of anti-Semitism' (B153).

10 HM Prison Service, IG28/1996.

11 We saw no evidence that Christian chaplains were exempted from normal security checks. On the contrary, chaplains seemed to be subject to the full panoply of them in the establishments that we visited.

5 'FACILITATION' OR 'DEPENDENCE'?

1 This was supported by another chaplain's claim that 'The Moslems are probably the ones who try hardest – usually among inmates from one of the ethnic minorities. Currently 28 per cent of these are registered as Christian and 61 per cent as Moslem' (D096).

2 A clear instance of this type of allegation occurred in a chaplain's account of the topics discussed at formal meetings with other Christian chaplains: 'how to manage the Moslems who attend chaplaincy on Friday afternoons to have "doss" ' (D076).

3 For example, some Visiting Ministers' statements about underlying tensions were very general in nature, such as 'I insist on the rules of religious practice being applied equally to all religions. This causes tension as minority religions are viewed as less important than Christianity' (B182) or (in the form of a list) 'Publicity of my work in prison. Finance and reimbursement. Lack of notification of Buddhist inmates. Lack of help generally. In fact, sometimes [chaplains] seem to be hindering my work' (B013).

4 For example, a Muslim wrote that he could not propose any better alternative 'as it would never work because of the ideology and the regulations' (B094).

5 Located at http://www.penlex.org.uk.

6 INCLUSION AND EXCLUSION

1 The decision to include Catholics and Methodists in the category of 'chaplain' was first formalised in 1971 as a mark of 'denominational unity' and as an attempt to erase the idea of Anglican superiority. A statement was issued that all chaplains were 'colleagues with no relationship of superiority or inferiority' and that all were 'independent in their pastoral work and in the way they organise their work'. This Christian ecumenical initiative was strengthened in 1983 when a formal Concordat was signed. It specified that the Chaplain General was head of the PSC and representative spokesman for all chaplains on condition that he consults the senior representatives of the Roman Catholic and Methodist chaplaincies. A further refinement insisted that the correct way of referring to chaplains was as 'Church of England (or Anglican) chaplain', 'Roman Catholic chaplain' and 'Methodist chaplain'. The point of this was to eliminate the old practice of calling only the Anglicans 'chaplains' and the others 'priests' or 'ministers'. See *Chaplain General's Newsletter*, June 1988, 28–27.

2 For a chaplain's endorsement of an 'inter-faith committee' representing all the religions found among inmates in a Toronto prison, see Gull (1985). He argued that no one religion was dominant in this part of Canada, 'so it has been essential for the inter-faith committee to evolve a clear stance on human rights and religious freedom'.

3 'It is sometimes observed that the time is long gone when the Chaplain was also the Deputy Governor. Equally, the effects of Fresh Start in its further weakening of the Chaplain's status in the Prison Service cannot be reversed' (Stokes 1988: 1) was one chaplain's rather resigned opinion.

8 CONCLUSIONS: STATE, CHURCH AND DIVERSITY

1 The (Presbyterian) Church of Scotland is also established in law.

2 For example, disputes have been provoked by attempts both to restrict *and* to maintain Parliament's right to determine certain aspects of the Church's liturgy and governance. See Medhurst & Moyser 1988.

3 Figures supplied in January 1995 by the Department for Education and Employment.

4 'Norman Tebbit's cricket test . . . challenged those who lived and were settled in England to support the English cricket team. If they could not, and supported India, Pakistan or the West Indies instead, then they should ask themselves whether they might be better off living in the country to which they had greater loyalty. In other words, the choice for black people in Britain was assimilation or repatriation/emigration' (Gabriel 1994: 31).

5 Prison Act (1952), Section 10 (3).

Appendix

The following people served as Consultants to the project on 'The Church of England and Other Faiths in a Multi-Faith Society'

Mr Imran Abbasi
Mr Hugh Adamson
Prof. Muhammad Anwar
Dr Rohit Barot
Mr Bashir Ebrahim-Khan
Preb. Marcus Braybrooke
Revd Robert Clarke
Prof. Douglas Davies
Revd David Everett
Dr Shirley Firth
Revd Martin Forward
Revd Dr Norman Gale
Revd John Hargreaves
Canon Peter Heartfield
Revd Roger Hooker
Revd David Horn
Mr Asaf Hussain
Mrs Angela Jagger

Dr Sewa Singh Kalsi
Revd Molly Kenyon
Dharmachari Kulananda
Dr Philip Lewis
Dr Peggy Morgan
Dr Eleanor Nesbitt
Revd Seye Olumide
Revd Edward Pogmore
Revd Nigel Pounde
Revd David Robinson
Mrs Doris Sadeghi
Dr H V Satyanaraya Sastry
Dr Derek Seber
Dr Natubhai Shah
Dr Kartar Surindar Singh
Mr S K Vadivale
Mr Paul Weller
Revd James Woodward

References

Ålund, A. and Schierup, C.-U. 1992, *The Paradoxes of Multiculturalism*, Aldershot: Gower

Anon. 1994, 'Religious Freedom Restoration Act (RFRA) now law of the land', *Correctional Law Reporter* 5 (5): 65–6, 72

Apichella, M. 1996, *Prison Pentecost. Has Revival Come to Our Prisons?*, Eastbourne: Kingsway Publications

Archbishop of Canterbury's Commission on Urban Priority Areas. 1985, *Faith in the City*, London: Church House Publishing

Asad, T. 1990, 'Multiculturalism and British identity in the wake of the Rushdie affair', *Politics and Society* 18 (4): 455–80

Austin, G. 1995, *Affairs of State. Leadership, Religion and Society*, London: Hodder & Stoughton

Avebury, Lord 1996, 'UK: calling for an inter-faith prison chaplaincy', *Dialogue* July: 7

Bauberot, J. (ed.) 1994, *Religions et Laïcité dans l'Europe des Douze*, Paris: Syros

Beckford, J. A. 1994, 'Religione e società nel Regno Unito', Aa.Vv. *La Religione degli Europei*, Turin: Fondazione Giovanni Agnelli, pp. 217–89

Beckford, J. A. and Gilliat, S. 1996, 'The Church of England and other faiths in a multi-faith society', Working Papers in Sociology, no. 21, University of Warwick

Bourdieu, P. 1984, *Distinction*, London: Routledge

Bruce, S. 1993, 'Religion and rational choice: a critique of economic explanations of religious behaviour', *Sociology of Religion* 54 (2): 193–205

Bruce, S. (ed.) 1992, *Religion and Modernization*, Oxford University Press

Butler, K. 1978, 'The Muslims are no longer an unknown quantity', *Corrections Magazine* 4: 56–59

Byrne, P. 1988, *The Campaign for Nuclear Disarmament*, London: Croom Helm

Carey, G. 1993, *Sharing a Vision*, London: Darton, Longman and Todd

Casanova, J. 1994, *Public Religions in the Modern World*, Chicago: University of Chicago Press

Champion, F. 1993, 'Entre laïcisation et sécularisation. Des rapports église-état dans l'Europe communautaire', *Le Débat* 77: 46–72

Church of England, Church Assembly, Prisons Commission 1960, 'The Church and the Prisoner', CA 1332

Church of England, General Synod, Standing Committee, Review and Estimates Sub-Committee 1974, *Memorandum*, July, pp. 7–10, GS Misc. 38.

Church of England, General Synod, Board of Social Responsibility 1996, 'Private Sector Involvement in Prisons', GS Misc 479

Church House Publishing 1992, *Multi-Faith Worship?*, London: Church House

Cohen, S. and Taylor, L.1972, *Psychological Survival. The Experience of Long-Term Imprisonment*, Harmondsworth: Penguin

Colley, L., 1992, *Britons. Forging the Nation 1707–1837*, New Haven: Yale University Press

Commission on British Muslims and Islamophobia 1997, *Islamophobia. Its Features and Dangers*, London: Runnymede Trust

Cook, A. *c.* 1913, *Our Prison System*, London: Drane's

Cornwell, P. 1983, *Church and Nation*, Oxford: Blackwell

Davie, G. 1990, 'Believing without belonging. Is this the future of religion in Britain?, *Social Compass* 37: 456–69

   1993, 'Religion and modernity in Britain', *International Journal of Comparative Religion* 1 (1): 1–11

   1994, *Religion in Britain since 1945*, Oxford: Blackwell

Denzin, N. 1970, *The Research Act in Sociology*, London: Butterworths

Dobbelaere, K. 1981, 'Secularization: a multi-dimensional concept', *Current Sociology* 29 (2): 1–216

Dobbelaere, K. and Jagodzinski, W. 1995, 'Religious cognitions and beliefs', in J.W. van Deth and Scarbrough, S. (eds.), *The Impact of Values*, Oxford: Oxford University Press, pp. 197–249

Duncan, C. 1992, 'The call for "separate" schools', in B. Drury (ed.), 'Education, the Education Reform Act (1988) and Racial Equality', Warwick University: *Occasional Paper in Ethnic Relations* no. 7

Feeley, M. M. and Hanson, R. A. 1990, 'The impact of judicial intervention on prisons and jails: a framework for analysis and a review of the literature', in J. J. DiLulio Jr. (ed.), *Courts, Corrections, and the Constitution*, New York: Oxford University Press

Finke, R. and Stark, R. 1992, *The Churching of America 1776–1990. Winners and Losers in our Religious Economy*, New Brunswick, NJ: Rutgers University Press

FitzGerald, M. and Marshall, P. 1996, 'Ethnic minorities in British prisons: some research implications', in R. Matthews and Francis, P. (eds.), *Prisons 2000*, London: Macmillan, pp. 139–62

Forest Hermitage 1996, 'Newsletter', 2539, April

Fox, L. 1952, *The English Prison System*, London: Routledge & Kegan Paul

Gabriel, J. 1994, *Racism, Culture, Markets*, London: Routledge

Genders, E. and Player, E. 1989, *Race Relations in Prison*, Oxford: Oxford University Press

Gilbert, N. (ed.) 1993, *Researching Social Life*, London: Sage

Goffman, E. 1968, *Asylums*, Harmondsworth: Penguin

Greeley, A. 1972, *Unsecular Man: the Persistence of Religion*, New York: Shocken

Grünhut, M. 1948, *Prison Reform*, Oxford: Oxford University Press

Gull, B. 1985, 'Prison chaplaincies abroad', *New Life* 3: 8–13

Habgood, J. 1983, *Church and Nation in a Secular Age*, London: Darton, Longman & Todd

   1988, *Confessions of a Conservative Liberal*, London: SPCK

Hastings, A. 1986, *A History of English Christianity, 1920–80*, London: Collins
  1991, *Church and State*, Exeter: Exeter University Press
Helsinki Watch 1982, *Prison Conditions in the United Kingdom*, London
Hooker, R. and Lamb, C. 1993, *Love the Stranger. Ministry in Multi-Faith Areas*, London: SPCK, 2nd rev. edn
Hornsby-Smith, M. and Lee, R. 1987, *Roman Catholics in England: Studies in Social Structure since the Second World War*, Cambridge: Cambridge University Press
Hutton, W. 1995, *The State We're In*, London: Cape
Ignatieff, M. 1978, *A Just Measure of Pain. The Penitentiary in the Industrial Revolution, 1750–1850*, Harmondsworth: Penguin
Jewson, N. and Mason, D. 1992, 'The theory and practice of equal opportunities policies. Liberal and radical approaches', in P. Braham, Rattansi, A. and Skellington, R. (eds.), *Racism and Antiracism*, London: Sage, pp. 218–34
King, R. and Morgan, R., 1980, *The Future of the Prison System*, Farnborough: Gower
King, R. D. and McDermott, K. 1995, *The State of Our Prisons*, Oxford: Oxford University Press
Kosmin, B. and Lachman, S. 1993, *One Nation Under God. Religion in Contemporary American Society*, New York: Harmony Books
Lloyd Rees, L. 1975, 'The role of the prison chaplain in the modern world', unpublished lecture to the Howard League, 19 June
Loucks, N. 1994, *Prison Rules. A Working Guide*, London: Prison Reform Trust
Lynne, P. J. 1975, 'The prison chaplain – search for a role', *Prison Service Journal* 19: 8–10
McConville, S., 1995, 'The Victorian prison. England 1865–1965', in Morris and Rothman (eds.), pp. 131–67
McGowen, R. 1995, 'The well-ordered prison. England 1780–1865', in Morris and Rothman (eds.), pp. 79–109
McLaughlin, T. *et al.* 1996, *The Contemporary Catholic School: Context, Identity and Diversity*, London: Falmer
Macquiban, T. 1995, 'Prison chaplains – their theology of ministry and mission', *New Life* 12: 1–13
Mathiesen, T. 1990, *Prison on Trial*, London: Sage
Matthews, R. and Francis, P. (eds.) 1996, *Prisons 2000. An International Perspective on the Current State and Future of Imprisonment*, London: Macmillan
Medhurst, K. and Moyser, G. 1988, *Church and Politics in a Secular Age*, Oxford: Clarendon Press
Modood, T. 1994a, 'Establishment, multiculturalism and British citizenship', *Political Quarterly* 65 (1): 53–73
  1994b, *Racial Equality. Colour, Culture and Justice*, London: Institute for Public Policy Research
Modood, T. *et al.* 1997, *Ethnic Minorities in Britain*, London: Policy Studies Institute
Montefiore, H. 1990, *Christianity and Politics*, Oxford: Oxford University Press
Moore, K. M. 1995, *Al-Mughtaribun. American Law and the Transformation of Muslim Life in the United States*, Albany, NY: State University of New York Press

Morris, N. and Rothman, D. T. (eds.) 1995, *The Oxford History of the Prison*, Oxford: Oxford University Press

Nye, M., 1996, 'Hare Krishna and Sanatan Dharm in Britain: the campaign for Bhaktivedanta Manor.' *Journal of Contemporary Religion* 11 (1): 37–56

Parekh, B. 1990, 'The Rushdie affair: research agenda for political philosophy', *Political Studies* 37: 695–709

Parekh P. and Bhabha, H. 1989, 'Identities on parade', *Marxism Today* June: 24–29

Potter, H. 1991, 'Speaking from the heart', *New Life* 8: 67

Poulat, E. 1990, 'En 1990, la laïcité pour une confession majoritaire: le catholicisme', in H. Bost (ed.), *Genèse et Enjeux de la Laïcité*, Geneva: Labor et Fides

Poulter, S. 1987, 'Ethnic minority customs, English law and human rights', *International and Comparative Law Quarterly* 36: 589–615

Pound, K., Atherton, R. and Davies, W. 1989, 'Six faces of a future chaplaincy', *New Life* 6: 53–6

Prison Service Chaplaincy 1993, *Directory and Guide on Religious Practices in HM Prison Service*, London: Prison Service, (2nd rev. edn)

nd, *Inside Faith*, London: Prison Service

Rex, J. 1986, *Race and Ethnicity*, Milton Keynes: Open University Press

1994, 'Ethnic mobilisation in multi-cultural societies', in J. Rex and Drury, B. (eds.) *Ethnic Mobilisation in a Multi-Cultural Europe*, Aldershot: Avebury, pp. 3–12

1996, 'National identity in the democratic multi-cultural state', *Sociological Research Online* 1 (2)

Robbins, T. 1988, *Cults, Converts and Charisma*, London: Sage

Robilliard, St. J. 1980, 'Religion in prison', *New Law Journal*, 4 September: 800–1

1984, *Religion and the Law: Religious Liberty in Modern English Law*, Manchester: Manchester University Press

Russell, D. 1979, 'Religious minorities in prison. Tolerated? Accepted?', *Prison Service Journal* July: 7–12

Séguy, J. 1973, *Les Conflits du Dialogue*, Paris: Cerf

Shaw, Richard D. S. 1995, *Chaplains to the Imprisoned. Sharing Life with the Incarcerated*, New York: Haworth Press

Sparks, R. 1996, ' "Penal austerity": the doctrine of less eligibility reborn?', in R. Matthews and Francis, P. (eds.), *Prisons 2000*, London: Macmillan, pp. 74–93

Stark, R. and Bainbridge, W. S. 1985, *The Future of Religion. Secularization, Revival and Cult Formation*. Berkeley, CA: University of California Press

Stern V. 1987, *Bricks of Shame. British Prisons*, Harmondsworth: Penguin

Stokes, R. 1988, 'The changing chaplaincy and some reflections', *New Life* 5: 1

Taylor, C. 1992, *Multiculturalism and 'the Politics of Recognition'*, Princeton: Princeton University Press

Tribe, L. 1982, 'Church and state in the Constitution', in D. Kelley (ed.), *Government Intervention in Religious Affairs*, New York: Pilgrim Press, pp. 31–40

Troyna, B. 1987, 'Swann's song: the origins, ideology and implications to "Education for All" ', in T.S. Chivers (ed.), *Race and Culture in Education*, Slough: NFER

US Department of Justice, Federal Bureau of Prisons 1993, *A Volunteer's Guide to the Bureau of Prisons*, Washington, DC

    1995a, *The Ministry of Chaplains: Technical Reference Manual*, TRM 014.01., Washington, DC

    1995b, *Religious Beliefs and Practices of Committed Offenders*, PS5360.06, Washington, DC

    1995c, *Common Fare Diet Program*, OM051–95 (5360), Washington, DC

    1996, *Program Review Guidelines*, 003–96 (5360), Washington, DC

Vertovec, S. 1994, 'Multicultural, multi-Asian, multi-Muslim Leicester: dimensions of social complexity, ethnic organisation and local government interface', *Innovation* 7 (3): 259–76

    1996, 'Multiculturalism, culturalism and public incorporation', *Ethnic and Racial Studies* 19 (1): 49–69

Wallerstein, I. 1990, 'Culture as the ideological battleground of the modern world-system', *Theory, Culture & Society* 7: 31–55

Ward, K. 1992, 'Is a Christian society a contradiction?', in D. Cohn-Sherbok and McLellan, D. (eds.), *Religion in Public Life*, London: Macmillan, pp. 5–16

Willaime, J.-P. 1996, 'La Laïcité et religion en France', in G. Davie and Hervieu-Léger, D. (eds.), *Identités religieuses en Europe*, Paris: la Découverte, pp. 153–71

Wilson, B. R. 1966, *Religion in Secular Society*, London: Watts

    1985, 'Secularization: the inherited model' in P. E. Hammond (ed.), *The Sacred in a Secular Age*, Berkeley, CA: University of California Press, pp. 9–20

Wolffe, J. 1994, ' "And there's another country . . .": religion, the state and British identities', in G. Parsons (ed.) *The Growth of Religious Diversity. Britain from 1945*, London: Routledge, pp. 85–159

Yuval-Davis, N. 1992, 'Fundamentalism, multiculturalism and women in Britain', in J. Donald and Rattansi, A. (eds.), *'Race', Culture and Difference*, London: Sage, pp. 278–91

Index